Freedom and Its Betrayal

Isaiah Berlin was born in Riga, now capital of Latvia, in 1909. When he was six, his family moved to Russia; there in 1917, in Petrograd, he witnessed both Revolutions – Social Democratic and Bolshevik. In 1921 he and his parents came to England, and he was educated at St Paul's School, London, and Corpus Christi College, Oxford.

At Oxford he was a Fellow of All Souls, a Fellow of New College, Professor of Social and Political Theory, and founding President of Wolfson College. He also held the Presidency of the British Academy. In addition to *Freedom and Its Betrayal*, his main published works are *Karl Marx*, *Russian Thinkers*, *Concepts and Categories*, *Against the Current*, *Personal Impressions*, *The Crooked Timber of Humanity*, *The Sense of Reality*, *The Proper Study of Mankind*, *The Roots of Romanticism*, *The Power of Ideas*, *Three Critics of the Enlightenment*, *Liberty*, *The Soviet Mind* and *Political Ideas in the Romantic Age*. As an exponent of the history of ideas he was awarded the Erasmus, Lippincott and Agnelli Prizes; he also received the Jerusalem Prize for his lifelong defence of civil liberties. He died in 1997.

Henry Hardy, a Fellow of Wolfson College, Oxford, is one of Isaiah Berlin's Literary Trustees. He has edited (or co-edited) many other books by Berlin, including the first three of four volumes of his letters, and is currently working on the remaining volume.

Enrique Krauze is editor of *Letras Libres*. His latest book is *Redeemers: Ideas and Power in Latin America* (2011).

For further information about Isaiah Berlin visit
<http://berlin.wolf.ox.ac.uk/>

ALSO BY ISAIAH BERLIN

*

Karl Marx
The Hedgehog and the Fox
The Age of Enlightenment
Russian Thinkers
Concepts and Categories
Against the Current
Personal Impressions
The Crooked Timber of Humanity
The Sense of Reality
The Proper Study of Mankind
The Roots of Romanticism
The Power of Ideas
Three Critics of the Enlightenment
Liberty
The Soviet Mind
Political Ideas in the Romantic Age

with Beata Polanowska-Sygulska
Unfinished Dialogue

*

Flourishing: Letters 1928–1946
Enlightening: Letters 1946–1960
Building: Letters 1960–1975

FREEDOM AND ITS BETRAYAL

SIX ENEMIES OF HUMAN LIBERTY

ISAIAH BERLIN

Edited by Henry Hardy

Second Edition

Foreword by Enrique Krauze

PRINCETON UNIVERSITY PRESS

PRINCETON AND OXFORD

Published in the United States of America, its Colonies and Dependencies, the Philippine Islands, and Canada by Princeton University Press, 41 William Street, Princeton, New Jersey 08540

Requests for permission to reproduce material from this work should be sent to Permissions, Princeton University Press

press.princeton.edu

First published by Chatto & Windus and
Princeton University Press 2002
Second edition published by Princeton University Press 2014

ISBN 978-0-691-15757-3

British Library Cataloging-in-Publication Data is available

This book has been composed in Garamond Premier Pro

Printed on acid-free paper ∞

Printed in the United States of America

1 3 5 7 9 10 8 6 4 2

To the memory of Anna Kallin
1896–1984

CONTENTS

FOREWORD

Isaiah the Prophet

Enrique Krauze

Freedom and Its Betrayal: Six Enemies of Human Liberty is a collection of six remarkable lectures (as edited by Henry Hardy) that Isaiah Berlin delivered on BBC Radio in the autumn of 1952. They are an impassioned political interpretation of what Berlin sees as the authoritarian legacy of six philosophers: Helvétius, Rousseau, Fichte, Hegel, Saint-Simon and Maistre. In response T. S. Eliot offered a left-handed compliment to Berlin's 'torrential eloquence'[1] and the philosopher Michael Oakeshott called him a 'Paganini of ideas'.[2] Hundreds of thousands listened to the series and Berlin received many enthusiastic letters.

Berlin had first treated this material earlier in the same year, when he delivered the Mary Flexner Lectures (at Bryn Mawr College in Pennsylvania) under the title 'Political Ideas in the Romantic Age'. Lelia Brodersen, who was briefly his secretary during his residence at Bryn Mawr, was present at the lectures. She would remember the 'furious stream of words, in

[1] In his 1955 lecture 'The Literature of Politics'. T. S. Eliot, *To Criticise the Critic and Other Writings* (New York, 1965), 137.

[2] When introducing Berlin at the London School of Economics on 12 May 1953 before the lecture that became 'Historical Inevitability'. LSE Archives, Oakeshott 1/3.

beautifully finished sentences' from the professor who in a 'true state of inspiration' drew his distinctions between various forms of freedom.

He had prepared himself with great energy for these lectures. According to his biographer Michael Ignatieff, in 1950–1 Berlin 'read furiously' the works of the eighteenth-century French philosophers (Diderot, Helvétius, Holbach, Voltaire) and the German Romantics (Schelling, Herder, Fichte).[1] But perhaps the 'fury' to which Ignatieff alludes had less to do with Berlin's academic commitment than with the sense that he was beginning to find his personal vocation and his own voice for a confrontation with history.

The highly positive reception of these lectures must have further strengthened his convictions. Their title reflects the moral fibre of Berlin's thought, which resembles that of the Russian thinkers who would later become his subject. Even today, read not heard,[2] they have the resonance of a solemn summons bolstered by those long loping sentences and cascades of precise and penetrating adjectives that sound eloquent and natural within Berlin's style. Ignatieff calls these lectures 'a landmark in British broadcasting [and] in Berlin's life'.[3] But how did Isaiah Berlin arrive at this point and these specific insights?

The post-war world imposed the need for political and moral definitions. Nazism had been destroyed, but Soviet totalitarianism remained, supported by the initial prestige of the Russian Revolution and by the progress, real or imaginary, of the Russian economy. It was all legitimised by the philosophy of Marxism, which presented a defiant challenge to its critics. Karl Popper had earlier responded to this challenge with his compendious

[1] *Isaiah Berlin: A Life* (London and New York, 1998), 201.

[2] Though a recording of the lecture on Rousseau survives, and may be heard at *<https://itunes.apple.com/itunes-u/isaiah-berlin-centenary/ id381701053?mt=10>*.

[3] op. cit. (note 1 above), 205.

philosophical refutation of totalitarian thought from Plato to Marx;[1] and George Orwell published *Animal Farm* and *1984*, after writing (before and during the Second World War) various criticisms of the Soviet State and its Western sympathisers. At the other end of the scale, some of Berlin's colleagues (including E. H. Carr and Christopher Hill) had reaffirmed their commitment to the Soviet Union and written their own histories of the Bolshevik Revolution. In 1945 Berlin had made a highly eventful trip to Moscow and Leningrad, during which he heard revelations from Boris Pasternak and Anna Akhmatova about the innermost workings of Stalinist repression. His experiences had helped to revive his interest in nineteenth-century Russian thought and literature and, at the same time, to establish one of the principal themes of his work, a criticism of the Soviet state based on the study of its intellectual precursors. But defining a position in the face of post-war realities was not the only dilemma Isaiah Berlin had to confront.

From 1940 to 1946, his diplomatic and intellectual contribution on behalf of the British Diplomatic Service, much of it in Washington, had earned him significant recognition in the higher spheres of American and British politics, but at the end of the war he was compelled to return to a cloistered academic life at New College in Oxford, a prospect for which he had little enthusiasm. And Berlin also had other concerns. Despite the solidity of his academic career and position, he felt himself to be a marginal person: a professional philosopher but with an inclination towards the history of ideas and towards literature; an exile from his native Russian culture set down at the intellectual heart of England; and, above all, a Jewish thinker divided (at times truly torn) between the will to integrate himself fully into English culture, history and society, and the call of his ancestors – their history, their culture, their identity.

[1] *The Open Society and Its Enemies* (London, 1945).

This last pressure was perhaps the most complex and also the most decisive of Berlin's problems. Light years away from his childhood Talmudic studies or his illustrious Hasidic ancestors, Berlin accepted his Jewish identity as an irreversible biological fact and a cultural heritage within which he recognised himself, at least in part, and to which he was loyal, largely because of his awareness of 'the unbelievable cost in blood and tears which has made the history of the Jews for two thousand years a dreadful martyrology'.[1] He was free of ideological or nationalist zeal but was sympathetic toward Zionism. During his years in Washington, he established a close relationship with Chaim Weizmann (so close and committed that, according to Ignatieff, Berlin even supplied him with some secret information he had learned from the British). In July of 1947, shortly before the declaration of independence by Israel, Berlin travelled with his father to the land soon to be designated as a homeland for the Jews. There he received continual invitations (from Weizmann and even Ben-Gurion) to burn his Oxford boats and establish himself in Israel, where he would be assigned a high political position. It was one possible path, a full return to Judaism, and one that his father urged upon him.

Two extremely influential writers of the time, Arthur Koestler and T. S. Eliot, had similar (though differently motivated) ideas about Jews and Israel. In an interview published in May of 1950,[2] Koestler argued that the Jews of the Diaspora, after the foundation of Israel, had only two rational paths open to them: either emigrate to Israel or assimilate irrevocably to the religion and life of the countries where they now resided. Eliot's argument, first proposed in a 1934 lecture but put into circulation once again

[1] 'Jewish Slavery and Emancipation', in *The Power of Ideas*, ed. Henry Hardy, 2nd ed. (Princeton, 2013), 198.

[2] Maurice Carr, 'Arthur Koestler's Renunciation', *Jewish Chronicle*, 5 May 1950, 15, 20. Cf. Koestler's *Promise and Fulfilment: Palestine 1917–1949* (London, 1949), 332–5.

on the establishment of Israel, pointed in a similar direction (though deeply tainted with the poet's anti-Semitism). The Jews could legitimately reassume their religious identity (returning to their ghettos) or they could totally assimilate. But, he emphasised, 'reasons of race and religion combine to make any large number of freethinking Jews undesirable'[1] in the societies that had accepted them.

Berlin felt the need to answer and oppose these assertions. Beyond the issue of Eliot's disgraceful bigotry, the either/or option seemed radically to limit Berlin's own personal freedom. The alternatives – emigration or assimilation – presupposed an act of freedom assumed to be positive and seen as liberation from a long-standing state of slavery. He could choose to be a liberated Jew in Israel (where, for the first time in nearly two thousand years, the historical anomaly – especially of the European Jew – as a kind of pariah in an alien and hostile environment had been resolved), or he could renounce his Jewish identity. Berlin responded in a long and impassioned essay, the autobiographical content of which – in my view – has not been sufficiently appreciated, and helps us to understand the manner in which Berlin found his true voice and his definitive vocation as a public intellectual. It was published in the autumn of 1951 in the *Jewish Chronicle* under the title 'Jewish Slavery and Emancipation' and it offered a third possibility, what Berlin would later call 'negative freedom', freedom to be a Jew in the manner each person might feel to be best, and in particular the author himself, Isaiah Berlin.

To illuminate the condition of the European Jew, Berlin invented a parable. Some travellers, by chance, insert themselves into the life of a tribe. In order to survive, they begin to learn the customs and habits of their environment and little by little come to understand it as well or even better than the members of

[1] *After Strange Gods: A Primer of Modern Heresy* (London, 1934), 20.

the tribe: They 'become primary authorities on the natives: they codify their language [...], they interpret the native society to the outside world. With each year their knowledge and love of it [...] become greater.'[1] But then something strange happens. Although the members of the tribe can appreciate the labour and loyalty of the strangers, they still can only see them as *the others*, and think that precisely in this otherness resides their capacity to see and interpret the real conditions of the tribe: 'their understanding is too sharp, their devotion too great, they are experts on the tribe, not members of it. They are its servants, perhaps its saviours, but they are not homogeneous with it.'[2] And the best proof of the fact that they are not part of the tribe is their excessive complacency: 'They are altogether too anxious to please; indeed, too anxious to be whatever it is that they protest so much – and to all appearances so plausibly – that they surely are.'[3] Within the tribe, this uneasy insistence of the foreigners results in bewilderment and distancing. Nevertheless the foreigners insist on their illusion – their fantasy––of thinking that they are (or can be if they try hard enough) members of the tribe. But everything that follows is useless: 'The more desperately the strangers argue, the more vividly their differences from the natives stand out; indeed, the anxiety to deny the difference is itself a barrier.'[4] They cannot be part of the tribe and preserve particular attributes (especially religious ones) that do not belong to the tribe. In effect they both are and are not tribesmen. They are present among them but not united with them.

The natives, Berlin explains, do not have any doubts about their identity but are comfortably at home within it. But the foreigners elaborately and continually examine this identity that eludes them: they express it, they recreate it, they celebrate it. Berlin points to the cases of Heinrich Heine and Felix Mendelssohn,

[1] op. cit. (xiv/1), 202–3. [2] ibid. 203. [3] ibid.
[4] ibid. 205.

two Germans of Jewish origin who construct their work 'with a particular kind of self-consciousness alien to a normal member of a recognised community'.[1] Both came from families that had converted to Lutheranism, but they never became truly native Germans like Goethe or Beethoven. Berlin asserts that this very marginality explains what he asserts is the inclination of Jews to interpretation (in the arts and humanities) rather than creation: 'the Jews, like the strangers seeking to lose themselves in the strange tribe, find themselves compelled to devote all their energies and talents to the task of understanding and adaptation upon which their lives depend at every step'.[2] This exhausting process leads, according to Berlin, to a genius 'for observation and classification and explanation' and toward a characteristic veneration for 'the heroes or institutions of the nations among which they live'.[3]

Strangely enough, Berlin in this essay hardly mentions the denouement of this long and tangled history: the extermination of most European Jews, including many of the highly educated Jews who in Germany considered themselves more German than the ethnic Germans. For Berlin, the 'astonishing event'[4] of the foundation of Israel had, in one blow, changed the historical condition of the Jews. The new Israel offered the possibility of freedom, of freely abandoning the tribes among whom they were guests and of putting down palpable roots within their own tribe. But this option – and here Berlin was at odds with militant Zionists – was not an imperative, and it may have been precisely here, with the resolution of his personal dilemma, with his passionate defense of a third alternative (to remain in an intermediate situation) that Berlin encountered his personal concept of freedom. He would later apply it to the human condition in general. A Jew could now determine his destiny in an entirely personal way. If he chose to continue living as a foreigner within

[1] ibid. 207. [2] ibid. 209. [3] ibid. [4] ibid. 215.

a tribe – which was up to a point Berlin's own situation and decision – he was perfectly free to do so and accept the eventual consequences. And the choice was a matter of personal freedom, not a prescription for happiness:

> If a man chooses, whether actively or passively, the discomfort, the insecure status, the social humiliations of living as a Jew, whether concealed or open, in a country which does not like Jews, that is to a large and increasing degree his own or his family's affair. We may despise him for insufficient pride, or denounce him for deceiving himself and predict disasters for him in the future, or congratulate him on a far-sighted utilitarianism or on bravely sacrificing himself to the future of his children, or on a commendable independence or disdainfulness of prejudice; that is our right. But it is no less his right to live the life he chooses, unless thereby he brings too much pain or injustice into the world.[1]

And, in an angry paragraph, he defends his option against the assertions of T. S. Eliot, incidentally associating Eliot with Plato's elitism and twentieth-century French Fascism. To be different, even irritatingly different, is not a crime, 'and neither Plato nor Maurras nor Eliot, nor any of their followers, have a right to place men, for this alone, beyond the borders of the city'.[2] Eliot received a copy of the essay and exchanged correspondence with the author, an interchange that Berlin would later deplore for his own obsequiousness.

Isaiah Berlin had taken a critical step. Before he came to postulate the concept of 'negative freedom', Berlin asserted his own right to choose and exercise 'negative freedom' within the Jewish tradition. It was a risky position, uncertain, uncomfortable, difficult and at times perhaps even (in the opinion of some) unworthy, but he had freely chosen it to be his.

[1] ibid. 219. [2] ibid. 224.

Berlin decided not to become an Israeli. It was a decision that not only freed him from his dilemma of identity but also allowed him freely to undertake the 'interpretative'[1] work which he considered typically Jewish. The BBC lectures that immediately followed this decision were his first great moment as a public figure, but there is more to be said about his style in these lectures. Eliot considered it 'torrential', but there is a more essential quality it possesses – a distinct prophetic tone. Though he came from a prominent Hasidic family and had Talmudic schooling in his childhood, Berlin tended to give these early experiences very little weight in his intellectual formation. But his own intellectual self-definition in 'Jewish Slavery and Emancipation' included attributes that he specifically associated with Jews (like the capacity 'for the analysis of the past, the present and sometimes the future also')[2] and that come very close to the qualities of a prophet. He himself had written that the foreigners in his parable of the tribe 'feel – not unjustifiably – that they are its best friends, its champions and its prophets'.[3] The predicament of the European Jew had helped define his commitment to human freedom. Now, with the voice of a prophet, he would have to lay claim to its universal relevance.

Central to this inclination toward prophetic utterance was his strongly felt intention to warn the public (to move it emotionally) toward a realisation of the oppressive power of very old and strongly rooted political ideas. Like his contemporary, Jacob Talmon, later author of the book *Political Messianism: The Romantic Phase*, Berlin wanted to reveal and denounce the 'theological' substratum of philosophies apparently objective and secular: 'This is a theological doctrine' he wrote about the nationalist metaphysics of Fichte, and Fichte clearly was in this sense a theologian, and so was Hegel, and no good purpose is

[1] ibid. 208–9. [2] ibid. 209. [3] ibid. 203

served by supposing that they were secular thinkers'.[1] In the same interpretative mode, referring to the years at the end of the eighteenth and the beginning of the nineteenth centuries (the specific period that saw the rise of those he termed 'enemies of human liberty'), Berlin notes 'the extraordinary density of megalomaniac Messiahs', men 'gifted with that unique power of penetration and imagination which was destined to solve all human evils',[2] and he goes on to condemn them.

In his angriest moment, Berlin provides a brilliant diagnosis of the Fichtean posture and the horrors to which it leads, but he does not directly refute these ideas. He simply describes and condemns them as antecedents to National Socialism. After quoting a passage in which Fichte summons Germany to its transcendental destiny, he finds his best answer in another prophet, Heinrich Heine, who, in his famous visions of Germany's future, writes that 'Armed Fichteans will come, whose fanatical will neither fear nor self- interest can touch. [...] A drama will be performed in Germany in contrast with which the French Revolution will seem a mere peaceful idyll'.[3]

Understandably, in his other five profiles Berlin's criticism does not reach the level of intensity found in his piece on Fichte. In each case, he follows the same method of exposition: he describes the logical and biographical development of a particular thinker's ideas, which always leads to a final synthesis in which the individual philosopher is judged to be opposed to human freedom. In Berlin's analysis of Rousseau, for example, the concept of radical liberty leads to the 'general will', that social 'we' which is not the sum of individual 'I's but a greater unity that integrates them and whose collective authority, in a final 'mystical' leap, Rousseau finally assigns to the State.[4] Berlin's

[1] 73 below (subsequent plain numbers refer to the pages of the present volume).

[2] 113. [3] 78. [4] 48.

revelatory portrait of Rousseau (whom he considers 'the most sinister and most formidable enemy of liberty')[1] is not without sympathy. Berlin grants him some credit for the genesis of participatory democracy and praises his spontaneous distrust of the Enlightenment elite whom Helvétius esteems.

He also sees valuable contributions in the philosophy of Hegel, such as the incorporation of the arts and sciences into his integral vision of history. His account of Hegel is schematic but clear: from the metaphysical spark of the concept of the dialectic to Hegel's notion of 'transhistorical heroes' as the protagonists of the inevitable march of history toward its final synthesis in universal reason as represented by the State. In the case of Hegel, Berlin's prophetic impetus is not so much revelatory as highly critical: he considers Hegel the creator of the most influential and oppressive 'theodicy'[2] in history.

It is noteworthy, at least from our distance in time, that Berlin includes two 'enemies' of individual freedom whose ideas – in the arena of history – do not seem opposed to liberalism, at least in their views on economics: Helvétius and his utilitarianism and Saint-Simon's productivism. Be that as it may, his portrait of Saint- Simon is probably the best in the book. Beyond his status as a prototypical secular 'Messiah', Berlin regards him as 'the greatest of all the prophets of the twentieth century'[3] for having been the first to discern the economic and technological forces of history. The essay on Maistre (on whom Berlin would later publish much wider investigations) shows a somewhat strange attraction to a personage very far from Berlin, to a man who was a firm apologist for monarchy, the Church, the past and the dictatorship of the sabre.

Those BBC lectures – writes Ignatieff – 'provided him with a platform and a new audience. He had become a public

[1] 52. [2] 108. [3] 113.

intellectual – in the Russian mould, but in an English idiom'.[1] And, it should be added, with the distinctive note of a Hebrew prophet.

For those who heard those 'torrential' radio lectures, Berlin succeeded in revealing the various and diverse antecedents of the cult of the State and at the same time defended the ideas of individual liberty that were an essential value of the 'tribe' to which this 'foreigner'[2] had incorporated himself, the 'tribe' of British culture. And he became a prophet far beyond the borders of his country.

Berlin, in 1948, wrote to Chaim Weizmann that his decision to remain at Oxford 'in an hour of crisis for our own people may seem unpardonable egoism and even a kind of levity'.[3] But there is no doubt that, on balance, this thinker who defended human freedom with the insight and tone of a Hebrew prophet, made the right decision. 'A prophet hath no honour in his own country.'[4] Yet not only outside but within his own adopted tribe, Isaiah Berlin was a clear exception.

Translated from the Spanish by Hank Heifetz

[1] loc. cit. (xii/3).

[2] op. cit. (xiv/1), 207.

[3] *Enlightening: Letters 1946–1960*, ed. Henry Hardy and Jennifer Holmes (London, 2009), 54.

[4] John 4: 44.

EDITOR'S PREFACE

FIFTY YEARS AGO, when the six hour-long lectures published in this volume were broadcast on BBC Radio, they created a broadcasting sensation. Never before had a speaker on this scale been allowed to dispense with a prepared script,[5] and the forty-three-year-old Isaiah Berlin was the right person to inaugurate this risky practice. His headlong delivery, his idiosyncratic voice (even though this made it hard for some to understand him), his extraordinary articulacy, his evident absorption in his topic, the unfamiliar but immediately exciting subject matter – all this combined to create an impact that those who listened at the time still remember today. People tuned in expectantly each week and found themselves mesmerised. John Burrow, then a schoolboy, records that the lectures 'excited me so much that I sat, for every talk, on the floor beside the wireless, taking notes'.[6] When the series was over, it was the subject of a *Times* first leader, which provoked a correspondence on the letters page to which Berlin contributed.[7]

The lectures consolidated Berlin's growing reputation as a man who could speak about intellectual matters in an accessible

[5] Though unscripted, the lectures were not broadcast live, but recorded and edited before transmission.

[6] John Burrow, 'A Common Culture? Nationalist Ideas in Nineteenth-Century European Thought', unpublished inaugural lecture as Professor of European Thought, Oxford, 7 April 1996, 3. See also Lelia Brodersen's description (xiv) of the earlier version of the lectures delivered in the USA.

[7] 'The Fate of Liberty', *The Times*, 6 December 1952, 7; letters, 9, 10, 12, 16 (Berlin), 18 December.

and absorbing way, and in his view they also laid the foundation for his appointment five years later to the Chichele Professorship of Social and Political Theory at Oxford.[1] There was a less flattering side to this celebrity too, one which was always a worry to Berlin: he was afraid he was regarded partly as a showman, a variety turn,[2] and indeed Michael Oakeshott introduced him at the London School of Economics the following year, when he gave the first Auguste Comte Memorial Trust Lecture[3] there, as 'a Paganini of ideas'.[4] There was some foundation to this fear, for he became a byword for rapid highbrow speech: 'the only man in Oxford who could pronounce "epistemological" as one syllable'.[5] But this aspect of his public image did no permanent damage to the kind of recognition that counted, recognition of his wide-ranging intellectual resources and his ability to deploy them with unique style, clarity and persuasiveness.

A somewhat crackly recording of just one of the lectures – that on Rousseau – survives, and may be listened to at the British

[1] In a piece on his appointment the *Sunday Times* referred to 'his famous broadcasts, rapid, vivid, torrential cascades of rich, spontaneous, tumbling ideas and images' (31 March 1957, 3).

[2] The *Radio Times* stressed this aspect of Berlin's appeal too strongly, in his view, observing among other things that he 'is renowned for his fluent and witty expositions of abstract ideas' and 'has a reputation as a conversationalist which extends far beyond Oxford' (24 October 1952, 3). Berlin wrote to his producer Anna Kallin on 26 October saying that this treatment was unacceptable, and that therefore he could not continue to work for the BBC. Evidently he later recanted, but he had been cut to the quick, writing with rare sternness: 'although I may be a mere jolly & garrulous vulgarisiteur [sic] this is not the capacity in which I thought I was being employed'.

[3] On 12 May 1953. The lecture was published in London in 1954 as *Historical Inevitability*.

[4] The handwritten text on which Oakeshott based his introduction survives. The relevant sentence runs: 'Listening to him you may be tempted to think that you are in the presence of one of the great intellectual virtuosos of our time, a Paganini of ideas.' LSE Archives, Oakeshott 1/3.

[5] C. M. Woodhouse, *Something Ventured* (London etc., 1982), 2.

Library in London.[1] This is the closest we can come to recreating today the effect the lectures had in 1952. But there are transcripts (if sometimes very imperfect) of all six lectures, and now that these have been edited it is possible once again to witness Berlin's exceptional expository fluency, and to feel the impact of this early account of his views on liberty, views made famous in 1958 in his inaugural lecture as Oxford's Chichele Professor of Social and Political Theory, *Two Concepts of Liberty*.[2] But *Freedom and its Betrayal* is by no means simply a crude forerunner of a more refined later development. The conception of freedom that infuses these early lectures is in its essentials already fully formed, and this much less dense treatment, especially since it is presented in terms of specific thinkers rather than as an abstract treatise, and includes a great deal that does not appear in the inaugural lecture, is a significant supplement to the work he published in his lifetime.

In my more flippant moments I have thought of subtitling this book 'Not the Reith Lectures'. Anna Kallin, Berlin's BBC Third Programme producer, had already been responsible for a number of talks of his. She knew he was preparing to give the Mary Flexner Lectures at Bryn Mawr College in Pennsylvania (as he did in February and March 1952), and she asked him to deliver a version of these on the radio. She was well aware that he would be hard to persuade – for he customarily resisted offers of the limelight – and she was ready to be disappointed. To her delight, however, he was willing. When she heard recordings (now lost)[3] of the Flexner Lectures she had no hesitation in offering him, in addition, the prestigious role of Reith Lecturer, to which he was ideally suited.

But when Kallin's superiors heard of her coup, they caused

[1] By prior appointment. The call number of the recording is T10145W.

[2] Oxford, 1958.

[3] If there was ever a transcript of the author's Flexner Lectures, this too has now disappeared.

her great embarrassment by ruling that Berlin was not a suitable Reith Lecturer. I have found no record of their reasons for this view. It may simply have been that Berlin was not sufficiently established at that time, and that the criteria for choosing Reith Lecturers were more conservative then than they are today. There is no evidence, at any rate, that anti-Semitism was at work. Whatever their reasons, the top brass were immovable, and Kallin had to break the news to Berlin. To her relief, he was not offended.[1]

A word should be said about Berlin's attitude to the publication of these transcripts. Broadly speaking, it was similar to his view of the publishability of his Mellon Lectures, delivered thirteen years later in Washington, DC, and published in 1999 as *The Roots of Romanticism*.[2] He knew that the transcripts ought to be heavily revised and no doubt expanded if they were to be brought to a state in which he could contemplate their appearance in book form in his lifetime. As he wrote to Kallin on 11 December 1951, 'You will easily perceive how it is one thing to say a lot of things in a general fashion to an audience and a very different one to commit words to cold print.' He certainly intended to publish a book based on the Bryn Mawr Lectures, and to do so within a year or two of their delivery, but, as in other cases, he never managed to complete the necessary work, and the

[1] I cannot now remember where I first heard this story: presumably from Berlin himself in conversation. But I checked it with him by letter in 1992, and in a letter dated 10 March 1992 he wrote: 'Anna Kallin did indeed wonder whether [the lectures] might make Reith Lectures – I was only too ready. She put it up, I had a letter inviting me to do them, followed by a letter two days later countermanding. That was that. I was asked to do the series seven or eight years later, and by that time said that I had nothing to say. That was before I thought of Romanticism.' Useful supplementary accounts of the genesis of the lectures and of Anna Kallin's role can be found in Michael Ignatieff, op. cit. (xii/1), 204–5, and Humphrey Carpenter, *The Envy of the World: Fifty Years of the* BBC *Third Programme and Radio 3, 1946–1996* (London, 1996), 127.

[2] London and Princeton, 1999; 2nd ed., Princeton, 2013.

long draft typescript on which both sets of lectures were based was laid aside and forgotten, despite the fact that he had revised it extensively. In 1993 I produced a fair copy of it for him, incorporating all his manuscript alterations and an introduction that he had written subsequently, but I do not believe he ever looked at it in any detail. Entitled 'Political Ideas in the Romantic Age' (the title under which the Flexner Lectures were delivered), it runs to over 110,000 words, and was finally published in 2006.[1]

I also gave Berlin an earlier draft of the edited transcript of the BBC talks that appears in this book, but this too he could not bring himself to inspect. I thought it almost certain that he would never turn to it, and once mentioned this belief to him, coupling it with an expression of regret. Perhaps out of kindness he said that I could not be certain that nothing would happen: "Who knows? In twelve years or so I might suddenly pick it up and feverishly revise it' (or words to that effect). But he was already well into his eighties, and this was not a task for a nonagenarian.

Despite his reservations, he did not think altogether badly of the lectures. He thought some were better than others, but he allowed, all the same, that 'tidied up' they 'might make a booklet'.[2] I thought they would do so even as they stood, and backed up my judgement by consulting experts who knew more than I do about the subject matter. They too found some lectures stronger than others, and some of the interpretations by now somewhat out of fashion; but there was general agreement on almost all hands that publication was highly desirable. I hope it goes without saying that the result is not to be taken as carrying Berlin's own full *imprimatur*; but I do believe that it fairly represents his views on these enemies of freedom, that it will help his readers to a

[1] *Political Ideas in the Romantic Age: Their Rise and Influence on Modern Thought*, ed. Henry Hardy (London and Princeton, 2006; 2nd ed., Princeton, 2014) (hereafter PIRA). I should perhaps make clear that this typescript played virtually no part in the construction of the text of the present volume.

[2] Letter to Henry Hardy of 28 March 1989.

fuller understanding of these views, and that it is no disservice to his reputation to add these remarkable lectures to his published *oeuvre*, so long as their provisional, extempore, informal nature is made crystal clear, and no greater claims are made for this volume than its origins justify.

The BBC lectures are not simply an abbreviation of the typescript prepared for the Flexner Lectures. Nor are they simply a re-run of the Flexner Lectures themselves, as the weekly summaries in Bryn Mawr's *College News*[1] make clear – though it is hard to itemise the differences in the absence of full transcripts or recordings of the earlier version. Berlin himself sometimes said that the two sets of lectures were more or less the same – for example, in a letter of 22 January 1953 to President Katharine E. McBride of Bryn Mawr College:

> I have thought of Bryn Mawr often when I delivered lectures substantially identical with those given under the auspices of Mary Flexner, over the radio in London, when instead of being faced with 100 faces, I looked at a neat functional table and cork-lined walls – and I fear preferred that on the whole: so terrified am I. These lectures have brought in the most astonishing volume of correspondence from the most extraordinary persons who appear to listen to such things and seem to be filled with inarticulate feelings and thought on the subject of history and politics which have come bursting out in the most surprising fashion, and to all of which I suppose I now have the duty of sending some kind of answer.

However, it is clear from the BBC and Bryn Mawr files that the lectures underwent considerable reorganisation before and after Berlin spoke in America, and it would in any case have been very uncharacteristic of him to deliver the same lectures twice, since

[1] 13 February to 19 March 1952. These summaries are reprinted in PIRA.

he was an obsessive reviser[1] and, besides, almost always created his lectures afresh on the podium, even if he drew on the same body of material on more than one occasion.

Berlin's description of his terror when facing an audience is a cue for the introduction of Lelia Brodersen,[2] who worked briefly as Berlin's secretary when he was at the College. She was doing graduate work there at the time, was therefore short of money, and was picking up earnings wherever she could find them. In a letter to a friend she gives the most vivid account of Berlin's lecturing style that I have seen:

> Monday evening I went to his lecture on Fichte & was appalled. He bowed hastily, established himself behind the lectern, fixed his eyes on a point slightly to his right & over the heads of the audience, & began as if a plug had been pulled out. For precisely an hour, with scarcely a second's pause & with really frightful speed, he poured forth what was evidently a brilliant lecture from the little I could catch of it. He never shifted the direction of his gaze once. Without a pause he swayed back & forth, so far that each time one was sure that he was going to topple over, either forward or backward. His right hand he held palm up in the palm of his left hand, & for the whole hour shook both hands violently up & down as if he were trying to dislodge something from them. It was scarcely to be believed. And all the time this furious stream of words, in beautifully finished sentences but without pauses except for certain weird signals of transition such as "... & so it is evident that Kant's idea of freedom was in some ways very dissimilar to the idea of freedom which Fichte held, well!" I was exhausted at the end, & yet I am sure that if ever I

[1] 'I am by nature a correcter and re-correcter of everything I do.' Berlin to Mrs Samuel H. Paul, Assistant to President McBride, 20 June 1951.

[2] Lelia Brodersen (1912–2006), later chief clinical psychologist of the child guidance clinic at Bryn Mawr College.

saw & heard anyone in a true state of inspiration it was then. It is really a tragedy that communication is almost impossible.[1]

To return to the history of the present text: the four chapters of the long typescript – and therefore also of PIRA – are entitled 'Politics as a Descriptive Science', 'The Idea of Freedom', 'Two Concepts of Freedom: Romantic and Liberal' and 'The March of History'. If further chapters were written as a basis for the last two lectures, they do not survive. Perhaps shortage of time prevented Berlin from drafting these, though in the case of Maistre he could make use of a typescript prepared some years before.[2] At any rate, what began as a treatment of six topics, though each topic was predominantly illustrated at Bryn Mawr (in most cases) by the ideas of two individuals, ended up focused on the six figures named in the present chapter titles. Before the final overall title was chosen the lectures are referred to in the BBC file as 'Six Enemies of Human Liberty', and I have adopted this as a useful subtitle. I have also separated out the first section of the first lecture as a general introduction to the whole series, since this is what it provides.

In many ways the editing of these lectures has been similar to that of Berlin's Mellon Lectures, though in this case there were more different versions of the transcripts, more authorial annotations

[1] Letter to Sheema Z. Buehne postmarked 2 March 1952. Another letter contains a highly recommended account of the experience of acting as Berlin's secretary. I am most grateful to the late Lelia Brodersen for sending me these letters, which are both posted at <http://berlin.wolf.ox .ac.uk/> under 'Letters on Berlin'.

[2] A revised version of this typescript, giving a fuller, and in some respects modified, account of Berlin's views on Maistre, appeared as 'Joseph de Maistre and the Origins of Fascism' in *The Crooked Timber of Humanity* (London, 1990; New York, 1991; 2nd ed., Princeton, 2013). The BBC lecture based on it also appeared, in advance of its inclusion in the present volume (and in a slightly adjusted form), as the Introduction to Joseph de Maistre, *Considerations on France*, ed. Richard A. Lebrun (Cambridge, 1994: Cambridge University Press).

of these, and more caches of relevant notes to rifle. I shall not repeat here what I said about the editorial process in my preface to *The Roots of Romanticism*. The main difference here has been the absence of recordings of all but one of the lectures. This has meant a greater role, here and there, for conjectural restoration of Berlin's words. The bulk of the book rests on uncorrected transcripts made by members of the BBC staff who, naturally enough, were not familiar with Berlin's voice or subject matter, and found the work hard going; at times they were defeated, and the transcript descends into near-gibberish. (To give just one example for fun, Saint-Simon appears as 'Sir Seymour'.)[1] Almost always, though, it is clear what Berlin was saying, even if the actual words are occasionally in doubt.

As usual, I have been helped by experts in my search for sources for Berlin's quotations, as I record in the preamble to the references.[2] But my greatest debt, and the reader's – apart, naturally, from that to the author – is to the late Anna Kallin, whose role in Berlin's intellectual career should not be underestimated. She determinedly pressed him, again and again, to speak on the radio. She cajoled and supported him through the lengthy process of recording, and where necessary re-recording, the lectures – a process which, characteristically, he found stressful (partly because it fed his lifelong self-doubt). She was a brilliant editor: 'you perform miracles of cutting, condensing, crystallising', writes Berlin in the letter to her from which I have already quoted, where he also refers to her 'magical hands'. Their correspondence makes clear how important the personal chemistry was between these two Russian-Jewish exiles. Berlin, then and later, needed an intellectual impresario to enable him to realise his full potential. Anna Kallin filled that role with providential effectiveness, and that is why I dedicated this book to her memory.

[1] See also 169, first note to 122.
[2] 269–70.

For the second edition I have added as an appendix a composite text of the early drafts of 'Two Concepts of Liberty' that provides readers with the earliest version of most of that celebrated and influential lecture, a lecture whose origins are to be found both in the lectures published in the present volume and in the longer version of the same material that appears in PIRA. I explain more fully in an introductory note to this appendix why I think these drafts worth publishing, and in a postscript I make use of them in an attempt to throw some light on three problems of interpretation that arise in the lecture's famous peroration.

Since this new edition has been reset, its pagination differs from that of the first edition. This may cause some inconvenience to readers who wish to follow up references to the first edition in the second. I have therefore posted a concordance of the two editions at *<http://berlin.wolf.ox.ac.uk/published_works/fib/concordance.html>*, so that references to one can readily be converted into references to the other.

In the second impression of the book I corrected a few errors in the first. I am grateful to Lady Berlin, George Crowder, Roger Hausheer and Noel Malcolm for drawing four of them to my attention. I have made further corrections in this new edition, and added some illustrations. The portrait of Félicien David on p. 138 is in the Collection Saint-Germain-en-Laye, Musée Municipal, and was photographed by L. Sully-Jaulmes.

Henry Hardy
Wolfson College, Oxford, May 2001
Heswall, September 2013

Introduction

THE SIX THINKERS whose ideas I propose to examine were prominent just before and just after the French Revolution. The questions they discussed were among the perennial questions of political philosophy, and, to the extent to which political philosophy is a branch of morals, moral philosophy also. Moral and political philosophy are vast subjects, and I do not here wish to analyse what they are. Suffice it to say that for our purposes we can, with a certain amount of exaggeration and simplification, reduce the questions to one and one only, namely: 'Why should an individual obey other individuals? Why should any one individual obey either other individuals or groups or bodies of individuals?' There are, of course, a great many other questions, such as 'Under what circumstances do people obey?' and 'When do they cease to obey?', and also questions apart from obedience, questions about what is meant by the State, by society, by the individual, by laws, and so forth. But for the purposes of political philosophy, as opposed to descriptive political theory or sociology, the central question seems to me to be precisely this one: 'Why should anyone obey anyone else?'

The six thinkers with whom I am concerned – Helvétius, Rousseau, Fichte, Hegel, Saint-Simon and Maistre – dealt with these questions at times not very distant from each other. Helvétius died in 1771 and Hegel in 1831; the period concerned is therefore not very much more than half a century. The six also have certain qualities in common in virtue of which it is interesting to consider them. To begin with, they were all born in what might be called the dawn of our own period. I do not know how to describe this period – it is often referred to as that of liberal democracy, or of the ascendancy of the middle class. At any rate, they were born at the beginning of a period of which we are perhaps living at the end. But whether or not this period is passing, as some people think, it is clear that these are the earliest thinkers to speak a language which is still directly familiar to us.

No doubt there were great political thinkers before them, and perhaps more original ones also. Plato and Aristotle, Cicero and St Augustine, Dante and Machiavelli, Grotius and Hooker, Hobbes and Locke enunciated ideas which in certain respects were more profound, more original, bolder and more influential than those of the thinkers I shall discuss. But these other thinkers are divided from us by history, we cannot read them altogether easily or with familiarity, they need a kind of translation. No doubt we can see how our ideas derive from the ideas of these earlier thinkers, but they are not identical with them, whereas I should like to maintain that the six thinkers in question speak a language which still speaks directly to us.

When Helvétius denounces ignorance or cruelty or injustice or obscurantism; when Rousseau delivers his passionate diatribes against the arts and the sciences and the intelligentsia, and speaks (or thinks he speaks) for the simple human soul; when Fichte and Hegel glorify the great organised whole, the national organisation to which they belong, and speak of dedication and mission and national duty and the joys of identifying oneself with other people in the performance of a common task; when Saint-Simon speaks of the great frictionless society of producers of the future, in which workers and capitalists will be united in a single, rational system, and all our economic ills, and with them all our other sufferings as well, will at last and for ever be over; when, finally, Maistre gives his horrifying picture of life as a perpetual struggle between plants and animals and human beings, a blood-soaked field in which men – puny, weak and vicious – are engaged in perpetual extermination of each other unless held back by the most vigorous and violent discipline, and only at times rise beyond themselves to some huge agony of self-immolation or self-sacrifice – when these ideas are enunciated, they speak to us and to our age.

This is another thing which is interesting about these thinkers. Although they lived towards the end of the eighteenth century and at the beginning of the nineteenth, the kind of situation to which they seem relevant, which they seem to have perceived, to have described with an uncanny insight, is often characteristic not so much of the nineteenth century as of the twentieth. It is our period and our time which they seem to analyse with astonishing foresight and skill. That, too, makes them worthy of our consideration.

When I say that they have these curious powers of prediction, I should like to say that they are prophets in another sense also. Bertrand Russell once said that the important consideration to keep in mind when reading the theories of the great philosophers (other than mathematicians or logicians, who deal with symbols and not with empirical facts or human characteristics) is that they all had a certain central vision of life, of what it was and what it should be; and all the ingenuity and the subtlety and the immense cleverness and sometimes profundity with which they expound their systems, and with which they argue for them, all the great intellectual apparatus which is to be found in the works of the major philosophers of mankind, is as often as not but the outworks of the inner citadel – weapons against assault, objections to objections, rebuttals of rebuttals, an attempt to forestall and refute actual and possible criticisms of their views and their theories; and we shall never understand what it is they really want to say unless we penetrate beyond this barrage of defensive weapons to the central coherent single vision within, which as often as not is not elaborate and complex, but simple, harmonious and easily perceptible as a single whole.

All our six thinkers had some such vision. What they did was bind it upon their disciples, their readers, and indeed even upon some of their opponents. For one of the ways in which a philosopher or a thinker can be great is by doing precisely that. One might almost say that thinkers may be divided into two kinds. In the first place there are those who answered questions which had previously been put, and which had tormented men before, and answered them with a degree of perception, of insight, of genius, in such a way that these particular questions never needed to be asked again, at least in the fashion in which they had been asked before. Newton, for example, was a thinker of this type. He answered questions which had puzzled many men before; he answered them with simplicity, with lucidity, and provided an answer of immense power and coherence. This could also be said of Berkeley and of Hume, and of thinkers who are not strictly professional philosophers, for example of Tocqueville, or of a novelist like Tolstoy. These are all people who answered the ancient, tormenting questions which had puzzled mankind for many centuries, and answered them in such a way that for some people at any rate this seemed to be the final solution.

But there are thinkers who are great in another way, namely, not by answering questions which had been put before, but by altering the nature of the questions themselves, by transforming the angle of vision from which the questions seemed to be questions; not so much by solving the problems as by so powerfully affecting the people to whom they talked as to cause them to see things 'in a very different light', in which what had been a puzzle and a question before no longer arose, or at any rate did not arise with quite such urgency. And if the questions are modified, the solutions no longer seem to be required. People who do this tamper with the very categories, with the very framework, through which we see things. This kind of tampering can of course be very dangerous, and can cast both light and darkness upon humanity. I have in mind thinkers like Plato and Pascal, Kant and Dostoevsky, who in some special sense are regarded as 'more profound', 'deeper' thinkers than other men of genius, because they penetrate to a level where they affect people in a way which transforms their entire vision of life, so that they come out, as it were, almost converted, as if they had undergone a religious conversion.

I do not wish to claim for the six thinkers that they were all, or all equally, men of genius, of dangerous genius, in this remarkable sense. What distinguishes them is that those who followed their views, those who were affected by them, were not affected by this argument or that argument, did not see such thinkers simply as the end of a long period of elaboration consisting of other thinkers of whom they were merely the leaders, or to whom they were merely superior in some way. Rather they were affected by them as one is affected by someone who suddenly transforms one's view of things by placing them in a different relationship from that in which they were before. In this respect, too, all six are thoroughly deserving of our close consideration.

There is another quality, and a more curious one, which is common to them. Although they all discussed the problem of human liberty, and all, except perhaps Maistre, claimed that they were in favour of it – indeed some of them passionately pleaded for it and regarded themselves as the truest champions of what they called true liberty, as opposed to various specious or imperfect brands of it – yet it is a peculiar fact that in the end their doctrines are inimical to what is normally meant, at any rate, by individual liberty, or political liberty. This is the liberty which was preached by the great English and French liberal thinkers, for example; liberty in the sense in which it was conceived by Locke and by Tom Paine, by Wilhelm von Humboldt and by the liberal thinkers of the French Revolution, Condorcet and his friends, and, after the Revolution, Constant and Madame de Staël; liberty in the sense in which the substance of it was what John Stuart Mill said that it was, namely the right freely to shape one's life as one wishes, the production of circumstances in which men can develop their natures as variously and richly, and, if need be, as eccentrically, as possible. The only barrier to this is formed by the need to protect other men in respect of the same rights, or else to protect the common security of them all, so that I am in this sense free if no institution or person interferes with me except for its or his own self-protection.

In this sense all the six thinkers were hostile to liberty, their doctrines were in certain obvious respects a direct contradiction of it, and their influence upon mankind not only in the nineteenth century, but particularly in the twentieth, was powerful in this anti-libertarian direction. There is hardly any need to add that in the twentieth century this became the most acute of all problems. Since the way in which these men formulated the problem, being among the earliest to do so, is particularly fresh, particularly vivid and particularly simple, the problem is often best examined in this pristine form, before it gets covered over with too many nuances, with too much discussion, with too many local and temporal variations.

Let us now return to the central question which all political philosophers sooner or later must ask: 'Why should anyone obey anyone else?' By the time Helvétius began writing, this question had been answered altogether too variously. He was living at a time when, in other provinces of human interest, in the sciences for example, enormous strides had been made, particularly in the late sixteenth century and the seventeenth century, by men like Galileo and Descartes and Kepler, and that group of distinguished Dutchmen whose names I shall not cite, and who contributed so much to the subject, although their unique merits are still relatively unrecognised.

But all these men were overtopped by Newton, whose eminence was unique in the annals of mankind. Among all the men of his age the radiation of his name and achievement really was the greatest. He was praised by the poets, he was praised by the prose writers. He was regarded almost as a semi-divine being. He was so regarded because people thought that at last the whole of physical nature had been adequately and completely explained. This was because Newton had triumphantly managed to express in very few, very simple and very easily communicable formulae laws from which every movement and every position of every particle of matter in the universe could in principle be deduced. Everything which had previously been explained by other means, sometimes theologically, sometimes in terms of obscure metaphysics, at last seemed bathed in the light of the new science. Everything was interconnected, everything was harmonious, everything could be deduced from everything else. The laws in terms of which this could be done were, again, very few and easily acquired by anyone who chose to take the trouble to learn them. One needed for this no special faculty, no theological insight, no metaphysical gifts, merely the power of clear reasoning and of impartial observation, and of verifying observations by means of specially arranged experiment wherever this was possible.

In the sphere of politics, in the sphere of morals, no such co-ordinating principle, no such authority, could apparently be found. If it was asked why I should obey the ruler or rulers of the State, why anyone should ever obey anyone else, the answers were altogether too many and too various. Because, as some said, this was the word of God, vouchsafed in a sacred text of supernatural origin; or perhaps by direct revelation to men whose authority in these matters is recognised through the medium of a Church; or perhaps given by direct revelation to the individual himself. Or because God had himself ordained the great pyramid of the world – that is what someone like Filmer said in the seventeenth century, for example, or the great French bishop Bossuet. The king must be obeyed because this is the order of the world, commanded by God, and perceived by both reason and faith, and the commands of God are absolute, and to ask for the source of their authority is itself impious. Because, said others, the command to obey the ruler is issued by the ruler, or by his agents. The law *is* what the ruler wills, and because he wills it, whatever his motive, it may not be examined at all. That is the theory of absolute monarchy.

Because, still other people said, the world has been created (or perhaps, as some said, exists uncreated) in order to fulfil a particular plan or purpose. This view is called natural teleology, according to which the universe is a kind of gradual unrolling of a divine scroll, or perhaps a self-unrolling of a scroll in which God is regarded as immanent. That is to say, the whole of the world is a kind of self-development, the gradual development of an incarnate architect's plan. In terms of this great plan everything in the universe has a unique place, that is, has a place which derives from its function, from the fact that it is needed by the plan to perform this particular task, live this particular life, if it is to fit into the general harmony. That is why everything in the universe is as it is and where and when it is, and acts and behaves as it does. I myself, since I am what I am, where I am and when I am, and in the particular circumstances in which I happen to be placed, must fulfil my function in such a place only by acting and being thus and thus, and not otherwise; by obeying this rather than that authority, because that is part of the plan, part of the scheme of things. If I do not do this, and of course in a minor way I may be able to obstruct the plan, then I shall be disturbing the harmony of the design, and frustrate others, and ultimately frustrate myself, and so be unhappy. In the end the plan is more powerful than I, and if I disobey it too far I shall be crushed by the gradual working out of the plan, which will sweep me away.

Some people modified this view and said it may not be absolutely indispensable that you fulfil your part of the plan, not quite inexorable, for the plan is not quite so tight and inevitable as all that, but perhaps it is the most convenient or economical or rational method of securing that necessary minimum which a man needs for the purpose of being happy, or being well, or anyhow in order that life should prove not too intolerable to him. There was still a plan, though you could live to some degree outside it, but not so well, not so comfortably, not so satisfyingly as by adjusting yourself to it.

These are by no means all the types of view which were expressed. Some said that I possess certain inalienable rights, implanted in me from birth by nature or by God (say rights to life or liberty or property), which were said to be inherent in me, clear for all considering men to see. These rights entailed the obligation to obey, and the right to be obeyed by, certain persons in certain ways on certain occasions. Again, there were people who said I must obey this or that king or government because I have undertaken to do it. This is the theory of the contract, the social compact, by which I have agreed to abide in my own interests, because I thought that unless I did so I should not obtain as much as I could in co-operation and collaboration with others. Or perhaps I never actually promised to do this myself, perhaps others promised this on my behalf. Or perhaps this promise never actually historically took place, but is 'implicit' in the way I behave. I behave as if it had taken place, even if it did not; and if I go back on it, then I shall be going back on my word, or somebody else's word on my behalf, and that is contrary to moral law, because promises ought to be kept. Others, again, said that I obey as I obey because I am conditioned to do so, by my education or by my environment, or by social pressure or by the fear of being made to suffer if I do not. There were still others who said that I was ordered to obey by something called the general will, or by an inner voice called conscience, or by something called moral sense, with which the general will is in some way identified, or of which it is a kind of socialised version.

There were, again, people who said that I obey because in doing so I fulfil the demand of the world spirit, or the 'historical mission' of my nation or my Church, or of my class or of my race, or of my calling. There were people who said I obey because

I have a leader and he has bound a spell on me. Or else I obey because I owe it to my family or to my friends, or to my ancestors or posterity, or to the poor and oppressed whose labours have created me – and I always do what is expected of me. Finally, it has been said that I obey because I wish to do so, because I like it, and I shall stop obeying when and as I please; or simply that I obey for reasons which I feel but cannot explain.

Some of these answers answer the question 'Why do I obey?' and some of them answer the question 'Why should I obey?', which of course is not the same question. Kant's very sharply drawn distinction between the two was destined to form a new period in the history of the entire subject. But what is important is that the entire topic had become a scandal in the eighteenth century. If scientific method could institute some degree of order in chemistry, in physics, in astrophysics, in astronomy and so forth, why did we have to be plunged into this dreadful chaos of conflicting opinions, with not a thread to guide us? Why should some assert one thing and others counter-assert another, some be faithful sons of the Church and some be atheists, some believe in metaphysics and others believe in a private conscience, some believe that the truth is to be found in a laboratory and others that it resides in some inspired teacher or prophet, so that nobody is able to institute the kind of order which Newton established in the great realm of nature? Naturally enough, men's wishes began to move towards the delineation of some simple single principle which would guarantee just such order and yield truths of just such an objective, general, lucid, irrefutable kind as had so successfully been obtained concerning the external world.

One of the people who made the most determined effort to do this is my first thinker, Helvétius.

Helvétius

Claude-Adrien Helvétius was born in 1715. He was a Frenchman of German origin – the family name had originally been Schweitzer, of which Helvétius is merely the Latin version. His father was physician to the Queen of France and he was himself a wealthy and gifted youth, who through his father and other connections obtained the patronage and friendship of some of the most talented and interesting men of his age – Voltaire, for instance, Montesquieu and Fontenelle. By profession he was a tax farmer; that is to say, he took a very prominent part in the financial administration of France and derived great profits from it. He was a man of charming and amiable disposition, and had many devoted friends. He became one of the leaders in his day of what came to be called the Enlightenment. His principal work is called *De l'esprit* ('On Mind'). He published it in 1758, but it was found to be so atheistical, so heretical, that it was condemned both by Church and by State, and was burnt by the public hangman. He had to make no fewer than three separate retractions of it. Nevertheless it is quite clear that, in spite of yielding to authority, in answer to the prayers of his wife and his mother-in-law, who were deeply upset by what had happened, he did not change his views. When his second book, which was called *De l'homme* ('On Man'), was published posthumously in 1773, it was found to contain precisely, or very nearly, the same impious doctrines.

Helvétius was very famous in his day. He travelled beyond France; he was well received by George II in England and by Frederick the Great in Germany, for he was much looked up to as one of the great leaders in the new enlightened movement of his time. His lifelong aim was the search for a single principle which was to define the basis of morality and really answer the questions about how society should be founded and how man should live and where he should go and what he should do, with the same degree of scientific authority that Newton had displayed in the realm of physics. And Helvétius thought he had found it, and therefore supposed himself to be the founder of a great new science, whereby he could put in order, at long last, this vast moral and political chaos. He thought himself, in short, to be the Newton of politics.

That the problem should have posed itself in that way is natural enough. Let me quote something from Condorcet, a radical Encyclopedist of very left-wing views born somewhat later than Helvétius, who died in one of Robespierre's prisons in Paris during the last year of the French Revolution:

> As one meditates about the nature of the moral sciences [and by that he of course means politics as well] one really cannot avoid the conclusion that since, like the physical sciences, they rest upon observation of the facts, they ought to follow the same methods, acquire a language no less exact and precise, and so attain to the same degree of certainty. If some being alien to our species were to set himself to study us he would find no difference between these two studies, and would examine human society as we do that of bees or beavers.

And then again he says:

> As mathematics and physics perfect the arts of supplying our simple needs, is it not part of the same order of nature that progress in the moral and political sciences should exercise the same effect on the motives which rule our actions and our feelings?

How was this to be done? Holbach, one of the other authors of the great Encyclopedia of knowledge, put it thus: 'Morality is the science of the relations which exist between the minds, wills and actions of men, in the same manner as geometry is the science of the relations that are found between bodies.' What is the geometry of ethics? What is the geometry of politics? How are we to reduce these sciences to the same degree of certainty and clarity as physics and geometry? Helvétius thought he had found the answer. Let me quote what he says. In the course of a dialogue between God and man (which, as Helvétius notoriously did not believe in God, is only a parable), he makes God say to man:

> I endow thee with sensibility. It is by this alone that thou, blind tool of my wishes, incapable of plumbing my aims, thou must, without knowing it, fulfil my purposes. Over thee I set pleasure and pain; the one and the other will watch over thy thoughts and acts, excite thy aversions, friendships, tender sentiments, joys, set on fire thy desires, fears, hopes, reveal to thee truths, plunge thee in error, and after causing thee to generate a million various absurd systems of morals and legislation, will one day disclose to thee the simple principles on the development of which depend the order and happiness of the moral world.

What is this but the first clear formulation of the principle of utilitarianism?

According to this principle, the only thing which men wish is pleasure, and the only things which men wish to avoid are pains. The pursuit of pleasure and the avoidance of pain are the only motives which in fact act upon men, as gravitation and other physical principles are said to act on inanimate bodies. At last we have discovered the central principle. If you want to know what it is that causes human beings to be as they are, that causes their characters to be what they are, that causes their acts to be as they are, that is responsible for their loves and their hates, their passions and their ideas, their hopes and their fears, it is this conscious or unconscious pursuit of pleasure and avoidance of pain.

This discovery excited Helvétius a great deal, because he thought it really gave him the key to the whole of social life. Not only did it give him the key to why men behave as they do, but it also seemed to him to give the key to the question: 'What are the proper ends for man?' For if men are capable of desiring only pleasure and avoidance of pain it is absurd to suggest that they should desire something other than what they can desire. If it is ridiculous to ask a tree to become a table, or to ask a rock to become a river, it is equally ridiculous to invite men to pursue something which they are psychologically incapable of pursuing. If it is a fact that they are conditioned by these two forces – love of pleasure and hatred of pain – then they will be happy if they go on pursuing pleasure, frictionlessly, efficiently and eternally.

The question, then, is this: 'Why are men not happy? Why is there so much misery, injustice, incompetence, inefficiency, brutality, tyranny and so forth on the earth?' The answer is that it is because men have not known how to obtain pleasure, how to avoid pain. They have not known this because they have been ignorant and because they have been frightened. They have been ignorant and frightened because men are not by nature good and wise, but their rulers have in the past seen to it that the great flock of men whom they have governed has been kept in artificial ignorance of the proper functioning of nature. This is a deliberate piece of chicanery on the part of the rulers, on the part of kings and soldiers and priests and other authorities whom enlightened persons in the eighteenth century so strongly condemned. The rulers are interested in keeping their subjects in darkness because otherwise the injustice, the arbitrariness, the immorality, the irrationality of their own rule will be altogether too easily exposed. So from the early beginnings of man an age-old conspiracy by the few against the many has been organised and kept going, because unless they do this the few cannot keep the many in subjection.

Man is entitled to happiness, to virtue, to truth. These three things go together, and men have been prevented from having them only by the wickedness of other men, by the weakness of their own nature, by their ignorance, by curable intellectual diseases of this kind. The first duty of the philosopher, therefore, is to apply a kind of social hygiene, to cure people of these easily remediable vices.

Ethics is a kind of technology, for the ends are all given. If you ask 'Why should we do what we do?' the answer is: 'Because we are made to do it by nature, because we cannot function otherwise.' If the ends are given there is no need to investigate those further. The only business of the expert, or the philosopher, is simply to create a universe in which the ends which men have to seek because they cannot help it are obtained with the least pain, most efficiently, most rapidly, most economically. Helvétius says as much. He says that the philosopher is really the architect of the edifice (he means the builder). The plan is there already, because it is discovered in nature; the plan is the seeking of pleasures and the avoidance of pain.

The 'physiocratic' philosophers, who were the leading economists of the eighteenth century, similarly say: Legislation is not the making of laws (that would be more properly called 'legisfaction'), legislation is the translation into legal terms of something which is to be found in nature: ends, purposes. The true ends of man are given; they can be discovered, as the laws of physics have been discovered; and the answer to the question why I should obey this or that king, this or that government, will simply be demonstrable in the way in which the laws of physics are demonstrable. If this or that course of action leads to greater happiness – if, that is, it conforms to the ends set for us by nature – then it is good, and if it detracts from happiness or frustrates it in some way, then it is bad. This is the simple rule of truth, and it ought to be applied everywhere.

Unlike some other thinkers of the eighteenth century, Helvétius did not have too high an opinion of human nature, in the sense of thinking man naturally benevolent. He thinks him neither benevolent nor malevolent, but infinitely flexible and pliable; a kind of natural stuff which nature and circumstances, but above all education, shape as they will. He therefore thinks that it is of no use merely to try to improve mankind by argument. The purpose of reform is to establish new institutions designed to maximise pleasure and minimise pain – to make people as happy as possible and eliminate all the causes of misery such as ignorance or injustice. But it is impossible to do this by precept. It is impossible to do it even by example. Preaching alone will not achieve much, because men are too ignorant, too blind; they are slaves to their passions, they are slaves to their own habits, they are slaves to meaningless and irrational loyalties. All the preaching of all the Christian preachers in the past has done little good because men are what they are, because of their evil education, their sad circumstances, their poverty, weakness, ignorance, fears – all the factors which have twisted them from their true purpose, which have made of them natural cripples.

How is this to be remedied? Only by artificial manipulation. Helvétius does not believe in automatic progress. Some celebrated thinkers of the eighteenth century did believe in that. The great minister Turgot and his friend Condorcet certainly believed in eternal progress: Helvétius did not. He supposes that there will be progress if a sufficient number of enlightened men with resolute wills and with a disinterested passion to improve mankind set themselves to promote it, above all if they convert the rulers of mankind – the kings, the ministers – and teach them the art of government, for government is certainly an art. It is the art of pursuing happiness. Like other arts it requires knowledge. Just as a man who wishes to build a bridge has to acquire a good deal of mathematics, mechanics, physics and so forth, so a man about to rule a State must know a considerable amount about anthropology, sociology, psychology, and indeed morals. Only when he discovers how men in fact function, what the laws which regulate conduct are, is he in a position to produce that which he wishes to produce. Without this he will make dreadful blunders and plunge mankind into miseries which are worse than his earlier state. In the late eighteenth century there was a reasonable hope that some of the rulers of the time would be amenable to this view of philosophical advice: Frederick the Great of Prussia, perhaps Catherine the Great in Russia, certainly Joseph II in Austria were obviously susceptible to this kind of enlightened teaching.

How is it to be achieved? What is the philosopher to do? How is he to transform the world? Not by preaching, because men will not listen. He must compass his purposes by much more drastic means. He must do so by legislation and by inventing a system of sticks and carrots for the human donkey. The philosopher, when he is in power, must create an artificial system of rewards and punishments which will reward men whenever they do what in fact leads to greater happiness, and punish them when in fact they do that which diminishes it. What human motives are is totally irrelevant. It does not in the least matter whether people contribute to happiness because they are benevolent and approve of it, or from some self-interested, base, mean motive of their own. It does not matter whether people prevent human happiness because they are malignant or vicious, or because they are ignorant blunderers or idealistic fools – the damage they do will be identical in either case, and so will the good. Therefore we must abandon all discussion of motives, which is really neither here nor there. It is of no use to try to operate against human prejudices, against human superstitions, because they can be cured only in some very long run. In the short run these things are too ingrained, and therefore, as the Italian thinker Pareto advised so cynically in the twentieth century, 'Do not fight prejudice; use it.'

That is precisely what Helvétius says. We, the enlightened reformers, must not try to convert people by reasoning, because their reason is not powerful enough, in the conditions of today, owing to the dreadful misgovernment of the past, to understand what it is that we tell them. We must substitute 'the language of interest', as he puts it, 'for the tone of injury'. Do not complain, appeal to interest.

'I do not care', said Helvétius, 'if men be vicious so long as they are intelligent. […] Laws will do everything.' Intelligent judges of their own interests, that is. That men principally pursue pleasure and avoid pain, and that the chief or only purpose of government is to make men happy – this, whether true or false, right or wrong, is a very ancient human doctrine, for which the eighteenth century can claim little originality. What is relatively new is the combination with this of the notion of using men's natural propensities without worrying about the moral or spiritual quality of these propensities or motives. This too is old: as old as Plato, the Assassins, or Machiavelli, or the practice of many religious sects and communities; but the alliance of it with rationalism, materialism, hedonism, belief in science, reason and a particular view of individualism is new. It is this that forms the heart of modern utilitarianism.

The legislator must use vices and weaknesses and play on vanities as well as the better feelings and worthier attributes of men. To get effective action he must make it worth men's while to do the things he wants them to do, not explain why he does it; make them do it whether they want to or not; and then, when, as a result of the social conditioning effected by the laws established by the enlightened philosophers, enough men have for a sufficient length of time done nothing but what contributes to happiness, then, in fact, they will insensibly acquire new and beneficent habits. It is their bad present habits which cause the misery, and it is their new good habits which will make them happy. They will not know how they will be making themselves happy; they may not, for a while at least, understand the working of their own new ways of living; but in fact they will be acquiring habits which will automatically produce happiness. The automatic production of happiness through the conditioning of society by men who have grasped the few, necessary rules about the right government of mankind, rules which can be obtained only by scientific observation, perhaps scientific experiment, and the application of reason to nature – that is the way to educate mankind.

After the proper coercive legislation has been established it is the turn of the educator. Now he need no longer be afraid of being stoned by his ignorant and outraged pupils. Once the laws protect him, he will be able safely to teach them virtue, knowledge and happiness. He will be able to teach them how to live. He will be able to explain to them why it is reasonable for them, for example, to pursue pleasure and avoid pain. He can explain to them why it is wrong to be an ascetic or a monk, why it is irrational, the product of misunderstanding of nature, to try to mortify the flesh or to be gloomy or to be melancholy. So gloom and melancholy will be driven from the earth: everybody will become joyous, harmonious and happy.

Helvétius gives precise instructions to his future educators. They must not waste time on history because history is nothing but the tale of the crimes and the follies of mankind. It may have certain lessons to teach us – one may teach history if it is only to show why it is that humanity, as a result of being ruled by knaves, as a result of being duped too much by its earlier rulers, has not done as well as it might. But to learn or to teach history for its own sake is surely absurd. Indeed, it is absurd to teach or do *anything* for its own sake. For the only end or purpose of action is to render people happy – which is, in brief, the doctrine of utilitarianism.

Similarly, the teaching of classical languages must be abandoned, for they are dead and of no practical interest to us now. All interest is practical interest. What people must be taught, consequently, are the sciences and the arts, and among the arts is that of being a citizen. There is to be no 'pure' learning; for nothing 'pure', without useful application, is desirable. 'Pure' learning is simply an old, medieval survival, something which derives from the days when ignorant men taught other ignorant men that there were certain things which were worth doing for their own sakes, for which no utilitarian reason could be given. Nowadays there is no need to do anything for which no reason can be given, and there must be a reason for doing whatever is to be done. The reason is the pursuit of happiness.

One of the direct consequences of this doctrine is an odd corollary about human rights. For generations men preached that every man has certain inalienable rights. It was one of the basic beliefs in the Christian tradition that man has an immortal soul, and because he has an immortal soul he must not be trampled on by other men. Men's souls – their reason – are sparks of a divine being, and in virtue of this they have certain 'natural' rights. They have the right to exercise their reason, and to enjoy certain things and be given certain things, in virtue of being sentient, being rational, and these rights are implanted in them by God or by nature. Eighteenth-century philosophers too talked a great deal about rights and indeed believed in them very strongly, but of course this is not consistent with a really thoroughgoing utilitarianism. To have a right which nobody may impinge upon, to have a right which nobody may trample, to have a right to do or be or have this or that, whether anybody likes it or not, is an obstacle to the transformation of society in the direction of the greatest happiness for the greatest number.

If I have what used to be called an imprescriptible right to, let us say, property, and even more to life itself, and to that limited degree of liberty which was usually recognised as being necessary for individuals – if I have such rights then the legislator, in trying to plan the world, may find himself faced with the obstacle of not being permitted to take something away from me which he needs to take away in order to produce a smooth, harmonious, completely frictionless society. But for a utilitarian this is clearly irrational. If the sole criterion of action is happiness and unhappiness, these odd rights which stick out in an obstinate way, and may not be smoothed over by the legislator, must be flattened out. Therefore, while of course Helvétius would maintain that everything which a human being naturally needs will be provided for in a benevolent State in which the legislator is the principal moving force, yet for him the persistence of rights which are absolute, which nothing may overcome, which are there whether other people like it or not, are made happy by them or not, are simply so many irrational survivals.

This is exactly what Bentham did eventually say. Bentham was a complete disciple of Helvétius, and although the word 'utilitarianism' is normally associated with him, I think it is fair to say that there is little – among the cardinal ideas, at least – in Bentham which does not stem directly from Helvétius. Bentham acknowledged intellectual debts very freely and generously, and he said that he had learned much from Helvétius. Even this seems to me to be an understatement.

How is the good, new society to be organised? Certainly it cannot be a democracy, for people are often stupid and often vicious, and we know that if we are guided by public opinion we shall seldom get anything done, because men have dwelt in darkness too long to be able to know what to do when they suddenly find themselves in the light of day. Men are liberated slaves, and for a long, long time must be guided by enlightened leaders, enlightened managers of human society. This is very much the view of the eighteenth-century liberals before Rousseau. 'Woe to us', says Voltaire, 'if the masses start reasoning'; and again, 'The people [. . .] are cattle and what they need is a yoke and a goad and fodder.' In the *Encyclopédie* – the great liberal encyclopedia which Diderot and d'Alembert edited, the most progressive document of its time, which got its editors into trouble with the clerical censorship in Paris – under the article entitled 'multitude' you will find the following passage: 'in intellectual questions [the masses'] voice is full of malignity, stupidity, inhumanity, perversity, prejudice. [... I]t is ignorant and idiotic [...] Beware of it in moral questions: it is incapable of noble or strong deeds: [...] heroism in its eyes is madness.' There is much praise for what was conceived, without much accurate knowledge of the facts, as the Chinese system, in which the mandarins, who alone are wise, do not listen to the masses, but gradually guide them towards a happier and freer and more enlightened existence by instituting laws which these masses do not understand, but by which they are insensibly drawn in a good direction, namely towards their own happiness.

The one principle to which Helvétius clings tenaciously is that education and laws can do anything. There was a great deal of discussion in the eighteenth century about what the factors are that most effectively condition men. Man is regarded by almost all the *philosophes* as an object in nature. They tend to look upon the notion of the immortal soul, which is something quite different from matter, as an obscurantist survival from an earlier period before the sciences had become dominant, when figments were invented to account for phenomena whose true causes had not yet been discovered. The soul is one of those figments and does not tell us what the real factors are which make men what they are. Some said that environment was the most important; others, the chemistry of the human body. Some, like Montesquieu, thought that climate was of cardinal importance, or kinds of soil or social institutions; and some, like Helvétius, declared that those factors had been much exaggerated, and that it was education which could transform anybody into almost anything. This became one of the central doctrines of the *philosophes*, whereby man is infinitely malleable, infinitely flexible. He is a piece of clay in the hands of the potter to mould as he pleases; that is why it is criminal irresponsibility to abandon man to his own devices and to let the ignorant and the malevolent deceive him into obedience, which does not in fact guarantee those ends which he really desires to achieve.

For Helvétius it is 'interest' alone that rules mankind; and this is very relative, for the interest of the ruler is not the same as the interest of the ruled, and the interest of men living in cold climates is not the same as the interest of those who live in warm ones. Nevertheless, it is always interest which is the central conditioning force. He brings this out in an amusing little parable. He asks us to imagine what the minute little gnats or flies who live in the high grass must feel about other animals which occur in their world. They see a large beast, to our eyes a sheep peacefully browsing in a meadow, and they say:

> Let us flee from this greedy and cruel animal, this monster in whose voracious jaws we and our cities will be swallowed up. Why can it not behave like lions and tigers? These kindly animals do not destroy our dwellings; they do not batten upon our blood. Just avengers of crime, they punish sheep for the cruelty sheep inflict upon us.

This is how the universe looks to a fly in the grass. This, no doubt, *mutatis mutandis*, is how the universe looks to every other creature in the universe from its own peculiar point of view. The business of the legislator is so to transform human beings that they shall no longer be preyed upon by ignorance, that their interest shall in fact coincide with what they think to be that interest, that their interest – which is the pursuit of pleasure and the avoidance of pain – shall in fact represent itself to them as such, and they shall not, in short, regard things as useful to them which are in fact useless. They shall not, indeed, suppose that sheep are cruel and bloodthirsty and tigers dignified and kind. They shall see things in their true light. They can see things in their true light only if, like scientists, they understand what the universe consists of, how it is governed, where it is going.

One thing is clear: in the kind of universe which Helvétius depicts there is little or no room for individual liberty. In his world men may become happy, but the notion of liberty eventually disappears. It disappears because liberty to do evil disappears, since everyone has now been conditioned to do only what is good. We have become like animals trained to seek only that which is useful to us. In this condition liberty, if it includes any licence to freewheel, the liberty to do now this, now that, to be able to choose even to destroy ourselves, if we want to – that kind of liberty will be gradually weeded out altogether by successful education.

Let me dwell a little on the presuppositions of this kind of system – this Brave New World (for that is what it comes to). To begin with, all questions of value are factual, and the answers discoverable by observation and reasoning. Ethics and politics are natural sciences. Some people are better at discovering their laws than others. There is such a thing as specific moral and political knowledge and skill, which specialists must have. These specialists should be given supreme power. Secondly, all ultimate ends are compatible with each other. They cannot clash. This proposition has often been refuted by human experience. For example, liberty, which is an ultimate purpose of some, has at times been found to be incompatible with equality, which is often an ultimate goal for others. It is difficult to see why honour should always and automatically be compatible with patriotism. The great tragedies – those written by the Greek dramatists as well as those of more modern days – are largely concerned with the fatal collision of values which cannot be reconciled. Precisely this was denied in the eighteenth century, because the most widespread belief of that age looked on nature as harmonious, and to say that nature was a harmony must mean to say that nothing real or valuable in it can conflict with anything else which is real or valuable.

In fact this belief rests on a false analogy from logic and geometry. Just as in logic and in geometry no true proposition can be incompatible with any other true proposition, so no value in the moral universe, if the moral universe is a harmony of which there is a science, can conflict with any other value, and Condorcet can say with great firmness that 'nature binds by an unbreakable chain truth, happiness and virtue'. From this it follows that whoever knows the truth completely is also virtuous and happy. Scientists know the truth, therefore scientists are virtuous, therefore scientists can make us happy, therefore let us put scientists in charge of everything. What we need is a universe governed by scientists, because to be a good man, to be a wise man, to be a scientist, to be a virtuous man are, in the end, the same thing. There is a great European tradition which supports this view, whereby scientific government is thought to be the best, and reformers are always, like H. G. Wells, asking angrily why we should not be governed by an elite of scientists. This attitude dates from the eighteenth century, when truth, happiness and virtue were regarded as incapable of conflict, since in the harmony of nature no values can conflict, and so all tragedy must be due to error. There is nothing inherently tragic in the world; all tragedy and conflict are curable and composable.

A further presupposition is that man is one with – continuous with – nature, and therefore there can be such a thing as a science of man; that man, like everything in nature, is malleable, plastic and alterable. This too may be questioned, but certainly the *philosophes* believed it. The Baron d'Holbach tells us that 'education is simply the agriculture of the mind': to govern man is like breeding animals. Hence, since ends are given and man is mouldable, the problem becomes a purely technological one: how to adjust men in such a way that they will live in peace, prosperity and harmony. Certainly men's interests do not automatically coincide. They will have to be adjusted, and this business of adjusting is the business of the legislator. As Helvétius says, the happiness of one man is not necessarily connected with the happiness of others. Social pressure and the philosopher – the enlightened philosopher – will link them. Hence the need for the despotism of an elite of scientists.

'And why not?' it may be asked. The great physiocrat Le Mercier de la Rivière did reason just like that: 'Euclid is a veritable despot, and the truths of geometry which he has bequeathed to us are truly despotic laws. The despotism of these laws and the personal despotism of the legislator are one and the same. They are the irresistible power of evidence.' If geometers may be despotic, why not philosophers? If we do not wish to escape from the truths of geometry, why from the truth of philosophers? Nature, and she alone, teaches philosophers what the true ends of men are. True, nature at all times speaks with too many voices. She said to Spinoza that she was a logical system, but to Leibniz that she was a congeries of souls. She said to Diderot that the world was a machine with cords, pulleys and springs, whereas to Herder she said that it was an organic living whole. To Montesquieu she talked about the infinite value of variety; to Helvétius of unalterable uniformity. To Rousseau she declared that she had been perverted by civilisations, sciences and the arts; whereas to d'Alembert she promised to reveal their secrets. Condorcet and Paine perceived that she implants inalienable rights in man; to Bentham she says this is mere '*bawling* upon paper' – 'nonsense upon stilts'. To Berkeley she reveals herself as the language of God to man. To Holbach she said that there was no God and Churches were conspiracies. Pope, Shaftesbury, Rousseau see nature as a marvellous harmony. Hegel sees her as a glorious field in which great armies clash by night. Maistre sees her as an agony of blood and fear and self-immolation.

What is nature? What is meant by 'natural'? It is a good question. Leslie Stephen tells us that an eighteenth-century English traveller in France once remarked that it was unnatural for soldiers to dress in blue, except, indeed, the Artillery or the Blue Horse. It is evident that nature speaks with too many different voices, and if we are taking instruction from nature we shall have too many conflicting lessons, and there will be no final solution, never the beginning of one. Helvétius was quite clear about what nature taught him. He *knew* that nature told him that the only thing which men could do and should do was to pursue pleasure and avoid pain, and upon this he erected the utilitarian system which, armed with the best will in the world, inspired by the purest of motives, directed as it was against injustice, against ignorance, against arbitrary rule, against all the horrors with which the eighteenth century was still filled, leads directly to what is ultimately a kind of technocratic tyranny. For the tyranny of ignorance, of fear, of superstitious priests, of arbitrary kings, of all the bogies fought by eighteenth-century enlightenment it substitutes another tyranny, a technological tyranny, a tyranny of reason, which, however, is just as inimical to liberty, just as inimical to the notion that one of the most valuable things in human life is choice for the sake of choice, not merely choice of what is good, but choice as such. It is inimical to this and in this way has been used as the justification both for Communism and for Fascism, for almost every enactment which has sought to obstruct human liberty and to vivisect human society into a single, continuous, harmonious whole, in which men are intended to be devoid of any degree of individual initiative. It is a very tight, well-built system; there is no room to move in it. Perhaps it can produce happiness; but it is not clear – it was not clear even in the eighteenth century, and certainly has not become clearer subsequently – that happiness is the sole value which men seek.

Rousseau

> Starting from unlimited freedom I arrive at unlimited despotism.
>
> Shigalev in Dostoevsky's *The Devils*

THE CELEBRATED HISTORIAN, Lord Acton, once observed about Jean Jacques Rousseau that he 'had produced more effect with his pen than Aristotle, or Cicero, or Saint Augustine, or Saint Thomas Aquinas, or any other man who ever lived'. And this observation, although obviously exaggerated, nevertheless conveys something which is not totally untrue. Against it may be cited the remark of Madame de Staël, who said: 'Rousseau said nothing new, but set everything on fire.'

What constitutes the greatness of Rousseau? Why is he regarded as an important thinker? What did he say? Did he make any new or original discoveries? Did he really say nothing new (is Madame de Staël right?), and if he did not, how is it that such words as Acton's can be applied to him at all?

Some say that his genius lies only in his wonderful eloquence, his hypnotic style, for example in the prose of the *Confessions*, a book very difficult for anyone to put down, a book which has had more effect upon readers than almost any similar work of literature. But was there then really nothing new in what Rousseau said? Was it really only old wine in new bottles? Some place his originality in the fact that, whereas previous thinkers addressed themselves to reason, Rousseau glorifies the passions. But this is scarcely true.

There is a great deal about passion and sentiment in Diderot and Helvétius, in Shaftesbury and Hume, who always say that, so far from suppressing men's feelings, as the more austere religions, and also philosophers like Plato and Spinoza, had demanded, man must not curb or maim his spontaneous nature. Certainly the emotions may have to be canalised or guided, but on no account must they be suppressed. On the contrary, more than any other thinkers who ever lived, the school of so-called empiricist thinkers in the eighteenth century stressed the value of feeling, of human spontaneity and warmth. No writer is more passionate, and indeed at times more sentimental, on that subject than Diderot.

If we look at Rousseau's writings, to all appearance the exact opposite is the case. Rousseau is not at all in favour of unbridled feeling. On the contrary, he says – and he has a great philosophical tradition behind him – that sentiments divide people, whereas reason unites them. Sentiments, feelings are subjective, individual, vary from person to person, country to country, clime to clime: whereas reason alone is one in all men, and alone is always right. So that this celebrated distinction, according to which Rousseau is the prophet of feeling against cold rationalism, is certainly, on the evidence of his writings, fallacious.

There are, according to Rousseau, certain questions about morals and politics, about how to live, what to do, whom to obey, to which many conflicting answers have been given by the accumulation of human feelings, prejudices, superstitions, played on by various causal – natural – factors, which have made men through the centuries say now this, now that. But if we are to obtain true answers to these questions, then this is not the way to do it. We must ask the questions in such terms as make them answerable; and that can be done only by means of reason. Just as in the sciences a true answer given by one scientist will be accepted by all other scientists who are equally reasonable, so in ethics and politics the rational answer is the correct answer: the truth is one, error alone is multiple.

This is all perfectly commonplace. Few philosophers have failed to say something of the kind, and Rousseau simply repeats the opinions of his predecessors in saying that it is reason which is the same in all men, and unites, and emotions which are different, and divide. What then was it that was so very original? Rousseau's name is, of course, associated with the 'social contract', but there is nothing new in that either. The notion that men in society, in order to preserve themselves, have had historically to enter some kind of compact; or if not historically, at any rate that they behave as if they had done so; that men in society, because some are stronger than others, or more malevolent than others, have had to set up institutions whereby the weak majority is able to prevent the strong minority from riding roughshod over them – that is an idea certainly as old as the Greeks.

What, then, is it, apart from minor variations, that Rousseau added to this theme? Some might say he effected a reconciliation between individual liberty and the authority of the community. But this was one question which had been discussed times out of number by his predecessors. Indeed, the central question which occupied thinkers like Machiavelli and Bodin, Hobbes and Locke, was this very question. Nothing is more familiar or more natural in the history of political thought than the question 'How is men's desire for liberty to be reconciled with the need for authority?' It is clear to all political thinkers that individuals wish to be free – that is to say, they wish to do whatever they wish to do, without being prevented from doing it by other people, or coerced into doing something they do not want to do – and that this freedom from coercion is one of the chief ends or values for the sake of which people are prepared to fight, one of the ends whose realisation is indispensable for leading the kind of life which most men wish to lead.

On the other hand, of course, there is the necessity for organised existence. Men do live in society, for whatever cause or reason; and because men live in society, individuals cannot be allowed to do whatever they like, because this may get in the way of other people, and frustrate their ends too much. Therefore some kind of social arrangement has to be made.

Among earlier thinkers this very central problem had led to various answers. It led to answers which varied in accordance with the view of the human individual taken by these different thinkers. Hobbes, who took a somewhat low view of human nature and thought that man on the whole was bad rather than good, savage rather than tame, thought that strong authority was necessary in order to curb the naturally wild, unruly and bestial impulses of man; and therefore drew the frontier between authority and liberty in favour of authority. He thought that a good deal of coercion was needed to prevent human beings from destroying each other, from ruining each other's lives, from creating conditions in which life would be perilous, nasty, brutish and short for the vast majority of society. Therefore he left the area for individual liberty rather small.

Locke, on the other hand, who believed that men were good more than wicked, thought that it was not necessary to draw the frontier quite so far in favour of authority, and held that it was possible to create a society in which some of those rights which, according to him, men possessed before they entered into societies – while they were in the 'state of nature' – were still retained by them even in civil society; and allowed men a good many more individual rights than Hobbes did, on the ground that they were more benevolent by nature, and that it was not necessary to crush them, coerce them and restrain them to quite the severe degree demanded by Hobbes in order to create that minimum of security which alone enables society to survive.

But the point I wish to make is that the argument between them is simply an argument about where the frontier is to be drawn, and the frontier is a shifting one. In the Middle Ages, when political thought was largely theological, this took the form of disagreement about whether original sin, which made man wild, wicked, voracious and unruly, was something stronger in him than natural or God-given reason, which made him seek after good and proper ends, implanted in him by God. In more secular ages, when these concepts became insensibly translated into secular terms, the same argument as to where the frontier was to be drawn took a more secular historical or psychological form. The question now was: 'How much liberty and how much authority? How much coercion versus how much individual freedom?' Some compromise had to be reached: and you simply arrived at the solution – at the estimation of where the frontier must be drawn – in accordance with what seemed to you to be the true constitution of human nature, in the light of, perhaps, such scientific data as the influence of climate, of environment, and other similar factors, which a thinker like Montesquieu, for example, takes into such great consideration.

The original aspect of Rousseau's teaching is that this entire approach will not do at all. His notion of liberty and his notion of authority are very different from those of previous thinkers, and although he uses the same words, he puts into them a very different content. This, indeed, may be one of the great secrets of his eloquence and of his immense effectiveness, namely that, while he appears to be saying things not very different from his predecessors, using the same kinds of sentences, and apparently the same concepts, yet he alters the meanings of the words, he twists the concepts in such a fashion that they produce an electrifying effect upon the reader, who is insensibly drawn by the familiar expressions into wholly unfamiliar country.

Rousseau says one thing and conveys another. He appears to be arguing along old-fashioned lines, but the vision which he projects before the reader is something totally unlike the schema which he appears to borrow from his predecessors. Let us take, for example, such central concepts in his teaching as the notion of liberty, the notion of contract, the notion of nature.

First, liberty. For Rousseau the whole idea of compromising

liberty, of saying 'Well now, we cannot have total liberty, because that will lead to anarchy and chaos; we cannot have complete authority, because that will lead to the total crushing of individuals, despotism and tyranny; therefore we must draw the line somewhere between, arrange a compromise' – this kind of thinking is totally unacceptable. Liberty for him is an absolute value. He looks on liberty as if it were a kind of religious concept. For him, liberty is identical with the human individual himself. To say that a man is a man, and to say that he is free, are almost the same.

What is a man for Rousseau? A man is somebody responsible for his acts – capable of doing good and evil, capable of following the path either of right or of wrong. If he is not free, this distinction becomes meaningless. If a man is not free, if a man is not responsible for what he does, if a man does not do what he does because he wants to do it, because this is his personal, human goal, because in this way he achieves something which he, and not somebody else, at this moment desires – if he does not do that, he is not a human being at all: for he has no accountability. The whole notion of moral responsibility, which for Rousseau is the essence of man almost more than his reason, depends upon the fact that a man can choose, choose between alternatives, choose between them freely, be uncoerced.

If a man is coerced, coerced by somebody else, by a tyrant, or even by material circumstances, then it is absurd to say that he chooses; for Rousseau he becomes a thing, a chattel, an object in nature, something from which no accountability can be expected. Tables and chairs, and even animals, cannot be regarded as doing right and wrong, for they either do not do anything, or know not what they do, and if they do not know they cannot be said to act; and not to act is not to be a human being. Action is choosing, choosing implies selection between alternative goals. Someone who cannot choose between alternative goals because he is compelled is to that extent not human. This would be the case if he is an object determined in nature, as the physicists had taught, simply a bundle of nerves and blood and bones, a collection of atoms, as much under the sway of material laws as the inanimate objects of nature. Alternatively, if he is determined not as things are determined in nature, but in another way – because he is bullied or coerced by a tyrant, because he is made the creature of somebody else who plays upon his fears, or his hopes, or his vanity, and is manipulated like a puppet – a creature like that is equally not fully capable of freedom, not fully capable of action, and is therefore not fully a human being.

There is no saying but what a man in this condition – for Rousseau, a slave – might not be happy, but happiness is not the goal of men: the goal is to live the right kind of life. Therefore, for Rousseau, the proposition that slaves may often be happier than free men does not begin to justify slavery, and for this reason he sharply and indignantly rejects the utilitarianism of people like Helvétius. Slavery may be a source of happiness: but it is monstrous all the same. For man to wish to be a slave may be prudent, but it is disgusting, detestably degrading. For 'slavery [...] is against nature', and the unanimity of servitude is quite different from the unanimity of a genuine assembly of men. 'To renounce liberty', declares Rousseau, 'is to renounce being a man, to surrender the rights of humanity, and even its duties. [...] Such a renunciation is not compatible with man's nature.'

This means that for a man to lose his liberty is for him to cease to be a man, and that is why a man cannot sell himself into slavery, for once he becomes a slave, he is no longer a man, and therefore has no rights, no duties, and a man cannot cancel himself out, he cannot commit an act whose consequence is that he can commit no further acts. To do this is to commit moral suicide, and suicide is not a human action – 'death is not an event in life'. Liberty, therefore, for Rousseau, is not something which can be adjusted or compromised: you are not allowed to give away now a little of it, now much more of it; you are not allowed to barter so much freedom for so much security, so much freedom for so much happiness. To yield 'a little' of your liberty is like dying a little, dehumanising yourself a little; and the belief which is most passionately held by Rousseau, one of the values to which he devoted more eloquence than to almost any other, is this notion of human integrity, the fact that the ultimate crime, the one sin not to be borne, is dehumanisation of man, degradation and exploitation of man. He spends a great deal of his passionate rhetoric on denouncing those who use other people for their own selfish purposes – not because they make the people whom they use unhappy, but because they deform them, they make them lose their human semblance. That is, for him, the sin against the Holy Ghost. In short, human freedom – the capacity to choose ends independently, autonomously – is for Rousseau an absolute value, and to say of a value that it is absolute is to say that one cannot compromise over it at all.

So far so good. Rousseau has made clear that his attitude towards man entails regarding liberty as the most sacred of human attributes – indeed not as an attribute at all, but as the essence of what being a man is. But there are other values too. It is impossible simply to declare that freedom, individual freedom, permission for men to do what they like, a situation in which anybody does anything, is the ideal condition of man. This is for two reasons. In the first place there is the empirical or historical reason. For one reason or another, for one cause or another, men do live in societies. Why this happens, Rousseau never quite clearly explains. Possibly it is because of the inequality of gifts, which makes some men stronger than others, and enables them to assert their power over others, and so enslave them. Perhaps also because of some inevitable law of social evolution, perhaps because of some natural instinct of sociableness which drives people to live together. Perhaps, again, for some such reasons as those which the Encyclopedists spoke of: division of labour and co-operation for the purpose of leading a life which satisfies a greater number of human wishes, and the wishes of more individuals, than the isolated life of savages could satisfy.

Sometimes Rousseau talks about the savage as if he was happy, innocent and good; at other times as if he was merely simple and barbarous. But be that as it may, men do live in society, and consequently have to create rules whereby human beings must so conduct themselves as not to get in each other's way too much, not frustrate each other excessively, not employ their power in such a way as to thwart too many of each other's purposes and ends. So now we are faced with the problem: How is a human being to remain absolutely free (for if he is not free, he is not human), and yet not be allowed to do absolutely everything he wants? Yet if he is stopped, how can he be free? For what is freedom, if it is not doing what he wants, and not being stopped from doing it?

Secondly, there is also for Rousseau a further and a deeper reason for coercion. Rousseau was, after all, a citizen of Geneva, and deeply affected by its Calvinist traditions; and therefore, for him, there is an ever-present vision of the rules of life. He is deeply concerned about right and wrong, about justice and injustice. There are certain ways of living which are right, and certain ways of living which are wrong. In common with the rest of the eighteenth century he believes that the question 'How should I live?' is a real question; and therefore, however we may come by it, by reason, or by some other route, that there is some answer to it.

Given that I have obtained this answer – or that I think I have obtained it – it will take the form of rules of life which, in effect, say 'Do thus: do not do thus', or statements of the form 'This is wrong: this is right. This is just: this is unjust. This is good: this is bad. This is handsome: this is ugly.' But once we have rules, once we have laws, principles, canons, once we have some kind of regulations which prescribe conduct, what is to happen to liberty? How can liberty be compatible with regulations, which after all hem man in, prevent him from doing absolutely anything he wants, tell him what to do and what not to do, forbid him to do certain things, control him to a certain degree?

Rousseau is very passionate about this. He says that these laws, these rules of life, are not conventions; they are not utilitarian devices invented by man simply for the purpose of achieving some short-term, or even long-term, subjective purpose. Not at all. Let me quote from him again. He speaks of 'the law of nature, the sacred imprescriptible law which speaks to the heart of man and to his reason', and says that it is 'graven on the hearts of men better than all the rubbish of Justinian'. The power of willing or of choosing the right path, he claims, is not explicable by any mechanical laws. It is something inherent in man, and the subject matter of no natural science. The moral laws which man obeys are absolute, something from which man knows that he must not depart. In this respect Rousseau's view is a secular version of Calvinism, for the one thing which he perpetually insists upon is that laws are not conventions, are not utilitarian devices, but simply the drawing up in terms suitable to the particular time and place and people of regulations embodying sacred truths, sacred rules which are not man-made, but eternal, universal and absolute.

So we have a paradox. We have two absolute values: the absolute value of freedom and the absolute value of the right rules. And we are not allowed to compromise between them. We are not allowed to do what Hobbes thought might be done, namely to establish a de facto regime allowing so much freedom, so much authority, so much control, so much individual initiative. Neither of the absolute values may be derogated from: to derogate from freedom is to kill man's immortal soul; to derogate from the rules is to permit something absolutely wrong, absolutely bad, absolutely wicked, to fly against the sacred source of the rules, called sometimes nature, sometimes conscience, sometimes God – but which in any case is absolute. This is the dilemma in which Rousseau is plunged, and it is very different from the problem of those previous thinkers who believed in adjustment, in compromise, in empirical devices as means for finding a solution which would of course not be ideal, but adequate; neither wholly good nor wholly evil, but more good than evil; something enabling human beings to carry on not too badly, reasonably well; something based upon common sense and due respect, moderate, decent respect for most of each other's wishes, so that people on the whole get, not indeed all they want, but protection for minimal 'rights', and more than they would get under some other system. This kind of outlook, typical of Hobbes and Locke, Helvétius and Mill, is for Rousseau totally unacceptable. An absolute value means that you cannot compromise, you cannot modify; and he puts this in a very dramatic fashion. He says that the problem for him is 'to find a form of association [...] in which each, while uniting himself with all, yet may still obey only himself alone and remain as free as before'.

This certainly puts the paradox in an appropriately paradoxical form. How can we at one and the same time unite ourselves with other people, and therefore found a form of association which must exercise some degree of authority, of coercion – very different from being entirely free or solitary in a state of nature – and yet remain free, that is, not obey these same people?

Rousseau's world-famous answer was given by him in the *Social Contract*, and it is that each man, 'in giving himself to all, gives himself to nobody'. This celebrated formula, evocative as it is, is as dark and mysterious now as it ever was. Rousseau loved paradox, but his strangeness as a thinker goes deeper than that. He was obviously deeply tormented by the dilemma of freedom versus moral authority, on neither horn of which he wished to impale himself. Then suddenly there came to him a blinding solution to it. In a letter to Malesherbes he gives a vivid account of how this revelation dawned upon him. He was on his way to visit his friend Diderot in prison when the solution of the problem of human vice and virtue came upon him with a blinding flash of inspiration. He felt like a mathematician who had suddenly solved a long and torturing problem, like an artist to whom a vision had suddenly been vouchsafed, like a mystic who had suddenly seen the truth, the transcendental beatific truth itself. He tells us how he sat down at the roadside and wept and was beside himself, and how this was the central event of his entire life. The tone in which he communicates the answers to the ancient puzzles, both in the *Social Contract* and in other works, is exactly that of a man possessed by a single idea, of a maniac who suddenly sees a cosmic solution vouchsafed to him alone, somebody who for the first time in history has suddenly found the answer to a riddle which had for centuries tormented the whole of humanity, which previous great thinkers, perhaps Plato, perhaps the founder of Christianity, had in some degree anticipated, but which he and he alone had at last found in its full richness, so that nobody need trouble to look for the solution again.

He is, at such moments, like a mad mathematician who has found a solution which is not merely true, but demonstrable, by rules of such iron logic that nobody will ever reopen the question. What is this solution? Rousseau proceeds like a geometer, with two lines which intersect each other at one point and one only. He says to himself: 'Here is liberty and here is authority, and it is difficult – it is logically impossible – to arrange a compromise. How are we to reconcile them?' The answer has a kind of simplicity and a kind of lunacy which maniacal natures are often capable of. There is no question of compromise. The problem must be viewed in such a way that one suddenly perceives that, so far from being incompatible, the two opposed values are not opposed at all, not two at all, but one. Liberty and authority cannot conflict for they are *one*; they coincide; they are the reverse and obverse of the same medal. There is a liberty which is identical with authority; and it is possible to have a personal freedom which is the same as complete control by authority. The more free you are, the more authority you have, and also the more you obey; the more liberty, the more control.

How is this mysterious point of intersection to be achieved? Rousseau's solution is that, after all, freedom simply consists in men wanting certain things and not being prevented from having them. What, then, do they want? What I necessarily want is that which is good for me – that which alone will satisfy my nature. Of course, if I do not know what is good for me, then when I get what I want, I suffer, because it turns out not to be what I had really wanted at all. Therefore those alone are free who not merely want certain things but also know what, in fact, will alone satisfy them.

If a man knows what will satisfy him, then he is endowed with reason; and reason gives him the answer to the question: 'What should I seek for in order that I may be – that my nature may be – fully satisfied?' What is true for one rational man will be true for other rational men, just as, in the case of the sciences, what one scientist finds to be true will be accepted by other scientists; so that if you have reached your conclusion by a valid method from true premisses, using correct rules, you may be certain that other people, if they are rational, will arrive at the same solution; or alternatively, if you feel sure of the rationality of your thought, but they arrive at some different solution, this alone shows you that they cannot possibly be rational; and you may safely ignore their conclusions.

Rousseau knows that, since nature is a harmony (and this is the great premiss, the great and dubious premiss of almost all of eighteenth-century thought), it follows that what I truly want cannot collide with what somebody else truly wants. For the good is what will truly satisfy anyone's rational demands; and if it were the case that what I truly want does not tally with what somebody else truly, in other words rationally, wants, then two true answers to two genuine questions will be incompatible with each other; and that is logically impossible. For that would mean that nature is not a harmony, that tragedy is inevitable, that conflict cannot be avoided, that somewhere in the heart of things there is something irrational, that do what I may, be I never so wise, whatever weapons of reason I employ, however good I am, however upright, however clear-headed and reasonable and profound and wise, I may yet want something when an equally wise, equally good and virtuous man may wish the opposite of it. There will be nothing to choose between us: no criterion of morality, no principle of justice, divine or human. Therefore tragedy will turn out, after all, to be due not to human error, human stupidity and human mistakes, but to a flaw in the universe; and that conclusion neither Rousseau nor any other prominent eighteenth-century thinker, with the exception, perhaps, of the Marquis de Sade, accepts. But Sade was a notoriously vicious madman, and when Voltaire and Hume hinted at something of the kind, this was put down to the cynicism of the one and the scepticism of the other, in neither case to be taken too seriously; indeed neither Voltaire nor Hume were any too anxious to stress this aspect of their thought.

Consequently, if nature is a harmony, then anything which satisfies one rational man must be of such a kind as to be compatible, at any rate, with whatever satisfies other rational men. Rousseau argues that all that is necessary is for men not to seek the kind of ends which conflict with the ends of others. Why do they now tend to seek such ends? Because they are corrupt, because they are not rational, because they are not natural; and this concept of nature in Rousseau, although in certain respects like the concept of nature in other thinkers, nevertheless acquires a tone of its own. Rousseau is sure that he knows what it is to be a natural man: to him to be natural is to be good, and if all men were natural, they would all be good; what they would then seek would be something which would make each and all of them satisfied, taken together, as a single harmonious whole. For the unanimity of rational beings, willing rational ends which, *ex hypothesi*, are one single end, though willed by many individual wills, is a very singular affair. Let me quote him again: 'As long as several men in the assembly regard themselves as a single body they have only a single will [...]. The constant willing of all the members of the State is the general will.' This 'general will' is something that 'penetrates into a man's innermost being, and concerns itself with his will no less than with his actions'.

We may well, at this point, ask what this general will is. What is there about these men in the assembly that generates something which can be called a single will which holds for them all? Rousseau's answer is that, just as all men who argue rationally reach the same truth about matters of fact (politics and morals apart), and these truths are always necessarily compatible, so men in the same condition of nature – that is to say, unperverted, uncorrupted, not pulled at by selfish interests, not pulled at by regional or sectional interests, not enslaved by fear or by unworthy hopes, men not bullied, not twisted out of their proper nature by the wickedness of other men – men in that condition must want that which, if it is obtained, will be equally good for all other men who are as good as they are. Therefore, so long as we are able somehow or other to regain, to recapture, what is for him the original innocent state of nature in which men were not yet prey to the many passions, to the many wicked and evil impulses, which civilisation has bred in the human breast, natural harmony, happiness and goodness will once more be the lot of human society.

Rousseau's notion of the natural man was, naturally, affected by the kind of man he was. Rousseau was a petit bourgeois from Geneva who lived his early life as a tramp, and who was at odds with the society of his time, and was the prey of many kinds of what nowadays are called inferiority complexes. Consequently his notion of a natural man is the idealised opposite of the kind of persons whom he particularly detested and disliked. He denounces not merely the rich, not merely the powerful: few moralists have failed to regard these two classes as the natural enemies of society. He denounced, and is almost the first to denounce, a very different set of persons, and by this means deeply affected the consciousness of the next century. For all that he was a composer and a musical theorist, he detested the arts and the sciences; he disliked every form of sophistication, every form of refinement, every form of fastidiousness. He is the first person to say quite explicitly and openly that the good man is not merely simple, not merely poor – sentiments which many a Christian thinker has held – he goes further and thinks that the rough is better than the smooth, the savage better than the tame, the disturbed better than the tranquil. Rousseau is filled with deep resentment of cliques, of coteries, of sets; above all he suffers from a deep resentment of intellectuals, of those who take pride in cleverness, of experts or specialists who set themselves up over the heads of the people. All those nineteenth-century thinkers who are violently anti-intellectual, and in a sense anti-cultural, indeed the aggressive philistines of the next two centuries – whom Nietzsche called *Kulturphilister* – including Nietzsche himself, are the natural descendants of Rousseau.

Rousseau's tormented and tortured nature made him look with eyes of hatred upon people like Diderot, d'Alembert, Helvétius in Paris, who seemed to him fastidious, sophisticated and artificial, incapable of understanding all those dark emotions, all those deep and torturing feelings which ravaged the heart of a true natural man torn from his native soil. The natural man, for him, was somebody who possessed a deep instinctive wisdom very different from the corrupt sophistication of the towns. Rousseau is the greatest militant lowbrow of history, a kind of guttersnipe of genius, and figures like Carlyle, and to some extent Nietzsche, and certainly D. H. Lawrence and d'Annunzio, as well as *révolté*, petit bourgeois dictators like Hitler and Mussolini, are his heirs.

It is difficult, and indeed gratuitous, to classify this as a right-wing or a left-wing phenomenon. It is mainly a kind of petit bourgeois revolt against a society from which the *déclassé* feels excluded. Rousseau makes common cause with the outcasts, the rebels, the free wild artists. That is what makes him the founder of romanticism and wild individualism, as well as the founder of so many other movements of the nineteenth century – of socialism and communism, of authoritarianism and nationalism, of democratic liberalism and anarchism, of almost everything save what might be called liberal civilisation, with its fastidious love of culture, in the two centuries which followed publication of the *Social Contract*.

Rousseau hates intellectuals, hates persons who detach themselves from life, hates specialists, hates people who lock themselves up into some kind of special coterie, because he feels that hearts ought to be opened, so that men may achieve emotional contact; that the simple peasant sitting under the ancestral oak has a deeper vision of what life is like, and what nature is like, and what conduct ought to be, than the buttoned-up, priggish, fastidious, sophisticated, highbrow person who lives in the city. Because he feels all that, he founds a tradition distinct from that of the romantic rebel, which then spreads all over Europe, and then to the United States, and is the foundation of that celebrated concept called the American way of life, in accordance with which the simple people of a society possess a deeper sense of reality, a deeper virtue and a deeper understanding of moral values than professors in their universities, than the politicians of the cities, than other people who have somehow become de-natured, who have somehow cut themselves off from the inner stream which is at once the true life and the true morality and wisdom of men and societies.

That is the kind of impression which Rousseau communicates when he talks about nature, and although we are told that there are at least sixty senses in which the word 'nature' is used in the eighteenth century, Rousseau's usage is unique. He goes further than anybody in identifying nature not merely with simplicity, but with a genuine loathing of civilised, elaborate, sophisticated artistic or scientific values. Neither artists nor scientists must guide society – that is why he dislikes Helvétius and the Encyclopedists so acutely. Society must be led by the man who is in touch with the truth, and the man who is in touch with the truth is somebody who allows this divine grace, who allows the truth which nature alone possesses, to pour into his heart. This may be done only in the bosom of nature, only if we live the simple life. At first the simple life in Rousseau is merely a description of the kind of conditions in which the true answer may be vouchsafed. To those who crave for it, gradually it becomes that truth itself: it becomes difficult to distinguish, both in *Émile* and *La Nouvelle Héloïse*, between the conditions for knowing the answers to questions, and the answers themselves. For Rousseau, ultimately, the answer resides in being a certain kind of person: in having one's heart in the right place. To have a certain kind of knowledge – that is the key to all the problems.

In theory Rousseau speaks like any other eighteenth-century *philosophe*, and says: 'We must employ our reason.' He uses deductive reasoning, sometimes very cogent, very lucid and extremely well-expressed, for reaching his conclusions. But in reality what happens is that this deductive reasoning is like a straitjacket of logic which he claps upon the inner, burning, almost lunatic vision within; it is this extraordinary combination of the insane inner vision with the cold rigorous straitjacket of a kind of Calvinistic logic which really gives his prose its powerful enchantment and its hypnotic effect. You appear to be reading logical argument which distinguishes between concepts and draws conclusions in a valid manner from premisses, when all the time something very violent is being said to you. A vision is being imposed on you; somebody is trying to dominate you by means of a very coherent, although often a very deranged, vision of life, to bind a spell, not to argue, despite the cool and collected way in which he appears to be talking.

The inner vision is the mysterious assumption of the coincidence of authority and liberty. The coincidence itself derives from the fact that, in order to make men at once free and capable of living with each other in society, and of obeying the moral law, what you want is that men shall want only that which the moral law in fact enjoins. In short, the problem goes somewhat as follows. You want to give people unlimited liberty because otherwise they cease to be men; and yet at the same time you want them to live according to the rules. If they can be made to love the rules, then they will want the rules, not so much because the rules are rules as because they love them. If your problem is how a man shall be at once free and yet in chains, you say: 'What if the chains are not imposed upon him? What if the chains are not something with which he is bound as by some external force? What if the chains are something he chooses himself because such a choice is an expression of his nature, something he generates from within him as an inner ideal? If this is what he above all wants in the world, then the chains are no longer chains.' A man who is self-chained is not a prisoner.

So Rousseau says: 'Man is born free, and yet he is everywhere in chains.' What sort of chains? If they are the chains of convention, if they are the chains of the tyrant, if they are the chains of other people who want to use you for their own ends, then these are indeed chains, and you must fight and you must struggle, and nothing must stand in the way of the great battle for individual self-assertion and freedom. But if the chains are chains of your own making, if the chains are simply the rules which you forge, with your own inner reason, or because of the grace which pours in while you lead the simple life, or because of the voice of conscience or the voice of God or the voice of nature, which are all referred to by Rousseau as if they were almost the same thing; if the chains are simply rules the very obedience to which is the most free, the strongest, most spontaneous expression of your own inner nature, then the chains no longer bind you – since self-control is not control. Self-control is freedom. In this way Rousseau gradually progresses towards the peculiar idea that what is wanted is men who want to be connected with each other in the way in which the State forcibly connects them.

The original chains are some form of coercion which the tyrant used to employ in order to force you to do his will, and it is this which poets have so wickedly embellished with their garlands; it is this which writers have so fulsomely and so immorally tried to camouflage by the encomia which they have paid to mere force, to mere authority. But what is wanted is something very different. What is wanted – I quote Rousseau again – is 'the surrender of each individual with all his rights to the whole community'. If you surrender yourself to the whole community, then how can you not be free, for who coerces you? Not X, not Y, not this or that institution – it is the State which coerces you. But what is the State? The State is you, and others like you, all seeking your common good. For Rousseau there does exist a common good, for if there were not something which is the common good of the whole society, which does not conflict with individual goods, then to ask 'How shall we live? What shall we, a group of men together, do?' would be senseless, and that is patently absurd.

Consequently Rousseau develops the notion of the general will. It begins in the harmless notion of a contract, which after all is a semi-commercial affair, merely a kind of undertaking voluntarily entered into, and ultimately revocable also, an act performed by human beings who come together and agree to do certain things intended to lead to their common happiness; but still only an arrangement of convenience which, if it leads to common misery, they can abandon. This is how it begins; but from the notion of a social contract as a perfectly voluntary act on the part of individuals who remain individual and who pursue each his own good, Rousseau gradually moves towards the notion of the general will as almost the personified willing of a large superpersonal entity, of something called 'the State', which is now no longer the crushing leviathan of Hobbes, but something rather more like a team, something like a Church, a unity in diversity, a greater-than-I, something in which I sink my personality only in order to find it again.

There is a mystical moment in which Rousseau mysteriously passes from the notion of a group of individuals in voluntary, free relations with each other, each pursuing his own good, to the notion of submission to something which is myself, and yet greater than myself – the whole, the community. The steps by which he reaches it are peculiar and worth examining briefly.

I say to myself that there are certain things which I desire, and if I am stopped from having them, then I am not free; and this is the worst thing which can befall me. I then say to myself, 'What is it that I desire?' I desire only the satisfaction of my nature. If I am wise, and if I am rational, well-informed, clear-sighted, then I discover in what this satisfaction lies. The true satisfaction of any one man cannot clash with the true satisfaction of any other man, for if it clashed, nature would not be harmonious and one truth would collide with another, which is logically impossible. I may find that other men are trying to frustrate me. Why are they doing this? If I know that I am right, if I know that what I seek is the true good, then people who oppose me must be in error about what it is that they themselves seek. No doubt they too think that they are seeking the good, they assert their own liberty to secure it, but they are seeking it in the wrong place. Therefore I have a right to prevent them. In virtue of what have I this right to prevent them? Not because I want something that they do not want, not because I am superior to them, not because I am stronger than they are, not even because I am wiser than they are, for they are human beings with immortal souls, and as such my equals, and Rousseau passionately believes in equality. It is because, if they knew what they truly wanted, they would seek what I seek. The fact that they do not seek this means that they do not *really* know – and it is 'truly' and 'really' which, as so often, are the treacherous words.

What Rousseau really wishes to convey is that every man is potentially good – nobody can be altogether bad. If men allowed their natural goodness to well out from them, then they would want only what is right; and the fact that they do not want it merely means that they do not understand their own nature. But the nature is there, for all that. For Rousseau, to say that a man wants what is bad, although potentially he wants what is good, is like saying that there is some secret part of himself which is his 'real' self; that if he were *himself*, if he were as he ought to be, if he were his true self, then he would seek the good. From that it is but a small step to saying that there is a sense in which he already seeks this good, but does not know this. It is true that if you ask him what it is that he wants, he may enunciate some very evil purpose. But the true man inside him, the immortal soul, that which would speak out if only he allowed nature to penetrate his breast, if only he lived the right kind of life, and viewed himself as he really is, his true self, seeks something else.

I know what any man's true self seeks; for it must seek what my own self seeks, whenever I know that what I am now is my own true self, and not my other, illusory, self. It is this notion of the two selves which really does the work in Rousseau's thought. When I stop a man from pursuing evil ends, even when I put him in jail in order to prevent him from causing damage to other good men, even if I execute him as an abandoned criminal, I do this not for utilitarian reasons, in order to give happiness to others; not even for retributive reasons, in order to punish him for the evil that he does. I do it because that is what his own inner, better, more real self would have done if only he had allowed it to speak. I set myself up as the authority not merely over my actions, but over his. This is what is meant by Rousseau's famous phrase about the right of society to force men to be free.

To force a man to be free is to force him to behave in a rational manner. A man is free who gets what he wants; what he truly wants is a rational end. If he does not want a rational end, he does not truly want; if he does not want a rational end, what he wants is not true freedom but false freedom. I force him to do certain things which will make him happy. He will be grateful to me for it if he ever discovers what his own true self is: that is the heart of this famous doctrine, and there is not a dictator in the West who in the years after Rousseau did not use this monstrous paradox in order to justify his behaviour. The Jacobins, Robespierre, Hitler, Mussolini, the Communists all use this very same method of argument, of saying men do not know what they truly want – and therefore by wanting it for them, by wanting it on their behalf, we are giving them what in some occult sense, without knowing it themselves, they themselves 'really' want. When I execute the criminal, when I bend human beings to my will, even when I organise inquisitions, when I torture men and kill them, I am not merely doing something which is good for them – though even that is quite dubious enough – I am doing that which they truly want, though they may deny it a thousand times. If they do deny it, that is because they do not know what they are, what they want, what the world is like. Therefore I speak for them, on their behalf.

This is Rousseau's central doctrine, and it is a doctrine which leads to genuine servitude, and by this route, from this deification of the notion of absolute liberty, we gradually reach the notion of absolute despotism. There is no reason why human beings should be offered choices, alternatives, when only one alternative is the right alternative. Certainly they must choose, because if they do not choose then they are not spontaneous, they are not free, they are not human beings; but if they do not choose the right alternative, if they choose the wrong alternative, it is because their true self is not at work. They do not know what their true self is, whereas I, who am wise, who am rational, who am the great benevolent legislator – I know this. Rousseau, who had democratic instincts, leaned not so much towards individual legislators as towards assemblies, assemblies which, however, were right only to the extent to which they resolved to do that which the reason inside all the members of the assembly, their true self, genuinely desired.

It is in virtue of this doctrine that Rousseau lives as a political thinker. The doctrine did both evil and good. Good in the sense that he stressed the fact that without freedom, without spontaneity, no society is worth having, that a society as conceived by the Utilitarians of the eighteenth century, in which a few experts organised life in a sleek and frictionless manner, so as to endow the largest number of people with as much happiness as possible, is repulsive to a human being, who prefers wild, unruly, spontaneous freedom, provided that it is he himself who is acting; prefers this even to the maximum of happiness if that results from being worked into an artificial system, not by his own will, but by the will of some superior specialist, some manager, some arranger of society in a set pattern.

The evil that Rousseau did consists in launching the mythology of the real self, in the name of which I am permitted to coerce people. No doubt all inquisitors, and all the great religious establishments, sought to justify their acts of coercion, which subsequently may have appeared, to some people at any rate, cruel and unjust; but at least they invoked supernatural sanctions for them. At least they invoked sanctions which reason was not allowed to question. But Rousseau believed that everything could be discovered by mere untrammelled human reason, by mere unobstructed observation of nature, of actual three-dimensional nature, of nature simply in the sense of objects in space – human beings and animals and inanimate objects. Lacking the aid of supernatural authority, he therefore had to resort to the monstrous paradox whereby liberty turns out to be a kind of slavery, whereby to want something is not to want it at all unless you want it in a special way, such that you can say to a man: 'You may think that you are free, you may think that you are happy, you may think that you want this or that, but I know better what you are, what you want, what will liberate you', and so on. This is the sinister paradox according to which a man, in losing his political liberty, and in losing his economic liberty, is liberated in some higher, deeper, more rational, more natural sense, which only the dictator or only the State, only the assembly, only the supreme authority knows, so that the most untrammelled freedom coincides with the most rigorous and enslaving authority.

For this great perversion Rousseau is more responsible than any thinker who ever lived. The consequences of it in the nineteenth and twentieth centuries need not be enlarged upon – they are still with us. In that sense it is not in the least paradoxical to say that Rousseau, who claims to have been the most ardent and passionate lover of human liberty who ever lived, who tried to throw off every shackle, the restraints of education, of sophistication, of culture, of convention, of science, of art, of everything whatever, because all these things somehow impinged upon him, all these things in some way arrested his natural liberty as a man – Rousseau, in spite of all these things, was one of the most sinister and most formidable enemies of liberty in the whole history of modern thought.

Fichte

MORE THAN ANY OTHER German thinker, Johann Gottlieb Fichte appears to me to be responsible for launching an idea of freedom which is in sharp contrast and disagreement with that notion of freedom or liberty normally held by Western – that is to say, principally English, French and American – thinkers in the late eighteenth century and the nineteenth century.

Suppose that you were travelling about Europe at some time between the years 1800 and 1820. You would have discovered, to your surprise, that although the word 'freedom' was on every lip from the East to the West – although, if anything, the Germans and Austrians talked about it with more passion and eloquence even than people in France and in England – yet the meaning attached to the word differed widely between the two parts of Europe. It bore a very different sense in Germany from that which it appeared to have for thinkers in the great Anglo-French tradition.

What does 'freedom' mean for the principal political writers of the West at this time, for Condorcet, say, for Tom Paine, for Benjamin Constant – three representative thinkers, all of whom felt passionately on this subject, and all writers whose ideas had a very considerable influence both on contemporaries and on posterity? Let me quote a specimen passage from Constant, a very moderate, sensible liberal whose political writings belong to the beginning of the nineteenth century and who spoke for a large body of liberal democrats of his time. In a lecture delivered in 1819, in which he compares what he calls the modern with the ancient notion of liberty, he asks what his contemporaries mean by 'liberty'. This is his definition:

> It is the individual's right to be subject only to law, his right not to be arrested or detained or put to death or maltreated in any way as the result of the arbitrary will of one or several persons. It is every man's right to express his opinion, to choose his craft and exercise it, to dispose of his property, even to misuse it if he wishes; to come and go without getting permission for it, and without having to give any account of his reasons or motives. It is each man's right to associate himself with others, whether to discuss his own interests or to profess his religion, if he wishes, with his associates, or simply to pass his days and hours in any manner that accords with his inclination or his fancy. Finally it is everyone's right to influence the conduct of the government whether by nominating some or all of its public servants, or by representations, petitions, demands, which the authorities are more or less compelled to take into its consideration.

Then he adds that in the ancient world it was not so; there, although in some sense the individual was sovereign in public affairs, he was much more controlled and restricted in his private life; whereas in modern States, even in democratic States, the individual seemed comparatively powerless to influence the decisions of the political authorities; and fought precisely for this right.

That is a fair sample of what the word 'liberty' meant to moderate defenders of it in the early nineteenth century. But you would find that it was very different in the Germany of this period.

Fichte was always saying that liberty was the only subject with which he was at all concerned. 'My system, from beginning to end, is merely an analysis of the concept of freedom, [...] no other ingredient enters into it.' Then he warns the reader – and warns him very clearly – by insisting that his doctrine is very dark, and the language is not to be understood by ordinary men; that a special act of transformation or conversion or illumination is needed before the deep significance of his inspired utterance can be understood at all.

> To men [Fichte declares] as they are in their ordinary education, our philosophical theory must be absolutely unintelligible, for the object of which it speaks does not exist for them; they do not possess that special faculty for which, and by which, alone this object has any being. It is as if one were talking to men blind from birth; men who know things and their relations only by touch, and one spoke to them about colours and the relations of colours.

The reason why it is so unintelligible to ordinary men is that they are not endowed with the special, profoundly metaphysical faculty of perceiving such invaluable truths, which are open only to a very few men in each generation. Fichte regards himself as one of these few. His grasp of the essence of freedom is due to this special penetration into the nature of the universe. Let me explain this a little further.

The principal preoccupation of many Western European thinkers was to guard the liberty of the individual against encroachment by other individuals. What they meant by liberty was non-interference – a fundamentally negative concept. Treated in that way, it is the subject of the great classical thesis – the essay *On Liberty* by John Stuart Mill, which to this day remains the most eloquent, the most sincere and the most convincing plea for individual freedom ever uttered.

This is what liberty meant to Condorcet. This is what it meant to the majority of those French rebels who raised revolutionary standards in order to liberate the individual, and then sent their armies across Europe in order to liberate other nations. The assumption is that each individual has certain tastes, certain desires, certain inclinations, and wishes to lead his life in a certain fashion. Certainly he cannot be allowed to do so wholly, because if he does he will interfere too much with the similar ends of others. But a certain vacuum round him has to be created, a certain space within which he may be allowed to fulfil what might be called his reasonable wishes. One should not criticise these wishes. Each man's ends are his own; the business of the State is to prevent collisions; to act as a kind of traffic policeman and nightwatchman, as the German socialist Lassalle contemptuously observed later in the century; simply to see to it that people do not clash with each other too much in the fulfilling of those personal ends about which they themselves are the ultimate authorities. Liberty means non-encroachment; liberty therefore means non-impingement by one person on another.

Rousseau put this very clearly when he said: 'The nature of things does not madden us, only ill will does.' Slavery means being a slave to a person, not to the nature of things. Of course, we use the word 'freedom' in various metaphorical senses also. We speak of people not merely as being literally slaves, in the sense in which Uncle Tom was a slave to Simon Legree in the novel *Uncle Tom's Cabin*, but also in the sense in which a man is said to be a slave to his passions, a slave to the bottle, a slave to this, that or the other obsession. This sense of being a slave, though widespread, is nevertheless a metaphor; it is quite clear that there is a more literal and concrete sense in which, if a man is tied to a tree or imprisoned, he cannot by any possible perversion of language be said to be free; whereas a man who simply suffers from other kinds of inability is not usually described as a *slave*. There are all sorts of things I may be unable to do, but this does not make me a slave. I cannot fly to the sky with wings; I cannot count beyond five million; I cannot understand the works of Hegel. There are all sorts of things which I say I cannot do. But because I cannot understand the works of Hegel, and because I cannot fly through the air at more than a certain velocity, I do not describe myself as a slave. To be a slave is not the same thing as to be unable to do something; to be a slave is to be *prevented* from doing something, not by the nature of things, but by other persons.

Even economic slavery, which is often referred to in socialist writings, simply means that it is idle to offer rights to people who cannot use them; idle to give the penniless and the starving the right to purchase food and clothes for which they have not got the money. This is usually put by saying that political liberty is useless without economic liberty; but the assumption behind it is that they cannot buy these things, not because of some natural disability, as a cripple cannot walk a long distance because he is a cripple, but because other persons are preventing them. So long as there is not this notion of prevention by persons, the notion of liberty does not arise. Liberty is being free from the intervention, from the interference, of other persons. When they interfere accidentally, the lack of freedom is due to bad luck or mismanagement; when they do it deliberately, it is called oppression.

All this may hold for the thinkers of the West, where the principal problem was to put an end to what were regarded as the arbitrary rules of certain individuals self-constituted as authorities over the vast majority. But there is also another notion of freedom, which blossomed among the Germans, and to this we must now turn our attention.

The Germans were worried evidently not so much by ill will, on which Rousseau laid stress, as by the nature of things, which Rousseau had pronounced irrelevant. To them freedom seemed to mean freedom from the iron necessities of the universe – not so much from wicked or foolish persons, or social mismanagement, as from the rigorous laws of the external world.

To some extent this is due to the political state of the Germans in the eighteenth century. The Germans were, throughout this period, suffering from the appalling humiliation inflicted upon them by the victories of Richelieu and Louis XIV of France in the seventeenth century; and from political divisions, economic impotence, and the general obscurantism and backwardness of the average German citizen in the century which followed the Thirty Years War. Another factor of genuine importance was the absolute dependence of the German on the arbitrary will of the Prince, which gave him a sense of being a humbler citizen of the universe than the triumphant French or the free and proud English.

To such a man, what does it mean to be free? If you are living in sad circumstances, the first thing which impinges upon your consciousness is that there are very few things you *can* do. Either you have not the material means, or your ruler is unjust, brutal or stupid. Or there are too many natural misfortunes which rain down upon you. Or there is some other way in which you are hemmed in: you are placed in situations where the number of things which you can do is very small. The thought of freedom becomes at once something which is in practice unrealisable and, as an ideal, deeply and passionately desirable.

The reaction to this situation, which often occurs in the history of humanity, was to say, 'If I cannot get what I want, then perhaps by depriving myself of the want itself I shall make my life happier. Evidently I shall not be made happy by pining to get what powerful persons or adverse circumstances will not let me have. But perhaps by killing within myself the desire for these things I shall achieve that calm and that serenity which is as good a substitute for owning the things which I want as can be found in this vale of tears.'

This was the mood in which, when the Greek city State was declining, the Stoics and the Epicureans argued. This was the mood in the first century AD in which the Roman Stoics of that period, and indeed the early Christians also, preached their great sermons. This is indeed a truth which became particularly vivid for the Germans of the eighteenth century. There are many things which I want, but circumstances will not let me have them. Well then, I must defend myself against this outer universe, I must somehow contract the area which is vulnerable to these adversities. Instead of trying to lunge forward and obtain things which I cannot get, and merely being defeated and destroyed in the process, I must make a strategic retreat. I must go to a place where the tyrant and evil fortune cannot reach me. If I do not expose so much of myself, so great a surface, to these adverse factors, perhaps I shall be safer.

This is psychologically, and indeed sociologically, in part responsible for the doctrine of the unassailable inner life. I try to contract myself into my private world. I say to myself, 'The tyrant wants to deprive me of every opportunity of advancement, the tyrant wants to destroy my substance; very well, let him do so – these things do not matter. What he can have, let him have; I shall cut these things off from myself, for they are of no value to me. If I do not want to keep them, I shall not miss them if they are taken away.' It is a curious, strategic retreat into an inner citadel. I say to myself, 'If I preserve my own spirit, my inward serenity, if I keep myself to my own inner thoughts, if I cultivate inner ideals, the tyrant cannot reach that realm. If my body is exposed to his power, let him have it; if my wealth is something which he can confiscate, let him have it. I shall concentrate upon what is out of his reach – my inner spirit, my inner self.' This is the source of the re-emergence of the doctrine, which has its roots deep both in Christianity and in Judaism, of the two selves: the spiritual, inner, immaterial, eternal soul; and the empirical, outer, physical, material self, which is a prey to every misfortune, which is subject to the iron laws of the material world, from which no man may escape.

For natural scientists in the seventeenth and eighteenth centuries, and for some of the *philosophes* of the eighteenth century, too (according to whom man is but a collection of molecules like every other object in nature, and subject to the unalterable laws which govern such molecules), to protest against nature is folly, for we cannot change the material laws of the universe, the physics of it, however oppressive we may find this. And there is no way out.

So there are two enemies from which I must escape. One is the inexorable material laws that govern matter; and the other is the arbitrary willpower of wicked men, the caprice of fortune, and unhappy circumstances. I escape these by what I should like to describe as a very sublime, very grand form of the doctrine of sour grapes. I say that if I cannot have these things, then I do not want them. If I can only kill the desire in myself, the non-satisfaction of it will not irk me. In short, it is a doctrine which says that a desire satisfied and a desire killed come to much the same thing. But this entails various paradoxes. Is a man happier if he has forty desires of which he satisfies only ten, or if he has only two desires and satisfies them both? If freedom means doing what I want, is not a man happier – and freer – who wants less, and therefore has less to do, than a man who wants more and can do far less of what he wants?

It is Rousseau, again, who said that that man is truly free who 'desires what he is able to perform, and does what he desires'. If I desire little, the area within which I can be frustrated is correspondingly smaller. If this view is pushed to the uttermost, it leads almost to suicidal conclusions – literally suicidal ones. I have a pain in my leg. There are two ways of curing it: one is by applying medicine, but the other is by cutting off my leg. The tyrant oppresses me. There are two ways of resisting him: by killing the tyrant, or by making myself impervious to his blows, by not thinking about him, by giving him all he wants, by losing all desire to keep anything of which conceivably, in a moment of the wildest aberration, he might want to rob me. That is essentially the doctrine of the inner self as something not open to any possible attack on or invasion of the outer self – a self about which I no longer care, and which indeed may hurtle on through space, governed by the laws of physics, and a plaything of wickedness or blind chance.

In Kant's case this led to certain very important consequences which had a profound influence on Fichte and on all the German Romantic philosophers and thereby on European consciousness generally. Among these is the doctrine that the only thing which is valuable in the universe is a certain state of this true inner spiritual self. Happiness is something which I may or may not get: it is out of my reach. It depends upon too many material circumstances. To say therefore that the human goal is happiness is to doom man to perpetual frustration and self-destruction. The true ideal cannot rest on something which depends on external circumstances; it must depend upon an inner ideal, and the living up to this inner ideal; upon fulfilling something which my true self commands me to do. The true ideal is to obey the laws of morality. If the laws are issued by some outside force, then I am not free, then I am a slave. But if I order myself to do these things, then, as Rousseau had already said, I am no longer a slave, for I control myself; I am the author of my own conduct, and that is freedom.

Kant's profound notion is that what matters, the only thing which is a supreme value for us (and by value one means an end pursued for its own sake, not as a means to something else), the goal which itself justifies everything else and needs no justification in its turn, that for the sake of which we do what we do, and abstain as we abstain, that for the sake of which we act as we act, and, if need be, die – such a sacred, ultimate principle, which governs our conduct, is ordained to us by ourselves. That is why we are free. Therefore, Kant says, the most sacred object in the universe, the only thing which is entirely good, is the good will, that is to say the free, moral, spiritual self within the body.

It is alone sacred, for what else could be sacred, what else could be valuable? I do what I do for the sake of fulfilling the law which I impose upon myself. Utilitarians say that the proper purpose of action is to make as many people happy as possible, and of course, if that is the goal, then it may be possible to sacrifice human beings, even innocent human beings, for the happiness of the rest. Others again say that I must do that which a sacred text, or a religion, or God has ordained, or do that which the king has ordered me to do, or that which I find myself desiring, or that which my moral system (which I inherit or acquire without questioning it) permits, makes possible.

For Kant this is a kind of blasphemy. For him the only ultimately valuable thing in the universe is the individual human being. To say of a thing that it is valuable is to say that it is an ideal of a human being, something which a human being – as a rational being, he adds – orders himself to do. To what could a human being be sacrificed? Only to something which is superior to, more authoritative, more valuable than, that human being. But nothing can be more valuable than the principle which a human being believes in, for to say of a thing that it is valuable is to say that it is either a means towards, or identical with, something which somebody seeks, for its own sake, wills for its own sake, wills as a rational being.

Kant did talk a great deal about how important it is to emphasise the element of rationality (though what he meant by that has always been very far from clear, at least to some among his students); and he thought that all rational men would therefore necessarily desire the same general kind of conduct. Whether he was right about that or wrong I shall not here ask: that would take us too far afield. What is important to remember in the doctrine is that to say of a thing that it is valuable is to say that it is an ideal for the inner self which must not be impinged upon, must not be ravaged, or enslaved, or exploited, or destroyed, by any outside force. Hence Kant's passionate defence of the individual as the individual. The only thing which is ultimately wrong for him, as it is for Rousseau (though Kant is much more explicit and violent on the subject), is to deprive a human being of the possibility of choice. The only thing which is an ultimate sin is to degrade or humiliate another human being, to treat another human being as if he were not the author of values; for all that is valuable in the universe is what people honour for its own sake. To deceive somebody, to enslave him, to use another human being as a means for my own ends – this is to say that this other human being's ends are not as rational, as sacred as my own; and this is false, because to say of a thing that it is valuable is to say that it is an end, the end of any rational human being. Hence this passionate doctrine, according to which I must respect other human beings, the only entities in the universe to whom I owe absolute respect, because they are the only beings which create values, fulfil values, the only beings whose activities are that for the sake of which everything else is worth doing, for the sake of which life is worth living, or, if need be, sacrificing.

From this it follows further that morality, moral rules, are not something which I can discover as I can discover factual states of affairs. The whole of the eighteenth century – and not merely the eighteenth century, almost the whole history of philosophy, with the exception of the theology of the Jews and the Christians – insists that moral questions can be answered in the way in which other factual questions can be answered. Indeed, I tried to explain earlier how Helvétius and all his friends preached exactly that. For Kant that is not altogether true, and for his successors it becomes less and less true.

To discover what I ought to do I have to hearken to the inner voice. The voice issues commands, injunctions; preaches ideals which I must live up to. To command, to order, to tell me what to do, to issue what Kant called the categorical imperative, is not to say that something *is* the case. It is no use looking in the outside world for moral goals. Moral goals are not things; moral goals are not states of affairs like a growing tree; they are not facts like the fact that Julius Caesar crossed the Rubicon. They are orders or commands, and commands are not true or false, they are not something which can be discovered by observation. Commands may be right or wrong, they may be profound or shallow, they may be wicked or virtuous, they may be intelligible or unintelligible, but they do not *describe* anything. They order, they enjoin and they stimulate.

This is a very important moment in the history of European consciousness. Morality is seen to be not a collection of facts to be discovered by special faculties for discovering moral facts, as many philosophers, from Plato to our own day, have believed to be true; morality is rather something which is ordered, and therefore cannot be discovered. It is invented, not discovered, made, not found. In this respect it becomes akin to artistic creation. Kant, who speaks of objective, universal rules in some sense discovered by the right use of reason, certainly does not draw that quasi-aesthetic conclusion; but he moves us towards it. He believes in universal rational criteria that hold for all men: but his thesis – the language of inner voices – can point elsewhere. By the time we get to the German Romantics of the turn of the century, this becomes more explicit. When the artist creates a work of art, what is it that he does? He obeys some kind of inner impulse, he expresses himself. He creates something in answer to some inner demand, he projects himself, he above all does something, acts in a certain way, behaves in a certain fashion, makes something. He does not learn, discover, deduce, calculate, think.

In the case of previous thinkers, you could say that to discover certain things to be true (for example, that happiness is the true goal of man, or that happiness is not a worthy goal for man; that life is material in character or spiritual in character, or whatever it might be) was achieved in a fashion analogous to that in which Newton discovered the physical laws which the universe obeys. But when an artist creates something, is he discovering? Where is the song before it is sung? Where is the song before it is composed? The song is the singing of the song, or the composing of the song. Where is the picture before it is painted? Especially if the picture is non-representative, as music is non-representative, where is the artist's image of his creation before he creates it? The act of the artist is a kind of continuous activity, it is a doing of something, and the justification of it is that it is in obedience to some inner impulse. This obedience to the inner impulse is the realisation of an ideal, that for the sake of which he lives, that to which he dedicates himself and which he regards as his mission and his calling.

It is important to remember that, although Kant did not draw this conclusion, he did lay the foundation of such a belief with regard to ethics. It has two central elements. The first is that morality is an *activity*. The French Encyclopedists and the great figures of the German Enlightenment maintained that first we discover the truth in such matters, then we apply our knowledge effectively. But according to this new view morality is not first theory, then practice, but itself a kind of activity. The second element is that this is what is meant by human autonomy. Human autonomy, human independence, means that you are not the prey of some force which you cannot control. I have already quoted Rousseau's dictum that 'The nature of things does not madden us, only ill will does.' But these men fear the force of things even more than the force of persons. Heteronomy, which is the opposite of autonomy, means that I am not independent. I am not independent because I am overcome by passions, because I am overcome by desires or fears or hopes which force me to do various things which I might not, in some deeper sense, wish to do, which I regret afterwards, which I repent of, which I say that, if I were at my best, if I were really I, I would not be doing. Heteronomy means that you are in some way subject to, a slave of, factors over which you have no control. Autonomy is the opposite. Autonomy means that you act as you act because this is your will; *you* are acting – acting, not being acted upon.

This 'you' which is acting is of course not the body, which is prey to every possible physical ill and every possible physical law; it is something else which moves in a free region. Autonomy means the successful self-detachment from any region in which hostile forces or blind forces, or forces for which I am in any case not myself responsible, such as physical laws or the whim of a tyrant, operate. Autonomy, true freedom, consists in issuing orders to myself which I, being free to do as I will, obey. Freedom is obedience to self-imposed injunctions. This is Rousseau's concept of moral freedom, and it is Kant's. Every human being is such a source of value, and for this reason should be venerated by every other human being. That is why tampering with human beings, 'getting at' them, shaping them, altering them, doing things to them in the name of principles which are objective (that is, outside – valid independently of – human wills), in the way in which Helvétius wanted to do things to them in the name of happiness, is forbidden. That is why all that counts is *motive*. The execution of the plan I am not responsible for, since that is something in which physical laws intervene. I cannot be responsible for doing something of which I am not in control. 'Ought' implies 'can' – if you cannot do something, you cannot be told that you ought to do it. Therefore, if I have duties, if there is a morality, if there are ends, if there are certain things which I ought to do, and others which I ought to avoid, they must be in some region which can be completely free from outside interference. That is why it cannot be my duty to seek happiness, for happiness is out of my control. My duty can be only that which I can wholly control, not the achievement, but the attempt – the setting myself to do what I deem right. I am free only in the fastness of my own inner self.

Certain consequences sprang from this view which had very considerable political effects. The first, immediate effect was a kind of quietism. If all that a man should be promoting is his own inner moral self-protection, if the only thing which counts is the motive, if all that a man can be responsible for is his own personal integrity, that he be honest, that he be truthful, that he at any rate does not cheat, then, whatever may happen to the outside world – the economic and political sphere, the region of material bodies in space liable to be interfered with by outside factors, whether physical or not – all that should be outside the realm of proper moral activity. This is, indeed, how Fichte, in his earlier period, thinks.[1]

Fichte maintained that the individual must be absolutely free. 'I am wholly my own creation,' he says; and 'I do not accept the law of what nature offers me because I must, I believe it because I will.'*[2] He says that the important thing is not *das Gegebene* (that which is given) but *das Aufgegebene* (that which is imposed upon me, that which is my duty, that which is ordained, that which is part of my mission). Fichte declares that this law is not itself drawn from the realm of fact, but from our own self, the pure, original form of the self, which is, he says, the creating, the shaping, the forming of things in the outside world according to my ideas and aims, for it is only then that I am their master, that they must serve me.* Hence springs the romantic notion that the most important thing in the world is integrity, dedication.

This is so important an idea that I should like to linger a little on it. In all previous ages of man – since Plato at least – the person who was admired, the person who was looked up to, was the sage. The sage was a man who knew how to live. Some people thought the sage was in contact with God, and that God told him what to do and what the truth was. Some thought the sage was somebody in a laboratory – Paracelsus or Dr Faustus – or again someone who discovered these things by means other than empirical investigation, by some sort of intuitive grasp, by a special insight. Morality was like other forms of knowledge, a process of discovery of certain truths; and the most important thing to aim at was to be in a position to know these truths. If

[1] But gradually another thought comes stealing over this original one: that man is not an isolated being, that man is what he is because he is made by society. Here perhaps the German philosopher Herder, about whom I say something later, had a considerable influence on him.

[2] [For the meaning of the asterisks in this chapter see 275.]

you could not perceive them for yourself, you consulted a specialist; and to be a specialist was admired. The prophet, the seer, the scientist, the philosopher, or whoever it might be, was the person to look up to, because he was the person who knew how to do things, because he knew what the universe was like. The chemist might one day be able to change base metals into gold or discover the elixir of life. The political expert was somebody who knew how to govern because he understood the psychology and physiology of human nature, and of society, and knew enough about the general constitution of the universe to be able to adapt his skill thereto. The person one admired and looked up to was the man who got things right, who could discover the correct answer, who knew.

There will be cases where it is necessary not merely to live for the sake of obtaining these goals that you want, in the light of the knowledge which you have, but also to die for them. Christian martyrs died; but what they died for was the truth. They died because they desired, by their example and by their testimony, to witness to those truths, that knowledge, that wisdom which had been vouchsafed to them or to the people in whom they trusted. But the mere act of self-sacrifice, the mere act of dying for your conviction, the mere act of immolating yourself to some inner ideal because it happens to be your ideal and nobody else's – that was not hitherto admired. If a Muslim were brave and died for his faith, you did not spit upon his corpse, you did not mock him. You admired his courage and resolution; you thought it was the greatest of pities that a man so brave, and perhaps naturally so good, should die for so absurd a set of beliefs. But you did not admire him for his dedication to those beliefs.

By the time we get to the early nineteenth century all this has changed. We find that what is admired is *idealism* as such. But what is meant by idealism? An idealist is a person who throws away everything that might attract baser natures – wealth, power, success, popularity – for the sake of serving his inner ideal, for the sake of creating that which his inner self dictates. This is the ideal hero of German romanticism, and of its disciples, Carlyle, Michelet and, in their youth, the Russian radicals. The great artistic figure of the nineteenth century, who impressed himself deeply upon the imagination of Europe, was Beethoven. Beethoven is visualised as a man in a garret, poor, unkempt, neglected, rough, ugly; he has thrown away the world, he will have none of its wealth, and although the rewards are offered, he rejects them. He rejects them in order to fulfil himself, in order to serve the inner vision, in order to express that which demands, with an absolute imperative force, that it be expressed. The worst thing that a man can do is to 'sell out', to betray an ideal. That alone is despicable – despicable because the only thing which makes life worth living (to go back to Kant), the only thing which makes values values, which makes some things right and others wrong, the only thing which can justify conduct, is this inner vision.

The important thing about this attitude, which reaches its height in the early nineteenth century, is that it is no longer relevant, indeed it no longer means much, to ask whether what these people are seeking is true or false.[1] What you admire is a man who hurls himself against the walls of life, who fights against immense odds without asking himself whether the result will be victory or death, and who does this because he cannot act otherwise. The favoured image is that of Luther: there he stands, he cannot move, because he serves his inner ideal. That is what is meant by integrity, devotion, self-fulfilment, self-direction; that is what is meant by being an artist, a hero, a sage and even a good man.

This is quite novel. Mozart and Haydn would have been exceedingly surprised if what was valued in them was an inner

[1] Kant spoke about reason and gave certain criteria for determining the difference between false and true moral commandments. But by the time we get to the nineteenth century this is no longer operative.

spiritual impulse; they were artists who produced musical works which were beautiful, and these works were commissioned by patrons and admired by audiences because they were beautiful. They were craftsmen who made things: they were not priests, they were not prophets, they were purveyors. Some purvey tables, others purvey symphonies; and if the symphonies are good symphonies, still more if they are works of genius, then the persons who write them are, or should be, admired.

By the time we get to the nineteenth century the artist becomes a hero and the act of defiance becomes the central act of his life. You defy the powerful, the rich, the wicked, the philistines, and the dry and critical and mean-spirited intelligentsia if need be – all the people against whom Rousseau hurled his early thunderbolts, followed by Carlyle and Nietzsche and D. H. Lawrence. You defy these people in order to assert yourself, say your word, be something autonomous, not be at the mercy of, guided by, conditioned by, things or circumstances other than those which you create out of your own inner self.

So long as it is confined to artists this is a noble ideal which no one today publicly spurns; indeed the moral consciousness of today is largely moulded by these romantic notions, in terms of which we admire idealists and men of integrity, whether we agree with their ideals or not, sometimes even when we think them foolish, in a way in which in the eighteenth century and in previous centuries they were not admired at all, and thought lovable but silly.* But it has a more sinister side to it. Morality now becomes something which is not found but invented; morality is not a set of propositions corresponding to certain facts which we discover in nature. Indeed, nature is nothing to do with it; nature for Kant, nature for Fichte, is simply a collection of dead matter upon which you impose your will. We have departed far indeed from the notion of copying nature, following nature – *naturam sequi* – being like nature. On the contrary, now you mould nature, you transform nature; nature is a challenge, nature is simply the raw material. If this is so, if morality consists in projecting yourself in some way, it may be that political activity is also a kind of self-projection. Napoleon, who projects his personality across the map of Europe, who moulds human beings in France, in Germany, in Italy, in Russia, as the artist moulds his material, as the composer moulds sound and the painter colours – Napoleon is the highest expression of morality,[1] for he is expressing his personality, he is asserting himself, he is serving the inner ideal which drives him on and on.

At this point there is a quantum leap in Fichte's thought – from the isolated individual to the group as a true subject or self. How does this arise?

I am free only if I do things which nobody can stop me from doing, and I do this only if it is my inner self which is active, not impinged upon by anything else.* A self is a spirit, but it is not an isolated spirit, and it is here that Fichte begins on that path which leads to such peculiar conclusions, that path which begins to move towards the notion that selves are not individual human beings at all, that the self is something to do with society, that perhaps the self, the human self, is really not only itself the product of history and of tradition, but also bound to other human beings by Burke's myriad indissoluble spiritual links, that it exists only as part of a general pattern, of which it forms an element. So much so that it becomes misleading to say that a self is an empirical individual born in a certain year, living a certain kind of life, in a certain physical environment, and dying in a certain place at a certain date.

Fichte begins to move towards a theological conception of the self; he says that the true, free self is not the empirical self which is clothed in a body and has a date and a place,* it is a self which is common to all bodies, it is a superself, it is a larger, divine self

[1] Though not, as it happens, for Fichte, who had a particular hatred for Napoleon as a false artist, alien to spiritual values.

which he gradually begins to identify now with nature, now with God, now with history, now with a nation.[1]

Starting with the notion of the isolated individual who serves some inner ideal which is out of reach of nature or the tyrant, Fichte gradually adopts the idea that the individual himself is nothing, that man is nothing without society, that man is nothing without the group, that the human being hardly exists at all. The individual, he begins to suspect, does not exist, he must vanish. The group – *Gattung* – alone exists, is alone real.

It begins innocently enough. The individual man must endeavour to repay his debt to society. He must take his place among men, he must strive in some respect to advance the rest of humanity, which has done so much for him. 'Man', he says, 'becomes man only among other men.' And again: 'Man is destined to live in society; he must do so; he is not a complete human being, he contradicts his own nature, if he lives in isolation.'*

Fichte gradually came to believe something of this kind. But he goes much further. The real self of Fichte's fully developed philosophy is not you, nor I, nor any particular individual, nor any particular group of individuals. It is that which is common to all men; it is a personified, embodied principle which, like a pantheistic divinity, expresses itself through finite centres, through me, through you, through other people. Its embodiment on earth is the true society, conceived as a collection of persons bound together metaphysically, like small flames issuing from some great central fire. It is the great central fire towards which

[1] There is a peculiar, special process of metaphysical insight which only a few chosen men in each generation – in particular Fichte himself – can use for the purpose of discovering what is the duty of man, given to this special active insight, the free self within me, the self which a tyrant cannot reach, which alone is free. To go through this process is for Fichte analogous to the procedure of the ancient mystics, the ancient seers and prophets who felt themselves in the presence of something greater than themselves, greater than their physical selves, greater than their empirical selves – in the presence of some vast power: God, nature, the real self.

each flame tends in the process of being aware of the moral orders – which are impulsions, flamelike strivings – of its inner self.* This is a theological doctrine, and Fichte clearly was in this sense a theologian, and so was Hegel, and no good purpose is served by supposing that they were secular thinkers. They were deeply influenced by the Christian tradition, and it might seem to some that they were heretics in it. But theologians they were, far more theological than what is called philosophical at the present time.

In this way Fichte gradually moves from the group to the notion that the true person, the true individual, whose act of self-assertion is the march of morality in history – the imposition of moral imperatives upon a pliant, flexible nature – this individual is not even the human being at his most self-conscious, but a collectivity: race, nation, mankind.* This was the substance of those celebrated speeches of his to the German nation delivered in Berlin in 1807–8, at a time when the troops of Napoleon were occupying the city, in which he told the Germans to arise and resist. Let me quote from these to show the kind of thing he had in mind, and how far he must have travelled. Fichte is speaking of the German character, and he says that there are two kinds of characters in the world:

> Either you believe in an original principle in man – in a freedom, a perfectibility and infinite progress of our species – or you believe in none of this. You may even have a feeling or intuition of the opposite. All those who have within them a creative quickening of life, or else, assuming that such a gift has been withheld from them, at least reject what is but vanity and await the moment when they are caught up by the torrent of original life, or even if they are not yet at this point, at any rate have some confused presentiment of freedom, those who have towards it not hatred, nor fear, but a feeling of love – all these are part of the primal humanity, and considered as a people they constitute the primal people. In short, the people. I mean the German people. All those,

> on the other hand, who have resigned themselves to represent only derivative, second-hand products, who think of themselves in this way, these become in effect such and shall pay the price of their belief. They are only an annex to life. Not for them those pure springs which flowed before them, which still flow around them; they are but the echo coming back from a rock of a voice which is silent. Considered as a people, they are excluded from the primal people, they are strangers, outsiders. A nation which to this day bears the name of German (or simply the people) has not ceased to give evidence of a creative and original activity in most diverse fields. The hour has come at last when philosophy, penetrated through and through by self-awareness, will hold to this nation a mirror wherein it will recognise itself with a clear perception, and at the same time will become quite clearly aware of the mission of which it has hitherto had but a confused premonition, but which nature herself has imposed upon that nation; an unmistakable call has been addressed to it today to labour in freedom calmly and clearly and to perfect itself according to the notions which it has framed of itself, to accomplish the duty which has been outlined to it.
>
> And everyone who believes this kind of thing will join with these people whose function, whose mission, is to create. All those who believe on the contrary in an arrested being, or in retrogression or in cycles of history; or else those who put an inanimate nature at the helm of the world, whatever be their native country, whatever be their language, they are not Germans, they are strangers to us and one should hope they will be utterly cut off from our people.

Then the great paean begins, the great nationalist chauvinist cry. Individual self-determination now becomes collective self-realisation, and the nation a community of unified wills in pursuit of moral truth. But this collective march forward would be directionless if the nation were not led, if it were not illuminated by the quasi-divine leadership of the *Zwingherr*. Fichte says, 'What we need is a leader; what we need is a man to mould us.' 'Hither!' – he suddenly cries – 'Zwingherr zur Deutschheit [the man who will compel us to Germanism]. We hope, of course, that it will be our king who will perform this service, but be he who he may we must await him till he comes and moulds us, till he comes and makes us.'

In short, we have come full circle. We started with the notion of an autonomous person, anxious not to be impinged upon, wishing for a life of absolute freedom, obeying only the inner workings of its own inner consciousness, of its own inner conscience. And now we say: Life is art, life is a moulding, life is the creation of something – self-creation – by a so-called 'organic' process.* There are superior beings and there are inferior beings, as there is within me a higher and a lower nature, and I can rise to great heights in a moment of crisis, and crush my passions and desires and perform heroic acts of self-immolation in the name of a principle which raises me; which, as he says, catches me up in a flow of life. If I can suppress that which is lower in me, then the leader or the race can suppress that which is lower in it, as the spirit does the sinning flesh.

Here it is at last, the famous and fatal analogy between the individual and the nation, the organic metaphor which leaves the field of theological imagery and is secularised by Burke and by Rousseau, and is very powerful in Fichte. Fichte contrasts *compositum*, which is a mere artificial combination, and *totum*, which is a total nation, which is something organic, single, whole, and in which the higher principle dominates, the higher principle which may take the shape of a great nation, or of history.* And the greatest agent of this force is a divine conqueror or leader whose business it is to play upon his nation as an artist plays upon his instrument, to mould it into a single organic whole, as the painter, the sculptor moulds his materials, as the composer creates patterns of sound.

As for freedom, individual freedom and individual conscience, and right and wrong, whether discovered or invented, what has become of those now? What of that individual freedom of which we spoke earlier, which the British and the French writers defended, the freedom of each man to be allowed, within certain limits at least, to live as he likes, to waste his time as he likes, to go to the bad in his own way, to do that which he wants simply because freedom as such is a sacred value? Individual freedom, which in Kant has a sacred value, has for Fichte become a choice made by something superpersonal. It chooses me, I do not choose it, and acquiescence is a privilege, a duty, a self-lifting, a kind of self-transcendent rising to a higher level. Freedom, and morality generally, is self-submission to the superself – the dynamic cosmos. We are back with the view that freedom *is* submission.

Fichte himself largely thought in terms of some transcendental, idealistic willpower which had relatively little to do with the actual terrestrial life of men, and only towards the end of his life did he perceive the possibility of moulding earthly life in conformity with these transcendental desires. But his followers translated it into more mundane terms. The transfer of emphasis from reason to will created that notion of freedom which is not the notion of non-interference, not the notion of permitting each man to have his choice, but the notion of self-expression, the notion of imposing yourself upon the medium, the notion of freedom as the removal of obstacles to yourself. One can remove obstacles only by subjugating them: in mathematics, by understanding; in material life, by acquisition; in politics, by conquest. That is at the heart of the notion that a free nation is a victorious nation, that freedom is power and that conquest and freedom are one.

To show what this has led to, let me quote a very shrewd observer, the German poet Heinrich Heine, then living in Paris. These were the lines which he wrote in 1834 in an attempt to warn the French not to minimise the force of ideas:

> The idea tries to become action, the word desires to be made flesh, and lo, a man [. . .] has only to express his thought, and the world forms itself [. . .] The world is but the outer manifestation of the word.
>
> Note this, you proud men of action, you are nothing but the unconscious tools of the men of thought, who in humble stillness have often drawn up your most definite plans of action. Maximilien Robespierre was nothing but the hand of Jean-Jacques Rousseau, the bloodstained hand that drew from the womb of time the body whose soul Rousseau had created. [. . .] the *Critique of Pure Reason* by Kant [. . .] is the sword with which deism was beheaded [. . .].

Fichte was once well paraphrased by the American philosopher Josiah Royce thus: 'The world is the poem [. . .] dreamed out by the inner life.' So, then, our worlds are literally different if we differ spiritually. A composer, a banker, a robber literally create their worlds. Whether or not he was thinking of this, Heine feels genuine terror before this attitude, and had a genuine vision of doom to come: 'Kantians will appear, who in the world of mere phenomena hold nothing sacred, and ruthlessly with sword and axe will hack through the foundations of our European life, and pull up the past by its last remaining roots. Armed Fichteans will come, whose fanatical wills neither fear nor self-interest can touch.' These men, these pantheists, will fight recklessly for their principles, for these principles are absolute, and their dangers seem to them purely illusory. *Naturphilosophen* will identify themselves with elemental forces, which are always destructive. Then the god Thor will wield his gigantic hammer and smash the Gothic cathedrals. Christianity was the only force which held back the ancient German barbarism with its naked violence; once that talisman is broken a terrible cataclysm will break out. 'Don't try [he says to the French] to suppress or to extinguish the flame, you will only burn your fingers.'

Above all, don't laugh at the dreamy poet and his revolutionary fancies.

> Thought precedes action as lightning precedes thunder. German thunder too is a German, and not in a hurry, and it comes rolling slowly onward; but come it will, and once you hear it crashing, as nothing ever crashed before in the history of the world, then know that the German thunder has finally hit the mark. At that sound the eagles will fall dead from the air and the lions in the remotest deserts of Africa will [...] creep to their royal lairs. A drama will be performed in Germany in contrast with which the French Revolution will seem a mere peaceful idyll.

The French are warned not to clap this great gladiatorial show, which will begin in Germany. 'For you', he says to them, 'liberated Germany is more dangerous than the whole Holy Alliance, with all its Cossacks and its Croats. For [...] we Germans forget nothing', and pretexts for war will be found. The French are warned, above all, not to disarm. Remember, he says to them, that upon Olympus, 'amidst the nude deities who feast upon nectar and ambrosia, there is one goddess who amidst all this merriment and peace keeps her armour and her helmet and a spear in her hand – the goddess of wisdom'.

This prophecy was destined to be fulfilled. It is idle to blame any one thinker, any one philosopher, for the actions of multitudes in history. Nevertheless it is odd to reflect that there is a direct line, and a very curious one, between the extreme liberalism of Kant, with his respect for human nature and its sacred rights, and Fichte's identification of freedom with self-assertion, with the imposition of your will upon others, with the removal of obstacles to your desires, and finally with a victorious nation marching to fulfil its destiny in answer to the internal demands given to it by transcendental reason, before which all material things must crumble. We have indeed travelled a long way from the Anglo-French notion of freedom which allowed each man his own circle, that small but indispensable vacuum within which he can do as he pleases, go to the bad or go to the good, choose for the sake of choosing, in which the value of choice as such is regarded as sacred.

These are the two notions of liberty which were spread over Europe at the beginning of the nineteenth century; to ask which of them is true, and which of them is false, is a shallow and unanswerable question. They represent two views of life of an irreconcilable kind, the liberal and authoritarian, open and closed, and the fact that the word 'freedom' has been a genuinely central symbol in both is at once remarkable and sinister.

Hegel

OF ALL THE IDEAS that originated during the period which I am discussing, the Hegelian system has perhaps had the greatest influence on contemporary thought. It is a vast mythology which, like many other mythologies, has great powers of illumination as well as great powers of obscuring whatever it touches. It has poured forth both light and darkness – more darkness perhaps than light, but about that there will be no agreement. At any rate, it is like a very dark wood, and those who once enter it very seldom come back to tell us what it is that they have seen. Or, when they do, like those who are addicted to the music of Wagner, their ear appears permanently attuned to sounds very unlike the older, simpler and nobler harmonies which once they used to listen to. As a result it is not always very easy to understand, through the new terminology which the system seems to induce in them, what their vision really consists of.

One thing is certain. Followers of Hegel claim that, whereas previously they saw things only from the outside, they now see them from the inside. Whereas previously they saw merely the outer surface, the shell, they now see the inner essence, the inner purpose; the essential end towards which things tend. They have an 'inside' as opposed to an 'outside' view, and this difference between outside and inside is crucial to the understanding of the whole system.

When we look at material objects – tables, chairs, trees, stones – all that we see is a variety of objects, and movements among these objects, and we can describe them and classify them, and concentrate our classifications into general formulae which enable us to describe and predict their behaviour, and perhaps say something about their past also. When one asks why things happen as they do, there are two senses of this word 'why'. In one sense natural science does answer the question. If I say, 'Why does the table not fly upwards, but on the whole stay on the ground?', a great many physical facts will be offered me about molecules and their relations, and I shall be told about the physical laws which operate on these molecules. All this does, however, is to give me very general laws about the characteristics of objects which resemble each other. Newton and Galileo showed themselves to be men of genius in reducing to a minimum the number of formulae in terms of which I can classify the behaviour of objects, so that I can do so as economically and manageably as possible.

But suppose I ask a very different sort of question. Suppose I say, 'I perfectly understand what you are telling me; you are describing what this table does; all you are telling me is that the table does not, for example, fly upwards, but stays on the ground, because it belongs to a class of entities which are in general subject to the laws of gravitation. But I want to know something rather different: I want to know why it does it, in the sense in which I ask what the meaning of its behaviour is, or rather what the purpose is of what it does. Why was the world arranged in such a way that tables do not, in fact, fly upwards? Why do trees, for example, grow while tables do not?' This 'Why?' is not answered by reciting what happens, nor even by providing very powerful laws in terms of which I can determine the position and movement of every molecule. I want to know why things happen in the sense of the word 'why' in which I ask the question, 'Why did such and such a man strike such and such another man?'

In that case you would not simply answer, 'Because certain molecules rotating in a certain manner produced a certain effect in his bloodstream which gradually affected his muscles in such a way that his arm rose', and so forth. In a sense all this is true, and you could say it, and yet it would not be an answer to the question which I am asking. You would be answering my question much more naturally if you said that he did it because he was angry, or in order to accomplish this or that end. He did it in order to avenge himself; he did it in order to obtain the satisfaction of giving pain to the person whom he struck. It seems quite clear that, whereas we can ask that kind of question about persons, perhaps a little less certainly about animals, much less certainly about, say, trees, it is not sensible to ask such questions about material objects, or about a great many entities in the universe which do not appear to be animate.

According to the great German Romantic philosophers, the crime of eighteenth-century science, and to some extent of seventeenth-century science too, or anyway of their philosophical interpreters, was to amalgamate these two kinds of explanation; to say that there was only one kind of explanation, namely the kind which applies to material objects; to say that, in asking the question 'Why?', we mean only to ask for facts. We are asking 'What happens? When does it happen? Next door to what does it happen? What happens after what, and before what?' and never 'What purposes does it pursue? What goals? Why does it do it?' in the sense in which I can ask 'Why does a person do something?'

That is why Descartes said that history was not a science – because there were no general laws which could be applied to history. The whole thing was much too fluid, the number of differences was far greater than the number of similarities, it was impossible to collect so unstable a subject matter, about which so little was known, where there were so few repetitions, so few uniformities, into any form which could be subsumed under a few powerful formulae. Therefore he regarded history as simply a collection, ultimately, of gossip, travellers' tales, something scarcely worthy of the name of science. Indeed, the general ideal of the seventeenth-century scientists was not to concern oneself overmuch with anything which could not be dealt with by lucid and systematic methods; and systematic methods meant the methods of natural science.

One of the great advances made in the late eighteenth century and the early nineteenth was to revise this conception. Perhaps this was not the last word which could be said; perhaps the question 'Why?' was more interesting than it had been made out to be. When, for example, Vico – an Italian thinker of the early eighteenth century who was unjustly neglected although he was a bold and original genius – began to write about history, he said that to treat human beings as objects, like tables and chairs and trees, was absurd; that we knew more about human beings, in a certain sense, than we knew about natural objects; and that the whole of the prestige of the natural sciences was founded on a mistake. In the case of tables and stones we could say only what they looked like to us, and also what at any given moment they consisted of, what there was before them and what there was after them, what there was next door to them – we could simply place them in a sort of inventory of the universe in time and space and number. But we could do more than this in the case of history. If we are asked why Julius Caesar acted as he did, we do not just give a physical description of his body and movements. We tend to talk about his motives. We cannot talk about the motives of tables and chairs, even assuming that we think they might have such motives, because we do not know what it is like to be a table or to be a chair, only what they look like. But according to Vico we know more than this about Caesar, by a species of imaginative insight. By analogy with ourselves we know that he possessed a will, emotions, feelings, that he was, in short, a human being. We can try to talk about historical personages as we would talk about ourselves, and explain not merely what they did, but also what their purposes were, what their ends were, what their 'inner feelings' were. It is this distinction between inner and outer which becomes of importance.

Similarly, the German eighteenth-century metaphysician Herder thought that if we try to describe the life of a nation, it is natural to ask 'What is it like to belong to such and such a nation?' Then it is natural to ask 'What does it mean to "belong" at all?' If I say 'So and so is a German', it is not enough merely to say that he was born in a certain country, in a certain climate, on a certain date, and that he has certain physiological or physical resemblances to certain other persons also called Germans. When I say that he 'belongs' to them, and still more when I say that he 'feels that he belongs' to them, that he 'feels himself to be a German', this means at least that he likes what other Germans like, likes German songs, likes the way in which Germans eat and drink, likes the way in which they live, the way in which they make their laws and the way in which they tie their shoes. To feel oneself a German is to have a certain connection with other Germans which cannot be exhausted by a mere material or physical description of outer behaviour, as a behaviourist would record it. When I say of someone that he is a German, and that he thrills to the sound of German songs, or that his heart rises when he sees a German flag fly, the very words 'German songs' are not to be analysed in a purely materialistic or scientific, physical fashion. To be a German song is to be produced in a certain way by certain people with certain purposes; and the song itself must, I will not say 'possess a certain flavour', but it must possess a certain kind of expressiveness; it must spring from or express a certain kind of character, outlook, attitude to life. This attitude to life, this specific character which a song expresses, will also be expressed by much larger and more permanent institutions – by the German system of legislation, by their political system, by the way in which they treat each other, by their accent, by the shape of their handwriting, and by everything which they do and are and feel.

What is this common quality which makes a people German? According to Herder it is belonging to a certain individual group.

What is meant by individual? Herder's point was that when you talk about purposes you need not and should not confine yourself to individuals. When you ask why so and so does this or that, you normally answer in psychological terms – 'Because he wants to', 'Because he proposes to.' But you can also ask about impersonal entities. You can say 'Why do the Germans write in Gothic script, whereas the French do not?' This kind of 'Why?' will be answered in a manner much more like the way in which I answer questions such as 'Why does so and so eat with a spoon, whereas somebody else eats with his fingers?' than like the way in which I respond when asked 'Why do these molecules have this effect, whereas other molecules have quite a different one?'

This means that we are trembling on the verge of the notion of impersonal or superpersonal or collective purposes. This, of course is the beginning of a mythology, but a very convenient mythology, for otherwise we certainly do not know how to speak about groups and societies. When we say that a nation has a peculiar genius – that the Portuguese genius is quite different from the Chinese genius – we are not saying that a given average Portuguese is a man of genius and different from a given Chinese man of genius. We are trying to say that the way in which the Portuguese build their ships, the way in which they express their views, have something in common, a kind of family resemblance or family face which pervades everything, and that it is quite different from the corresponding resemblance among the Chinese; and this indication of the family face, the analysis of what it consists in, we call historical explanation. When someone says 'Why does so and so write as he does?' we do take it for an answer if you reply that it is because he belongs to the Portuguese family of nations, because he belongs to a particular group of persons who live in Brazil or Portugal or Goa and who have a certain outlook, certain kinds of values, who feel familiar with certain kinds of experience but feel that certain other kinds of experience are wholly alien to them. This is an answer to the question 'Why?'

which is quite different from the answer given by the sciences, and this is the kind of 'Why?' which Vico and Herder dealt with. It is this which Hegel tried to generalise, his view being that all questions about the universe could be answered in this 'deeper' sense of 'Why?'

He formulated this by saying that the universe was really the self-development of the world spirit. A world spirit is something like an individual spirit, except that it embraces and is identical with the whole universe. If you can imagine the universe as a kind of animate entity possessing a soul in roughly the same sense as, but no doubt grander than, that in which individuals possess souls, intentions, purposes, wills, then you can ask 'Why do things happen as they do?' They happen as they do because they are part of a vast spiritual movement which has purposes, intentions and a direction, very much as human beings have purposes, intentions and a direction. How do we know what that direction is? Because we are parts of it. Because every individual is a finite element in an infinite whole which, collectively speaking, possesses a certain purpose and a certain direction.

But, you may say, what is the evidence for this? Certainly Hegel does not provide anything which can be called empirical or scientific evidence. Ultimately it turns out to be a case of metaphysical insight or an act of faith. If what he says were not so, he claims, then there would be too many 'brute' facts. You would be asking why stones are as they are, why plants are as they are, and the answer would be, 'In your sense of the word "why", namely, if you are asking who intended them for what, we cannot answer the question.' Vico had already said that only those who make things can truly understand their nature. The novelist understands everything there is to be understood about his characters because he creates them; there is nothing there which he does not know, because he has made them. In this sense of understanding, only God can understand the universe, for he has made it, and we can understand only those finite things which we make. A watchmaker understands a watch as a novelist understands his characters.

But now you may ask, 'What about other human beings? Can we not understand them?' There is obviously a sense in which, when they talk to us or when they show certain moods, when they look gloomy or dejected or happy or gay or fierce, we are able to understand what they are at, in a different sense from that in which we understand stones and tables. We do not enquire about the outlooks or purposes of tables. In short, we do not think that tables are 'at' anything; they are what they are. The question 'What is a table at?' seems absurd because it appears to make the table an animated entity; it appears to make it sentient, when in fact we suspect that it is not. But we *can* ask this about other human beings, and Hegel – and the Romantics generally – suppose that this is because in some sense we participate in this one general 'spirit' of which all human beings are finite centres, and we have a species of metaphysical grasp of – quasi-telepathic insight into – what people are like, because we are human beings ourselves. Therefore history is solely an account of the experiences of human beings. Tables and chairs have no history because they have no experience. History is the story of human creation, human imagination, human wills and intentions, feelings, purposes, everything which human beings do and feel, rather than what is done to them. Human history is something which we create by feeling, by thinking, by being active in some fashion, and therefore, by creating it, we are able to understand it, which is why the understanding of history is an 'inside' view, whereas our understanding of tables and chairs is an 'outside' view.[1]

This being so, Hegel is able to say that, since the whole universe is an enormous sentient whole, we are able to understand what each part of it is doing, provided that we have a sufficiently clear

[1] With the justice of this distinction I do not here wish to deal: it would take us too far afield.

degree of metaphysical insight, such as is possessed, for instance, by the most powerful minds, the most penetrating intelligences. If it were not so, then there would be 'mere' facts which could not be explained at all. If I asked 'Why is this stone lying on the ground, whereas that stone is falling through the air?' I should have to reply that that sort of 'Why?' is not asked in the case of stones; it just is so, it is a brute fact. But for Hegel and for all the metaphysicians of his way of thinking the brute fact is an offence to reason. We cannot 'accept' brute facts because they are not to be explained, and just lie there as a challenge to our understanding. Unless we can relate them to a purposive system, unless they can be fitted into a pattern, they remain unexplained. But what is a pattern? A pattern is something which a plan has. The painting has a pattern because somebody planned it that way. The symphony has a pattern because that alone is what causes its various parts to 'make sense'; because there is a total purpose which the symphony subserves, whether in the mind of the composer who composed it, whether on the part of the musicians who play it, or on the part of the audience which listens to it, a purpose in terms of which the various elements of the symphony, namely the various sounds, function together in a pattern. Unless we can grasp the pattern, we do not 'understand'.

This is the special kind of understanding which means perception of patterns. This is the sense in which we understand what it is to be a German, what it is to be a Frenchman. To be a German is to be part of a general German pattern, a pattern which includes undergoing German experiences, German hopes and fears, the way in which a German walks, the way in which he gets up, the way in which he holds his head – everything about him. If we then ask 'Well, what part does he play in the larger pattern of which the entire universe consists?' the answer is that this can be discovered only by somebody who sees the whole. But only the whole, if it were conscious of itself, would see itself as a whole. We are confined to seeing parts. Some see greater parts, some smaller ones, but it is in perceiving things as parts of larger things that any degree of understanding is achieved.

Here arises the further question, 'How in fact does the spirit work? What is the mechanism, what is the pattern?' Hegel thought he had found the answer to that. He said that it worked according to what he called the dialectic. The dialectic for him really makes sense only in terms of thought or artistic creation; and he applies it to the universe because he thinks that in the universe is a kind of act of thought, or a kind of act of self-creation; *self*-creation, for there exists nothing else.[1] In what way does the dialectic work? It works in a way rather like that in which people work when they try to think of answers to questions. First, an idea occurs in my mind, then this idea is qualified by other ideas and does not stay. Other ideas come into collision with it and then, out of the collision and conflict of an idea and the qualifications – the idea and the criticism of the idea, the idea and other ideas which come falling upon it, impinging upon it – something else is born which is neither the first idea, nor the idea which is in opposition to the first idea; rather it is something which retains elements of both but, as he says, rises above them, or transcends them – a synthesis. The first idea is called *thesis*, the second *antithesis*, the third *synthesis*.

So for example (though Hegel does not use this particular metaphor) in a symphonic work you have a theme consisting of a phrase of music or a melody, then you have a melody which as it were runs against it, and something happens which cannot be called the cancellation of the first theme by the second nor the continuation of the first into the second, but is rather some kind of fusion which destroys the first two ideas and produces something which is half familiar because it grows in some way out of the collision and conflict of the first two and yet is something new.

[1] For him there is no personal deity. If he was a Christian, he was a very heretical one, because he believed in the identity of the creative principle, that is God, with the whole of the universe.

This, according to Hegel, is how the universe works. It works like this because that is how patterns work in thought and in every kind of conscious activity of which we know anything – and he distinguishes the universe into conscious and self-conscious and unconscious ingredients.

Plants and animals are conscious; that is to say they have purposes of some kind, they have low-grade volitions – low-grade thoughts perhaps. Human beings alone are self-conscious, because they not only have thoughts but can watch this dialectical process in themselves. They can see this development, this collision of ideas, the irregular line which their lives follow; how they first do one thing, then half not-do it, and then the doing and the not-doing fuse themselves into a new kind of doing. They can follow this twisting, spiral process in themselves. He tries to explain whole civilisations in these terms. His point is that in the eighteenth century people were able to explain differences but not change. For example, Montesquieu was very convincing and subtle in explaining how climate affected people, Helvétius may have been very penetrating in explaining how education or environment affected them; other eighteenth-century thinkers, by making over-close analogies between human beings and insentient entities, explained how human beings came to be what they were, to some degree, certainly how their bodies came to be what they were, perhaps their nervous systems, perhaps other aspects of them. But how are we to account for change? After all, Italy in Roman days and Italy now are physically much the same country. The seas which wash it affect it in the same way, its climate has not altered abruptly, nor its vegetation. Yet modern Italians are utterly different from ancient Romans.

The characteristic thinkers of the eighteenth century maintained that this was due to human development. It was the result of education and government; and it was because (people like Helvétius thought) human beings were governed, or rather misgoverned – a great many knaves, or perhaps a great many fools, misgoverned a great many fools – that the disasters occurred of which all history up to the beginning of the rational period of human existence was so full. This, for Hegel, is plainly not good enough. If human beings are as much under the influence of external causes as eighteenth-century science, needing to be materialistic, must maintain, then the vast differences, the growth and the development, cannot be explained. This can be explained only by the dialectic, namely by some process of movement, by a dynamism of some sort. This collision of thesis and antithesis, this perpetual clash of forces, is what is responsible for progress. These forces are not merely thoughts in people's heads; they 'incarnate themselves' in institutions, in Churches, in political constitutions, perhaps in vast human enterprises, in migrations of peoples, in revolutions, for example, or in vast intellectual developments, where the thesis and antithesis in their state of continual mutual inner tension grow to a climax. There is an outburst, and the synthesis comes to be born, like a kind of phoenix, from the ashes of the thesis and antithesis.

This need not take concrete physical forms. It need not take the form of a bloodstained revolution. It may take the form only of a vast cultural awakening, like the Renaissance, or some enormous artistic or intellectual or spiritual discovery. But always it takes the form of a leap forward. The process is not continuous, it moves in jumps. First the growing tension of the force and its opposite, then the climax and the enormous jump, the vast spring which the human mind – not necessarily only the human mind, but the whole of the universe – takes on to some new level, on to a new shelf. Then once more the process begins; the new creation is eaten out by its own inner opposing forces until the tension again grows to a climax and the next leap occurs. For Hegel, that is history, that is what explains the discontinuities and tragedies. The tragedies of life consist in this inevitable conflict, but unless there were these conflicts, between nation and nation, between institution and institution, between one form of art and another, between one cultural movement and another, there would be no movement; unless there was friction, there would be death.

That is why there is something shallow, for him, something inadequate in the eighteenth-century explanation of evil, sorrow, suffering and tragedy as simply due to mistakes, bad arrangements, inefficiency, so that in the efficient universe all this would be smoothed out, and there would be complete harmony. But for Hegel conflict is the very symptom of development, growth, something occurring, the stream of life beating against the shell of some earlier experience, from which it will presently burst, thus relegating the shell to the slag-heap of those bits of experience, those bits of history, which are done with and are now consigned to some dead past.

Sometimes this development occurs in the form of national activities; sometimes there are individual heroes who personify these leaps – Alexander, Caesar, Napoleon. Certainly these individuals destroyed much; certainly they caused a great deal of suffering. That is the inevitable consequence of any kind of advance. Unless there is friction, there is no progress. Before Hegel, Kant, and before him Mandeville, and to some extent Vico, had already said something of this kind.

Now the question arises: 'What is meant by saying that history is a rational process?' For Hegel, to say that a process is rational is to say that when you grasp what it is, in the only way you can ever really understand anything, that is, by means of a faculty he calls reason, then you see that the process is inevitable. It cannot happen otherwise than as it does. Hegel's train of thought goes somewhat as follows. How do we ever learn a truth, say that twice two equals four? At first it faces us like a brute fact. The schoolboy has to learn the multiplication table by heart in the beginning; he does not understand why two times two must equal four. Hence it is a burden upon his intellect and memory, a dogma which it is his task to learn and remember. Only when he has learned the axioms and the rules of arithmetic does he realise that two times two not merely *is* four, but cannot be other than four. He need not repeat it by rote: it has become part of his natural skill in adding or multiplying.

So, when we study history, Hegel supposes, we reach a sufficiently rational level, we rise to a certain stage of illumination in which we begin to understand that historical events not merely happened as they did, but *had* to happen as they did, necessarily; not in the sense of the mechanical causality with which physics deals but rather, for example, in the sense in which we follow the stages of a mathematical argument, where there are rigorous rules; or perhaps even of a symphony, where there are not quite such fixed rules, but we can say that each successive portion is, as it were, inevitable, or, as Hegel might say, a 'rational successor' of the previous portion, so that we say the earlier stage 'does not make sense' unless the later stage is there to complete it, in the way in which the pattern of the carpet can be traced. When we have learned arithmetic and music in this way, we move freely in the mathematical or musical world. The pattern becomes identified with our own mode of thought and feeling and action. We no longer feel it to be external or oppressive to us, or that there are grim de facto laws hemming us in to which we must adjust ourselves, but which are not part of what we are, what we want – of our own lives.

According to Hegel, the usual way in which one approaches the external world is by distinguishing between what you want – your intentions, your policies, what you are after – and, on the other hand, what is outside: the things and persons who, just by being there, obstruct the full, free development of your personality. But when you discover why everything is as it is – *must* be so – in the very act of understanding this you will lose the desire for it to be otherwise. When you learn not merely that two times two equals four, but also why, you can no longer wish it to be otherwise. You do not want twice two to be five. Twice two not merely *is* four, but you want it to be so; it is part of the rational pattern of your thought. The rules of arithmetic become assimilated into the general rules of reasoning, into the way in which you think and act.

This notion of assimilation is vital in Hegel, because he thinks of laws not in the way in which science and even common sense tend to think of them, namely as generalisations of what happens, but rather more as rules, patterns, forms, in the sense in which arithmetic – or logic, or architecture, or music – proceeds by rules. To think of a general law as something which you do not want to be otherwise than as it is, is to think of it as a rule with which you identify yourself, the method in terms of which you naturally think, or which you naturally apply, and not as an iron law discovered to operate outside you, an unbreakable, inescapable barrier against which you beat in vain. But rules and methods presuppose users of them – persons. You employ rules, or apply them, or live by them; and if the universe obeys rules, it is not far from this to the idea of it as a vast drama in which the characters fulfil parts assigned to them. But then there must be a dramatist; and if you can now imagine the characters in the confidence of the dramatist, understanding his intentions, you will arrive at something like the Hegelian notion of how the world functions.

It is an old theological or metaphysical belief that laws, which at first seem barriers, something you cannot overcome, gradually work themselves into your very self, once you understand their purposes, and you begin using them easily and freely yourself. Thus, when you become a mathematician, you think in mathematical terms almost unconsciously; and likewise you write correctly after you have assimilated the rules of grammar, without feeling that a terrible external straitjacket of despotic rules and regulations has been imposed upon you. If you can get on such terms with nature, consciously identify with her workings so closely that her laws coincide with the rules and patterns of your own reasonings and volitions and feelings, then you obtain the inside view. You are then said to be 'at one' with nature in her purposes, her intentions. This union, this being at one with the universe, has always been, in one way or another, the goal of all the great mystics and metaphysicians. Hegel expounds this notion in ponderous, obscure and occasionally majestic language. From it he derives his notorious paradox that liberty is the recognition of necessity.

One of the oldest problems of politics, as it is in life, in metaphysics and morals and everything else, is this: if I am completely determined, if some omniscient observer can foresee every single move which I make, how can I possibly be said to be free? If everything I have done in the past, am doing in the present and will do in the future can be accounted for by somebody who knows all the facts and all the laws which govern them, what is the sense of saying that I can do what I want? Am I not a wholly, rigidly determined element in some block universe? Hegel thought that this perennial problem was one which he had solved. The world, according to him, as we have seen, is something which develops, now gradually and cumulatively, at other times by explosions. The forces whose conflicts create movement, whose final clashes are cataclysmic leaps into the next phase, take the form sometimes of institutions – Churches, States, cultures, legal systems – sometimes of great inventions, discoveries, artistic masterpieces, sometimes of individuals, groups, parties, personal relationships. This is the dialectical movement.

But if I understand it, how can I oppose it? If I understand an art or a science – logic or music or mathematics – how can I want something which goes against it? To understand is not merely to accept, but actively to want what is understood, because to be understood is to become part of him who understands, part of his purposes, his goal and his development towards his goal. Of course, this is not an empirical hypothesis, not a scientific theory; no facts can falsify this Hegelian pattern. It is a vast metaphysical vision in which everything is accommodated either as a thesis or as an antithesis. Everything can be fitted in, nothing can be excluded, because every event and person and element in the world either accords or fails to accord with every other person, event and element – and whichever it does, it fits in either by being harmonious with something or by being in discord with it. There can be no evidence against such a view, for anything which might seem contrary can be absorbed as the necessary element of contrariety.[1] For this reason it is not a scientific or rational explanation in the sense in which, say, the Darwinian or Newtonian systems are rational, because one could conceive of evidence against them; they can be tested, but the dialectic cannot; it is a kind of framework of things in general.

In this metaphysical vision, what happens to human freedom? Hegel is very triumphant on this point. What is freedom but doing what I wish to do, getting what I want to get, obtaining from life what I am seeking for? I can get this only if I do not run against the laws which govern the world. If I defy them I shall be inevitably defeated. To wish to be something is the first principle of rationality. It is irrational to wish to be annihilated, to wish to cause a state of affairs in which there are no further wishes, no further goals. If I want to do mathematics, it is self-defeating to behave as if twice two did not make four. If I want to build an aeroplane, it is suicidal to defy the laws of aerodynamics. If I wish to be effective historically, I must not set myself against the laws which govern human beings and institutions. This non-defiance is not an acquiescence which I consciously adopt with resignation, although I would rather be free. To understand why things cannot be otherwise is to want them not to be otherwise, because to understand things is to understand the reasons for them. To want things to be other than what they rationally must be is to be

[1] As someone once remarked, facts which do not fit Hegel's hypothesis can always be fitted into the category of what does not fit in, a special sort of waste-paper basket category of the not-fitting.

mad. To want the universe to be other than what it is, for Hegel, is like wanting twice two to be seventeen.

If the laws of history are assimilated into the essence of my own thought, as the rules of arithmetic are, then to want them otherwise is like wanting myself to be myself and also different from what I am, to be guided by rules and not to have them, to think and not to think. If you understand Shakespeare, you cannot want Hamlet to have the character of Falstaff, for that is not to understand Shakespeare's intentions, not to understand why he created Hamlet and Falstaff as he did. To want Charlemagne to live after Louis XIV, and to think that Cromwell could well have lived in the nineteenth century, and Bismarck in the seventeenth, is not to understand how the world is made – to want a contradiction, to be irrational. Therefore I always want to be that which I am anyway forced to be; and to have what one wants is to be free. For everything to go as you want, for nothing ever to cross you, is absolute freedom, and the only thing which has that is the absolute spirit – everything there is. The world as a whole is totally free, and we are free to the extent to which we identify ourselves with the rational principles of the world. A free mathematician is a person who naturally thinks mathematically, and a man free in history is a man who naturally proceeds according to the rational laws which govern human lives, which govern history.

To be happy, to be free, is to understand where one is and when one is; where one is on the map; and to act accordingly. If you do not act, you are acted upon, you become historical stuff, you become, as Seneca said, a slave dragged by the Fates, and not the wise man who is led by them. In Hegel, we do see history through the eyes of the victors, certainly not through the eyes of the victims. We see history in the way in which those who, in that sense, understood history have seen it; the Romans were victors, they won, and to win means to be on the right side of the historical flow. Perhaps the Cappadocians whom the Romans defeated thought very differently about things, understood the universe differently, but if they had understood it correctly they would not have been defeated, and because they were defeated they must have misunderstood it.

Therefore to understand things correctly, to be victorious, to survive, to be, in Hegel's sense of the word, real are in some way identified. Certainly history is full of crimes and tragedies from the point of view of a given generation. That is the way of the dialectic. History, says Hegel, is not a smooth progression, not the happy fields, the bubbling brooks of Rousseau's nature – that is a very false conception. History is the 'slaughter-bench', as he calls it, 'to which the happiness of peoples, the wisdom of States and the virtue of individuals have been brought as sacrifices'; 'history is not the theatre of happiness; periods of happiness are blank pages in it'. How is history made? It is made by the few, of course, and by human beings, who are the highest rational creatures. But it is not necessarily made by their conscious wishes and desires.

The great heroes of history, the people who occur at the climaxes, at the moments of synthesis, are people who may think that they are merely pursuing their own particular ends. Caesar, Alexander were ambitious men, and their principal desire was to aggrandise themselves, or to defeat their enemies, but history is wiser than they; history uses them, uses them semi-consciously, as its weapons. This Hegel calls 'the cunning of reason'. He says it is history that 'sets the passions to work for itself, while that which develops its being through such impulsion pays the penalty and suffers the loss'. In short there is a vast, single, all-embracing reason, or what he calls 'the spirit', the development of which is all that occurs. It is a development of the spirit because there exists nothing else; it is a self-development because nothing else can develop it. If we understand it we are its willing tool. If we do not understand it we struggle against it and are lost.

Not to like what you see to be rationally determined, to resist it, is mere suicidal mania, ultimate stupidity, a kind of un-grown-up-ness, a failure to be adult. 'Subjective' for Hegel is an extreme term of opprobrium. Who cares what a schoolboy thinks of the theory of Euclid or the propositions of Newton or of Einstein? To dislike the universe, to denounce it, to resist it, to find it not to your taste, to complain about it, to say that the facts are against you, that there is a brute mass of resistance to you which you cannot pierce, to be frustrated by this, to bleed as the result of falling upon the thorns of life – that is, for Hegel, a form of being inferior, being blind, not understanding, of stupidity and, ultimately, vice.

Let me try to explain this a little more clearly. For Hegel, understanding history is really understanding the nature of things in general, and that is why it is automatically a kind of conscious self-identification with their pattern, so that to be free and to be rational are the same; to be rational is to understand; to understand is to assimilate into one's own being; to be unfree means to be resisted by outward obstacles. When you have captured the obstacle it becomes yours, just as, when a piece of property is out of bounds to you, then by purchasing it, or by invading it, you make it yours and it is not out of bounds, and you are free.

There is something absurd and crazy, for Hegel, in praising or in condemning the vast process in terms of which everything is explicable. To be aware of the whole objective march of history, and then to praise some parts of it because we like them, and to condemn others because they may seem to contain cruelty or injustice or waste, is a mere indulgence in subjective moods. That is an inability to rise beyond what he calls 'civil society', constituted by the economic desires of men, the ordinary private desires of men for prosperity or comfort or a happy life, which is the level at which shallow thinkers like Locke remained. To see a vast human upheaval and then to condemn it because it is cruel or because it is unjust to the innocent is for Hegel profoundly foolish and contemptible. It is like condemning the fact that the number three has no rational square root. Who can wish to know what this or that man feels about events of cosmic importance? These dissatisfactions are trivial facts about someone's passing feelings. To be truly worthy of the occasion is to rise to its level, to realise that something immense and critical is taking place, to have a sense of a historic occasion, when perhaps a new level is being attained by humanity which will automatically transform contemplation of both facts and systems of values.

In Hegel there is a great distinction, which runs through his entire work, between on the one hand the subjective, the emotional, the personal, the utilitarian, the middle-class, the individualistic, which may be a necessary stage in human development, but which is transient and by the early nineteenth century is certainly superseded; and on the other hand the objective, the demonstratively rational, the powerful, the inexorable, the decisive, the concrete – what he calls 'the world-historical'. He is fascinated by the concept of a great man who is a maker and a breaker of societies, the being in whom for the moment history has concentrated her powerful and irresistible strength, who is at once an instrument and a goal of the remorseless march of history. For him, such questions as whether the great man, the earth-shaker, is good or virtuous or just are absolutely meaningless, and indeed petty, for the values implied by these words are themselves created and superseded by those very transformations of which the great man is the Herculean agent. For him the question of whether such a man is just or unjust belongs to the particular system of values, to the particular sphere of action, to the particular moment which is occurring in history at a given time. These are values which great men themselves have made in the past; but the martyrs of one generation are often the lawgivers of the next. Therefore to say that something is bad, wretched, wrong, monstrous, indignation-provoking in a given age is to say that it is so at the level which the great rational process has reached at that particular moment. But by the very transformation of that process by some immensely heroic act, by a revolution, by a war, by the appearance of some vast hero who alters the thoughts and acts of mankind, the values of the previous age become automatically superseded, and what seems abominable in one generation seems virtuous in the next. Therefore let us wait, for it is only what history will make real that is going to be valuable. A value, after all, if you want it to be real, must be objective, and 'objective' means that which the world – reason, the world pattern – intends, that which it supplies next in the irresistible development, the unrolling of the scroll, the inexorable march, what Hegel calls 'God's march through the universe', which for him ultimately is the activity of the State.

The pattern matters more than the individual. For what is the individual? The individual taken by himself is as unintelligible as would be a patch of colour, an isolated sound, a word divorced from the sentence of which it is a part, for words make sense only when combined in sentences, and colours and sounds, whether in nature or in art, when seen in the unique setting in which they in fact occur. Why should this be different in the case of human beings? There are no laws which apply to a man in isolation. I am what I am, because I am uniquely situated in the social setting of my time and place. I am connected by a myriad invisible threads to my fellow beings, to members of my family and my city, of my race and religion and country, to the living and the dead and those yet unborn. I am a kind of nodal point, the focus of an infinite number of strands which centre in, and radiate from, me and everyone else who enters with me into combinations and patterns, groups of lesser or greater tightness or looseness – the great society of the living and the dead of which Burke had spoken. To understand a man, you must understand his milieu, his friends and relations, his superiors and inferiors, what he does and what is done to him, and by what and by whom, not merely because this throws light on him, but because he literally does not exist except as part of this total pattern, any more than a sound in a tune exists (except in some uninteresting sense as a mere physical event) save as a particular ingredient of that particular tune, played on a particular instrument in the particular context in which the music is played. Hence Hegel's celebrated reduction of the individual to an abstract element of a 'concrete' social pattern; his denial that such patterns are mere arrangements of society, that the State and the laws are artificial devices designed for the convenience of individuals; and his insistence that they are networks of which the individuals, whether they will it or not, are the organically fused-together elements. Hence the celebration of the authority and the power and the greatness of the State as against the whims or individual inclinations of this or that citizen or subject.

There is no doubt much plausibility in the view advanced by Hegel's contemporaries, the historical jurists, who said that legal institutions are not so many arbitrary orders of kings or assemblies, or utilitarian devices consciously invented to procure this or that benefit for this or that person or class, but rather part of the unconscious or semi-conscious growth of societies, and expressive of their attitude to life, their half-articulate thoughts and wishes, their ideals and fears and hopes and beliefs and interests, at once the symbol and the substance of what they are and seem to themselves to be. Yet ultimately, driven to its extreme by Hegel, this view becomes a sinister mythology which authorises the indefinite sacrifice of individuals to such abstractions – for all that he calls them 'concrete' – as States, traditions, or the will or destiny of the nation or the race. The world is, after all, composed of things and persons and of nothing else. Societies or States are not things or persons, but ways in which things and persons are or come to be arranged; social patterns have no likes, no wills, no demands, no destinies, no powers. But Hegel does speak as if patterns, like States or Churches, are more real than people or things; as if it is not the houses that make the street, but the street that somehow creates the houses – which it does in a celebrated fairy tale by Hans Christian Andersen.

Among all the patterns the State is supreme. It is the highest of all the patterns because, like the iron ring of which Fichte spoke, it integrates them all; because it is humanity at its most self-conscious, at its most disciplined and its most orderly, and if we believe the universe to be a march, we must believe it to be marching in an intelligible direction, we must believe it to be a patterned order; and the State is the most ordered thing there is. Whatever resists it is bound to be annihilated. Rightly, because what is right and wrong is what history promotes or rejects. The sole objective source of right is the direction of the facts themselves, not individual judgement; not any particular code of laws, not any set of moral principles, but the imperative of history itself, the demands of history. There is in Hegel perpetual talk about what history demands and what history condemns, and the way we talk today about how such and such a nation or such and such a person has been condemned by history is a typical piece of Hegelian realism. This is the imagery and worship of power, of the movement of force for its own sake. This force is, for him, the divine process itself, crushing whatever is meant to be crushed, enthroning that whose hour to dominate has struck – and this, for Hegel, is the essence of the process. This is the source of Carlyle's heroes or Nietzsche's superman, of openly power-worshipping movements such as Marxism and Fascism, both of which (in their different ways) derived morality from historical success;[1] it is the source of the great contrast which Hegel is perpetually tracing between great men and ordinary human beings, between fighters who hack their way and raise humanity to a new level and the mere ants of the human anthill who perform their task without effectively questioning whether to carry such burdens is necessary. It survives in the distinction we ourselves still draw between (what we call) realistic and

[1] Marxism is a little more faithful to Hegel, perhaps, because it assumes that it is classes that exercise power, and class is a super-human institution, whereas Fascists allow greater scope for the violent and imperious individual will.

unrealistic. 'Realistic' often means harsh and brutal, not shrinking from what is usually considered immoral, not swayed by soft sentimental moral considerations.

Hegel is very strong about the necessity for violent action which may be condemned by the more prudish moralists in history. 'Gangrene', he says, 'is not cured with lavender water.' Progress is the work of heroes; heroes who stand above the conventional morality, because they embody the human spirit at its highest; at so high a level, at so mighty a pinnacle, that ordinary human beings can hardly discern what goes on at so lofty a height. They draw, he says, 'not from the peaceful time-hallowed tradition [...] but from a spring whose contents are hidden, [...] from an inner spirit still concealed beneath the surface'. Hence ordinary virtues do not apply here. Sometimes he grows sentimental about heroes: Alexander dies young, Caesar is assassinated, Napoleon is sent to St Helena. Sometimes he exults in their brutal strength. What he says about heroes, he also says about peoples. Peoples are always performing the enormous tasks which history places upon them, and when history has done with them, she rejects them. Peoples are like the garments which the great world-historical process now dons, now doffs, and casts about at will. Having quaffed the bitter draught of world history for which it yearned with infinite thirst, a people apprehends its purpose, and then it dies. A people which insists on surviving after its part is played is a mere political nullity and a bore.

History is a vast cataclysmic objective march, and those who do not obey it are wiped out by it. But why should we condone all these cruelties? Why should the mere fact of a thing having happened in the way that it did automatically justify it? *Are* we so very much against the losers, the victims of history – against Don Quixote? Against the people who are crushed by the wheels of progress? Do we think it so wicked of Don Quixote to have protested against the vulgarity, the smallness, the immorality, the shoddiness of the facts, and to have tried, however foolishly, to erect a more noble ideal? Hegel does not burke this problem. For him the visions of the martyrs are not merely pathetic, not merely weak, not merely contemptible; for him they are vicious too, in a sense. The only thing which is bad is to resist the world process. For the world process is the incarnation of reason – when he says incarnation he means it in the literal sense – and to oppose it is immoral. Therefore he despises the utilitarians, the sentimentalists, the woolly, benevolent philanthropists, the people who want people to be happier, who wring their hands when they see the vast tragedies, the revolutions, the gas-chambers, the appalling suffering through which humanity goes. These persons are for him not merely contemptibly blind to the movement of history but positively immoral, because they resist that which is objectively good by pitting against it their subjective good; and subjective good is like subjective mathematics, it is absurd nonsense. It may obstruct the process for a little but it will be wiped out and pulverised.

Power alone is what Hegel celebrates in his dark, semi-poetical prose. There is a passage which makes this particularly clear. In 1806 Hegel was looking over the last pages of his first great contribution, the *Phenomenology of Spirit*. He was living in Jena at that time and saw the campfires of the French on the eve of the great battle of that name. It suddenly dawned upon him that there it was – history in its objectivity. Still more did he think so when he saw Napoleon riding through the city a few days later. He said, 'the Emperor – that world soul – I saw him ride through the town [...]; it is really an odd feeling to see such a personality physically concentrated in a unique point of space, seated on horseback, while his imperious thought roams and radiates over the entire world' – a vast mind, vast strength, a great bully crushing men and things with its mailed fist. This is Hegel's conception of objective history.

What is one to say about this? One can say only that this curious identification of what is good and what is successful is precisely what the average human being rejects. It is not what we mean by the good and the right. It is impossible to say to us that merely to pit oneself against superior force is in itself immoral. Hegel does not think it is immoral if you are ultimately going to win, if the martyr of today is the hero and the lawgiver and the dictator of tomorrow; but he thinks that to be good and to be successful, in the ultimate, vast, world-historical sense, are identical. This kind of political pragmatism, this kind of success-worship, revolts our normal moral feelings; and there is no genuine argument in Hegel which is really effective against that revulsion. It is merely that in Hegel's vision there is a vast coherent spectacle of history, with which he identifies his own worship of what are for him true values. True values for him are those which are effective; history is the big battalions, marching down a broad avenue, with all the unfulfilled possibilities, all the martyrs and visionaries, wiped out; and morality is really a specific form of bowing before the facts.

This identification of what works with what is good, of what is right with what succeeds, with that which crushes resistance, with that which deserves to crush resistance – this is the sure hallmark of the Hegelian system, whenever it is applied to politics. An unsuccessful rebellion is always bad. That is why it is not perhaps very surprising that he should have approved of the censorship decrees by which Metternich controlled the right to free speech in German universities, nor that he should have been sent for to Berlin by the King of Prussia, who certainly had no desire for any liberal in that particular post at that particular time.

Yet we must not be unfair to Hegel. He did a very great deal for the advance of civilisation. Almost single-handed he created institutional history. Although Herder and even Vico had adumbrated it, it was Hegel who impressed this truth vividly upon the imagination of his generation: that human history was the history of institutions at least as much as the history of kings, generals, adventurers, conquerors, lawgivers. Moreover it was really he who made it plain that what people looked for in history was the individual and the unique, not the general, and that in this respect history was deeply and genuinely different from the natural sciences. Hegel's remarks on the natural sciences are often ludicrous – both ignorant and grotesquely dogmatic. But he did show great insight in conveying the idea that the natural sciences always search for that which is common to all the objects under observation, so that by finding what is uniform in many different things, atoms, tables, elephants, earthquakes, they can formulate laws which apply to an infinite number of similar instances of atoms, tables and the rest. Yet this is the last thing that one seeks from history.

When I read about Robespierre or Napoleon, I do not wish to be told what it is that Napoleon had in common with all other adventurers or with all other emperors; I do not wish to know exactly how Robespierre resembled all other lawyers and revolutionaries. What I wish to discover is that which is uniquely important about and characteristic of these two men. I want Robespierre and his life and character and acts 'brought to life' before me in their unique individuality. When I read about the French Revolution or the Renaissance, I am interested only in a minor way in what these great episodes of human civilisation had in common with developments in Babylon or among the Aztecs. This may be of interest to sociologists, it may indeed be intrinsically illuminating, but the business of historians is to convey differences more than similarities, to paint a portrait of a unique, absolutely specific set of events and persons – a portrait and not an X-ray.

Hegel applied this notion to institutions as well as to individuals. Certainly nobody before the nineteenth century conceived it possible to write the biography of an army, of a civil service, of a religious development. Hegel's treatment of history as if it were the self-development of a vast and infinite world spirit contributed greatly, for all its mythology and darkness, to the rise of a new history, the history of the interconnection of all things. Perhaps Hegel's most original achievement was to invent the very idea of the history of thought: for certainly nobody before him had written, or conceived it possible to write, the history of philosophical or any other thought, not as a loose succession – first one sage and his system, then another – but as a continuous development of ideas from one generation of thinkers to the next, and intimately related to economic or social or other kinds of changes in a society or culture. All this is now so much taken for granted that Hegel's originality can scarcely be realised today.

Moreover, Hegel seemed to place immense stress on history and the value of history, and the fact that everything in it matters and nothing else matters at all. More emphatically even than Herder he spoke as if facts could not be clearly distinguished into the historically relevant and irrelevant; since the way in which people wear their clothes or eat their food, sail the seas or sing their songs, their handwriting, their accent, may be more illuminating than many of their more official acts – their wars, their treaties, their constitutions. There is no telling what may not be useful towards explaining the total process of history, in which this or that people played its part, appeared on the stage at its destined moment and duly left it after its hour had struck.

Hegel's attack upon the old moralising history which looked to the past mainly to learn about errors and vices, his condemnation of blame and praise, his invitation to rational men to identify themselves with the great moving forces as such, while they may have led to the worship of power, to a peculiarly brutal form of political realism, did also contribute to making all historical facts appear of equal and incalculable value. For the solution to all questions now seemed to lie in history – a priori history, it is true, and spiritual history, but still history. History was now as important in telling men how to live as theology once was. It was the new theodicy – the interpretation of the ways of God to men. And in this way it discredited eighteenth-century history, which classified facts in terms of some subjective criterion of good and bad, and it weighted the scales in favour of that scrupulous factual history which treated all facts as being on the same level, and was prepared to look for them in the most unlikely corners. History was supremely important; everything in it deserved notice, for it might throw light by laying bare the essence of that unique network, that concatenation of elements which forms the individual personality, in this case the universe, of which men are elements and limbs.

Furthermore, Hegel drew attention to unconscious factors in history: the dark forces, the vast impersonal urges, what he liked to think of as the semi-conscious strivings of reason seeking to realise its being, but which we may call simply the half-unconscious forces, the occult psychological causes which we now think at least as important as the conscious intentions of generals or kings or violent revolutionaries. This too helped to de-personalise and, if I may put it so, de-moralise history.

There is a further respect in which Hegel's method is valuable, namely in its application to works of art, to the sense of artistic greatness and beauty, and to the aesthetic field generally. He thought he was reducing the confused language of the Romantics to something disciplined and rigorous. This was an illusion. The form acquired a specious kind of technicality but the content remained thoroughly dark. Despite all his efforts the concepts remain loose. All the Romantic terminology which he and other German metaphysicians and poets of this period employed – the notions of transcendence and integration, of inner conflict, of forces which at once destroy and fuse with and fertilise each other; the notion of a unity which is at once the purpose and the principle, the pattern and the goal, and the essence of something which is at the same time an entity and a process, a being and a becoming – all this, which has led to such vagueness, and often nonsense, when applied in logic or history or the sciences, has a unique part to play in describing the indescribable: beautiful objects, psychical processes, works of art.

Romantic terminology generally is best at describing not easily analysable experiences precisely because it is evocative, imprecise, indefinite, and has a rich vagueness of association and a rich use of imagery and metaphor. How are we to describe a poem, a symphony, an aesthetic experience of almost any kind? Perhaps it is best to say nothing: but if we wish to speak, then the lucid, intelligible public language used by really clear elegant thinkers such as Hume and Voltaire, or even Helvétius, is of little use here. In music, for example, it does sometimes make a kind of sense to speak of a dialectical growth – a tune which clashes with and flows into other musical phrases, leading to their mutual annihilation and yet not: also to their transcendence, to the integration of the conflicting forces into something richer and, if you like, higher, more perfect than the original ingredients. Here one can speak of the obscure semi-conscious growth of forces which burst out suddenly in some splendid, golden shower. The turbid and infinitely suggestive language of Hegel, and still more of other Romantic philosophers, of Schelling, the brothers Schlegel, Novalis, and indeed of Coleridge and to some degree of Carlyle, really does at moments penetrate by its use of musical and biological imagery to something like the heart of the creative process.

Such language can do something to convey the essence of what the development of a pattern is like, the impalpable yet very real interrelation of sounds and feeling – and even moral purposes – in a symphony, or an opera, or a Mass; and with a greater risk of clouding the issue, such a semi-poetical way of talking may give a far more vivid sense of the contours of a culture, of the ideals of a school of artists or philosophers, the attitude of a generation – something not to be analysed by the more precise, more logically coherent, more tough-minded terminology which alone, with its standards of integrity and scholarship, guarantees truth and clarity in fields amenable to more exact treatment. In literary criticism and in the history of art, in the history of ideas and the analysis of civilisation, in every discipline in which there is poetry as well as prose, the Hegelian prescription – the thesis–antithesis method, the description of everything as perpetually passing into its opposite, as an unstable equilibrium of mutually conflicting forces – genuinely transformed both the European sensibility and its modes of expression.

Hegel's real error was to suppose that the whole of the universe – everything – was a kind of work of art which was creating itself, and therefore that this kind of half-biological, half-musical terminology was what described it best. As a result he imposed upon mankind a great many erroneous views; for example, that values were identical with facts, and that what was good was what was successful – which all morally sensitive persons, long before and after his day, have rejected, and rightly rejected. His great crime was to have created an enormous mythology in which the State is a person, and history is a person, and there is the one single pattern which metaphysical insight alone can discern. He created a school of a priori history which ignored the ordinary facts because the philosopher, armed with superior insight, can deduce what happens by a species of rational double vision, a kind of clairvoyance which enables him to tell in a mathematically certain way what has occurred, as opposed to the sadly empirical, imperfect, fussy way in which the ordinary historian has to proceed.

In spite of all his vices Hegel created an immense system which for a long time dominated the minds of mankind. As for liberty, there can be none in a tight pattern. There can be no liberty where obedience to the pattern is the only true self-expression, where what you call liberty is not the possibility of acting within some kind of vacuum, however small, which is left for your own personal choice, in which you are not interfered with by others. Hegelian liberty simply consists of conquest or possession of that which obstructs you, until you have conquered and possessed everything, and then you are identical with the master of the universe. Until you have done that, the best that you can do is to try to understand why you must be as you must be, and instead of groaning and moaning and complaining about the appalling burdens upon you, welcome them joyously. But the joyous welcome of burdens is not liberty.

There have always been people who have wanted to be secure in some tight establishment, to find their rightful secure place in some rigid system, rather than to be free. To such people Hegel says a word of comfort. Nevertheless, fundamentally this is a vast confusion, a historically fatal identification of liberty, as we understand it, with security – the sense of belonging to some unique place where you are protected against obstacles because you can foresee them all. But that is not what we call liberty: maybe it is a form of wisdom, of understanding, of loyalty, of happiness, of holiness. The essence of liberty has always lain in the ability to choose as you wish to choose, because you wish so to choose, uncoerced, unbullied, not swallowed up in some vast system; and in the right to resist, to be unpopular, to stand up for your convictions merely because they are your convictions. That is true freedom, and without it there is neither freedom of any kind, nor even the illusion of it.

Saint-Simon

COMTE HENRI DE SAINT-SIMON is the greatest of all the prophets of the twentieth century. His writings and his life were confused and even chaotic. He was regarded in his own lifetime as an inspired lunatic. He wrote badly – with flashes of intuition mingled with immense tracts of naive and fantastic imagining. His reputation grew posthumously. The fact that Karl Marx, who borrowed so much from him, relegated him to the ranks of utopian socialists, so called, did a great deal to create the impression that, although a gifted man, he was too naive and too foolish and too monomaniacal to be worth close study. Yet if prophecy is laid along prophecy and the predictions of Karl Marx are compared to those of Saint-Simon, the balance will turn out to be more than favourable to Saint-Simon.

All his life, Saint-Simon was possessed with the idea that he was the great new Messiah who had at last come to save the earth, and he lived at a time when a great many people were under that peculiar impression. There never was a period to compare with the end of the eighteenth and the beginning of the nineteenth century for the extraordinary density of megalomaniac Messiahs. Everybody at that period seemed to think that he at last had been gifted with that unique power of penetration and imagination which was destined to solve all human evils. If you read Rousseau, you get the impression that although he thinks he has predecessors it is only he to whom the final light has been vouchsafed. Similarly with Fichte: you feel that he is saying that, although naturally Luther was important and Christ was important, and the great Greek philosophers were important, yet the final illumination may be obtained only from him – that it is his mission, his dedication, to open to humanity those gates which no doubt have been prised half or a quarter open by previous thinkers, but which it was his privilege to fling open finally and for ever.

You get exactly the same impression when you read Hegel, who felt that he was the summation, the complete synthesis, of all the thought that had gone before, finally, in an immense harmonious composition which at last was the sum of all human wisdom, of all human knowledge, so that, after him, all that his disciples, and indeed humanity, would have to do was simply to work out the results and apply them. Similarly in France, with the so-called utopian socialists, Saint-Simon, Fourier and even their successors Bazard and Leroux, you get the impression that they say: 'Well, of course, there are predecessors; there was Moses, there was Socrates, there was Christ, there was Newton, or Descartes, or other important thinkers, even geniuses. But all these people merely adumbrated, they merely hinted; they merely obtained a corner of the truth. The final revelation is what I now have to say to you.' In spite of that, Saint-Simon remains an important, and indeed marvellous, thinker.

Let me try to enumerate some of the doctrines of which he was as much an originator as anyone. It is very difficult ever to attribute a doctrine or an idea to one person and one person only in so inexact a subject as the humane sciences. Nevertheless, one can without great fear of contradiction say that Saint-Simon is the father of European historicism far more than the Germans; that he is the person who really criticised the unhistorical methods of the eighteenth century and put forward an interpretation of history of his own which was at the root of the great French historical school of the early nineteenth century, and which really provided those weapons in terms of which concrete history came to be written, rather than those much more shadowy ideological schemata which the German idealists provided at the same time.

He is not only the father of historical writing – at any rate in France, and arguably in Western Europe. He is also the father of what I should like to call the technological interpretation of history. This is not quite the same as the materialistic interpretation of history which we associate with the name of Marx, but it does lie at its root, and in certain respects is a much more original and tenable view. Saint-Simon is the first person to define classes in the modern sense, as economic social entities, dependent in a direct way upon the progress of technology – the progress of machinery, the progress of the ways in which people obtain and distribute and consume products. In short, he is the first person to draw serious attention to the economic factors in history. Moreover, wherever there is talk about a planned society, about a planned economy, about technocracy, about the necessity for what the French call *dirigisme*, anti-laissez-faire; wherever there is a New Deal; wherever there is propaganda in favour of some kind of rational organisation of industry and of commerce, in favour of applying science for the benefit of society, and, in general, in favour of everything which we have now come to associate with a planned rather than a laissez-faire State – wherever there is talk of this sort, the ideas which are bandied saw the light originally in the half-published manuscripts of Saint-Simon.

Again, Saint-Simon more than anyone else invented the notion of the government of society by elites, using a double morality. There is of course something of that in Plato and in other previous thinkers, but Saint-Simon is almost the first thinker who comes out and says that it is important for society to be governed not democratically, but by elites of persons who understand the technological needs and the technological possibilities of their time; and that, since the majority of human beings are stupid, and since they mostly obey their emotions, what the enlightened elite must do is to practise one morality themselves and feed their flock of human subjects with another. So the notion of the double morality, of which we have heard so much in, for example, the hideous Utopias of Aldous Huxley or Orwell, has its origin in the golden, optimistic view of Saint-Simon, who, so far from thinking such a double standard immoral or dangerous, thinks that it is the only way to progress, to advance humanity towards the gate of that paradise which, in common with the thinkers of the eighteenth century, he thinks it best deserves and is on the point of attaining – if only it will listen to his views.

He is one of the most trenchant attackers of such eighteenth-century shibboleths as civil liberty, human rights, natural rights, democracy, laissez-faire, individualism, nationalism. He attacks them because he is the first person to see – as the thinkers of the eighteenth century never did quite clearly see – the incompatibility between the view that wise men ought to direct society and the view that people ought to govern themselves; the incompatibility, in short, between a society which is directed by a group of wise men who alone know towards what goal to move and how to get humanity to move towards it, and the notion that it is better to govern oneself, even than to be governed well. He chooses, of course, in favour of good government. But he is perfectly aware that this means the impossibility of self-government. He is the first person to make that clear, and that is why his attack on all the cherished liberal ideas of the eighteenth century, and indeed of the nineteenth and twentieth centuries, has not only a modern ring, but something truly original about it. It is as if he were the first person to feel the logical consequences of the beliefs which seem to be held so comfortably together with their opposites in the far shallower and apparently far clearer thought of the great thinkers of the eighteenth century, both in France and in Germany.

Finally, Saint-Simon is the first originator of what might be called secular religions – that is to say, the first person to see that one cannot live by technological wisdom alone; that something must be done to stimulate the feelings, the emotions, the religious instincts of mankind. He is the first person – not cold-bloodedly, because he did it with a great deal of enthusiasm and warmth, which were natural to him – to invent that substitute for religion, that secularised, humanised, de-theologicalised variant of Christianity of which so many versions began to circulate in the nineteenth century and after – something like the religion of humanity of Kant; something like all the pseudo-religions, all the moralities with a faint religious flavour, which were regarded as a substitute, for rational men, for the blindly dogmatic and anti-scientific theological darkness of the past. That alone gives Saint-Simon a claim to be regarded as one of the most seminal, one of the most original, and one of the most influential thinkers – if not the most influential thinker – of our own day; and like other thinkers whom I have been discussing, he is more relevant to our own century than he was to the nineteenth, as I propose to show.

Let us begin with the notion of historicism, for which, as I say, he was largely responsible. The problem which occupied Saint-Simon and his contemporaries was the failure of the French Revolution. Saint-Simon was born in 1760 and died in 1825, and I ought to say something about his life in order to explain how his views came to be what they were. He was a member of the great family of Saint-Simon, which had produced, about a hundred years before, the famous Duke, the author of the *Mémoires*, and he was very proud of that. He even traced his descent from Charlemagne. Let me quote him on the subject:

> I write because I have new ideas. I express them in the form in which they have taken shape in my mind. I leave it to professional writers to polish them. I write as a gentleman, as a descendant of the Counts of Vermandois, and as the literary heir of the Duke of Saint-Simon. All the great things that were ever done and said were done and said by gentlemen: Copernicus, Galileo, Bacon, Descartes, Newton, Leibniz – they were all members of the gentry. Napoleon too would have written down all his ideas

> instead of practising them, had he not happened upon a vacant throne.

This is a fair example of Saint-Simon's bombastic style. It was said that he got his valet to wake him every morning with the words: 'Rise, M. le Comte – you have great things to achieve.' When he was a young man, being of a restless disposition and imaginative temperament and warm heart, he went to America, where he entered into American service and took part in the siege of Yorktown under General Washington. After the American War of Liberation he went down to Mexico, where, being already possessed by ideas of the necessity of reforming society by vast technological schemes, he tried to persuade the Spanish Viceroy of Mexico to pierce the Isthmus of Panama and dig a canal, which he thought would revolutionise trade in those waters. At that time the idea was very premature and nobody took the slightest notice of it. From there he went to Holland, where he tried to stimulate an attack on British colonies; from there to Spain, where he tried to get a canal dug between Madrid and the sea. He was preoccupied with the notion of making nature serve mankind, getting something for nothing – getting a canal dug and then letting the water, nature herself, perform the work which was so laboriously and so wastefully performed by human beings. None of this came about; indeed the Spanish canal, which nearly went through, was overwhelmed by the French Revolution.

In the Revolution, of course, he sympathised most warmly with the reformers. He had been a pupil of the great mathematician and essayist, the editor of the Encyclopedia, d'Alembert. He knew some of the Encyclopedists of the end of the eighteenth century quite well personally and he was, at that time, set to complete the cycle of the century's enlightened men. He needed to drop the title of Count, and he called himself Monsieur Bonhomme. He took part in the Revolution on the side of the rebels, of the Gironde. Presently the Revolution developed into the Terror, and Saint-Simon, as an aristocrat, was almost arrested – a warrant went out in his name. Somebody else was arrested by mistake and Saint-Simon, very characteristically, as soon as he learnt this, gave himself up in order to liberate the man who was innocently incarcerated. He miraculously survived the Terror, and when he emerged threw himself with undiminished zeal into the stream of life, his great theory being that he wanted to reform humanity. Something was obviously gravely wrong with the affairs of men if all these admirable ideas conceived by men of such high character and such omniscience, such exquisite wit and such penetrating intelligence, such scrupulous attention to the truth, nevertheless ended in the slaughter of the guillotine.

But in order to reform mankind one must know, one must learn, one must study all the sciences and all the arts; and more than that, one must quaff the cup of experience, one must understand the true nature of virtue and of vice, and in order to do that one must have as many and as varied experiences as possible. One must touch life at as many points as possible. In short, one must live. In order to do this one must have money. But Saint-Simon's estate had been sequestrated by the Revolution. Consequently, he threw himself into financial speculation, took part in the sales of the confiscated estates of the nobility, made an enormous fortune, was cheated out of it by his German partner Baron Redern, and ended as he had begun in the Revolution – penniless.

By this time he had lived. He had given enormous dinner parties to which he invited those he regarded as the most interesting men of the time – the physicists, the chemists, the physiologists, the mathematicians – from all of whom he hoped to learn about the secrets of their craft. Some mathematics he already knew through d'Alembert. He complained in later life that these scientists consumed his food and talked about everything under the sun except the sciences about which he wished to question them. Nevertheless he did pick up, here and there, fragments of this and that, and became a typical imaginative autodidact. His head was a perpetual buzz of the most extraordinary confusion and chaos. In his writings the ideas of the greatest depth and brilliance alternate with absolute nonsense.

You begin, for example, reading an early treatise about the freedom of the seas, about which he had political theories, and suddenly, without knowing where you are, you find that you are in the midst of a disquisition on gravitation, and not just on gravitation in Newton's sense, but a quite mystical gravitation which affects the intellectual as well as the physical sphere. You think that you are reading about historical facts of the Middle Ages and you are suddenly told that humanity is like a single man – an idea already found in Pascal – and then that the age of mankind today is about forty – between thirty-five and forty-five – and in another place that the age of the French people is about twenty-one. You read pages of the greatest interest about his views on the development of mankind in the classical age and into the Christian Middle Ages, and suddenly you are told that Homer, who invented polytheism, also invented democracy, because there was democracy on Olympus, and that is how there came to be democracy on earth.

But let us leave out all the fantastic, naive and ludicrous aspects of Saint-Simon. His hypothesis about why the French Revolution had failed was perhaps the most original by then put forward. Everyone had explained the disaster in accordance with his own views. Why did the Revolution fail? The liberals said, because of the Terror, in other words, because the Revolutionaries were not liberal enough – did not respect human rights sufficiently. The orthodox and religious and conservatives said, because men had broken away from tradition, or from the word of God, and the spirit of God was sent to visit those who had preferred their own unaided human reason to the divine faith. The socialist fanatics – people like Babeuf – said, because the Revolution had not gone far enough, because equal distribution of property ought to have occurred, because, in short, though there may have been liberty, that liberty was nothing without economic equality. Many other explanations were also put forward.

Saint-Simon's explanation in a sense resembled Hegel's explanation, but was infinitely more concrete, infinitely more to do with actual living human beings and real history as opposed to the vast shadowy metaphysical ideas, like the shadows of a great Gothic cathedral, in which Hegel seemed permanently to dwell. Saint-Simon said this was because he was not understood, and in his early writings he begins to put forward his own view of what history is. He is really the father of the quasi-materialist explanation, as I said before. For him, history is a story of living men trying to develop their faculties as richly and many-sidedly as possible. In order to do this, they exploit nature; in order to exploit nature, they have to have tools or weapons. Consequently their imagination, their inventiveness, everything that they have with which to think and to will, is directed upon the discovery of the optimum weapons for the subjugation of nature and the procuring to themselves of what will satisfy their desires, their inclinations and what he likes to call their interests.

The very invention of weapons in this way creates what is called technological advance, and the technological advance itself creates classes. It creates classes because the people who have the weapons can dominate those who have not. This very simple, basic idea Marx borrowed from Saint-Simon, if not totally, then certainly more than from anyone else. Once you have a class association on the part of the able, the gifted, the superior, who have invented tools and weapons by which they can procure more, by which they can extract more from nature than others, the others gradually find themselves dominated by this superior elite. They are not dominated for long, because ultimately they become rebellious, they become discontented, they think that they too, if only they allowed their imaginations and their reasons to work, can invent something with which they can not only get more from nature than they are getting, but perhaps overthrow the elite. The elite gradually, as with all elites, becomes obsolete, their ideas become ossified, they do not realise that invention and discovery are going on underneath them, among the lower class; and gradually, because they cling for too long to weapons of production (if one can speak in such terms), or anyhow to economic forms of life which are no longer suitable to the new weapons, to the new technological advances which the recalcitrant, indignant, active, imaginative, ambitious slaves are in the meanwhile perfecting, they are duly overthrown by this lower class, which itself then comes to power, only gradually to be ousted and made obsolete by the persons whom they exploit, whom they use.

In a way this looks exactly like the Marxist, materialist view of history, but Saint-Simon does not say what Marx says, namely, that all ideas are dominated by the conditions of distribution or production, by economic factors. He does think ideas are born only at the time when they satisfy an interest. In that sense people make inventions and discoveries, and think thoughts, and invent mathematics or poetry or whatever it may be, only in response to the general conditions of their time – only when this kind of thing satisfies their particular impulses, which are themselves conditioned to some degree by the economic environment and by the way in which people live. But he thinks that these ideas have a vast independent influence far greater than Marxists accord them, and therefore he thinks that inventions are as much the products of ideas, and in particular that classes are as much the products of ideas, as they are of technological evolution as such.

For example, he thinks that slavery is an idea which was born at a certain period when people realised they would have much more leisure if they could make slaves do their work; similarly, the abolition of slavery was not so much the result of the pressure of economic circumstances, because it had become uneconomic to use slaves, which is the typical Marxist interpretation of this event, but because of the rise of Christianity. Christianity itself may have something to do with the economic world in which it was born; nevertheless it was Christian ideas – which were primarily religious, spiritual, ethical – that actually abolished slavery, when it need not have been abolished but for the birth of these ideas. Hence Saint-Simon's tremendous emphasis on the role of genius in history, on the fact that unless there are men of genius and unless they are given an opportunity of functioning, unless, in short, the great ideas of great men who perceive and understand the circumstances of their own time with a deeper insight and greater imagination are given scope, progress will be retarded. Progress is by no means automatic, by no means depends on some kind of inevitable machinery of the clash of classes or technological advance.

From this he developed the notion that history must be understood as a kind of evolution of mankind in the satisfaction of its various needs, and for that reason where the needs are different the satisfaction will be different. Therefore the dogmatic judgements which the eighteenth century was so fond of passing upon the Middle Ages or upon earlier periods as periods of darkness, ignorance, prejudice, superstition, ages of emptiness, and indeed contemptible and detestable in comparison with the dawning light of the rationalism of the eighteenth century – that was a profoundly unhistorical and totally untenable view.

Everything must be judged in its proper context. This idea, so familiar to us now, so simple, was not at all familiar to the people of the beginning of the nineteenth century. Everything must be judged in its context: Saint-Simon makes this idea much clearer than Herder. The Middle Ages, which we call dark, were not dark to themselves. The Middle Ages were a period when human needs were very different from ours, and an age ought to be approved of or disapproved of, praised or blamed, thought great or small, progressive or reactionary, in accordance with whether it satisfied the needs of its time, not the needs of some later period completely alien to its own time. Saint-Simon says: We always hear about this idea of progress, but what are we told about what progress is? What is this inevitable progress by which the eighteenth century is better than the seventeenth, and the seventeenth better than the sixteenth, and the sixteenth better than all the preceding ages? We are told that it is because men learn from nature, and because men apply reason, and something about more being done for the common good – but these, he says, are very vague terms; we do not know what people mean by reason, what they mean by nature. Let me give you some criteria for progress, he says, which will be concrete and which we may be able to use in writing history properly. He is as good as his word. He gives four criteria of progress, and very interesting they are.

The first is this: The progressive society is that which provides the maximum means of satisfying the greatest number of needs of the human beings who compose it. Anything is progressive which does this, which satisfies the maximum number of needs – that is the central idea of Saint-Simon from the beginning to the end. Human beings have certain needs – not necessarily for happiness, not necessarily for wisdom, for knowledge, for self-sacrifice or whatever it may be – and what they want is to satisfy them. These needs should be indulged, without asking why, and anything which gives a rich and many-sided development to these needs, which assists the greatest growth of personality in as many directions as is possible, that is progress or progressive.

The second criterion is this: Anything that is progressive will give the opportunity to the best to reach the top. The best, for him, are the most gifted, the most imaginative, the cleverest, the most profound, the most energetic, the most active, those who want the full flavour of life. For Saint-Simon there are very few classes of men: those who enhance life and those who are against it, those who want to get things done and want to provide things for people – who want a thing to happen, who want to satisfy needs – and those who are in favour of lowering the tone, making things quieter, allowing things to sink, who are against all the bustle, who want things, on the whole, to descend, decline and ultimately approach the condition of complete nullity.

The third criterion of progress is the provision of the maximum unity and strength for the purpose of a rebellion or an invasion; and the fourth criterion is conduciveness to invention and discovery and civilisation. For example, leisure conduces to these, and that is why slavery was seen, in his own time, as a progressive institution – or the invention of writing, or whatever it may be.

These are concrete criteria and, Saint-Simon says, if you judge history in terms of these the picture changes very deeply from that which has been presented to us by the dogmatists of the eighteenth-century Enlightenment. The dark ages cease to be dark if you think of what, for example, Pope Gregory VII or St Louis did in their day. These men, after all, built roads, they drained marshes. They built hospitals, they taught vast numbers of men to read and to write. Above all, they preserved the unity of Europe, they held back the invaders of the East, they civilised sixty million people, and sixty million people lived in a unitary manner, under roughly the same regime, and were able to develop harmoniously together. This is by no means a dark age; this is an age far less broken, far less turbid, far less frustrated for those who lived in it than the ages which followed. An age is progressive in which the largest number of people can do as much of what they want at that particular moment as is possible for them. The so-called dark ages were a period of the richest possible development of mankind at that time and in that condition of technological advance.

Of course, all these things pass, these institutions become obsolete, because they are superseded. New inventions occur, new discoveries are made, new men of genius arrive who automatically, by stirring people's minds, create new needs. The old institutions cannot satisfy the new needs, or become vested interests; they press against those needs, they try to repress them, restrain them, stop them, and they become a drag upon progress. Ultimately they become obsolescent, and somebody arises who destroys them, throws them over. That is a revolution. A revolution always means that somebody or other must arise for the purpose of clearing out what has become a completely antiquated, no longer useful institution which has outlived any possible good which it might conceivably once have done. Therefore history for Saint-Simon is a kind of rhythm of what his disciples called organic and critical periods.

Organic periods are periods when humanity is unified, when it develops harmoniously, when the people who are in charge of it on the whole foster progress – progress in the sense of providing the maximum number of people with the maximum of opportunities for satisfying the maximum number of their needs, whatever they are. Critical periods are periods when these arrangements are becoming obsolescent, when the institutions themselves become obstacles to progress, when human beings feel that what they want is different from that which they are getting, when there is a new spirit which is about to sunder the old bottles in which it is still imprisoned – when, for example, as Saint-Simon thought of his own day, we have an industrial age which is still ludicrously and artificially confined within obsolete feudal frameworks.

The critical age is an age when destruction predominates over construction. It is something inferior in Saint-Simon's eyes, but nevertheless it is inevitable and necessary. For example, in his discussion of the eighteenth century and what made the French Revolution he says the French Revolution was really made by lawyers and metaphysicians. These are fundamentally destroyers. What do lawyers do? Lawyers employ such concepts as absolute rights, natural rights and liberty, and liberty is always a negative concept. The invocation of liberty means that somebody is trying to take something away from you which you then try to invent some reason for keeping. In short, a situation has arisen in which humanity, or the greater part of it, does not have enough to live by, and you feel hemmed in, you feel repressed. So you engage professionals called lawyers, or professionals called metaphysicians, for the purpose of doing something which you cannot do yourself, namely somehow or other to extract out of the ruling class something which you are too weak to force them to deliver by sheer violence on your own part. So lawyers are people who are engaged in inventing good and bad reasons for circumventing the old, worn-out machinery of government, the old obsolete tradition which is stifling vast sections of the population; and metaphysicians are people, particularly in the eighteenth century, who perform the very necessary task of undermining the old religions.

Christianity, says Saint-Simon, was a great thing in its own day, as was Judaism, but it must develop, it must advance. If it remains static, it will burst, it will be overthrown. That is why, of all the great religious reformers, he dislikes Luther the most. Luther to him is a man too riveted to his particular faith, which was no doubt necessary for the purpose of overthrowing Catholicism, which Saint-Simon thought was becoming somewhat old-fashioned, obsolete, oppressive in Luther's day. For that Luther substituted devotion to the Bible, a single book. No doubt the Bible was all very well for a semi-nomadic Jewish tribe living in a small country in the eastern Mediterranean, but it cannot cope with the development of nations. Flexibility is wanted, perpetual change, perpetual advance. The Roman Church, whatever may be said against it, has a flexible element. No doubt it is reactionary in some ways, repressive and oppressive in others, but by means of endless legal fictions, by asserting that the source of authority is not an unalterable printed text but an altering human institution, which after all consists of generations of men, each of which is a little different from those of the past, it made itself sufficiently flexible to be able to guide humanity through the Middle Ages with immense success. This is precisely what Luther put an end to. He broke the European unity, he tied religion to something unaltering, he asserted private, absolute principles. If there is anything which Saint-Simon detests it is the notion of absolute principle – nothing is stable, nothing is absolute, everything evolves, everything responds to the movement of the times, to the evolution of humanity, to the new inventions, new discoveries, new minds, new souls, new hearts which it is gradually producing. Consequently he is on the whole pro-Catholic and anti-Protestant; but towards the end he is not an orthodox Christian at all.

As for the French Revolution, what was that? That was simply a revolution which occurred at the end of a period of long elaboration. The development of industry and commerce, and economic changes of a very violent and upsetting kind, had been occurring since at any rate the beginning of the seventeenth century. Too little notice had been taken of this by those whose business it was to govern mankind. Duly, as a result of mismanagement on the part of people who lived in the traditional past and did not understand that a new industrial age was dawning or that the middle classes were now the persons with the real power (and Saint-Simon is nowhere more eloquent or more penetrating than when he is discussing what he means by real power, and the people who really win it), the French government, like those of other nations, did not proceed in accordance with these changes, did not shift their arrangements accordingly. Consequently the Treasury had gone bankrupt when they called upon the State to assist them. The Third Estate, in whose hands by this time the real power was, though it did not know it, suddenly realised that it did not need to compromise. It had the power: all it had to do was to use it. Why should they pay for what they could take? Why should they use persuasion when they could use force? And the Revolution occurred.

In short, Saint-Simon interprets the Revolution as the rising of the middle class to class-consciousness, consciousness of its real place and the fact that it could satisfy its demands by simply blowing away the few simple rules, the completely hollowed-out earlier classes – the clergy and the aristocracy and the army – which had been sitting on their shoulders, suppressing them, with no *raison d'être* that applied in the new world. And the lawyers, what part had they played? They supplied arguments, slogans to the new bourgeoisie; but any slogans become obsolete in time, and their slogans – 'All Power for the People', 'Human Liberty' and so forth – were just as hollow as the slogans of the reactionaries whom they opposed. No doubt they performed a very necessary task, the task of termites, in boring under the old building, which had to collapse. They are the scavengers, the gravediggers, who are expected to remove the semi-ruined old regime, but they are not going to build a new citadel – that will need creative persons, constructive abilities, not people trained in circumventing, in pettifogging, in writing pamphlets under conditions of censorship in which you say one thing and mean another, not sly, cunning, ultimately small-minded lawyers with minds not attuned to the big constructive task of the future. But since the lawyers were the only people the lower classes trusted, because it was they who wrote the revolutionary pamphlets and put them in power, the revolution was lost. The revolution ought to have been conducted by the people who really were the new men, by the great new merchants, the great new captains of industry, the great new bankers, the people who belonged to the modern world.

Here one of Saint-Simon's most original, penetrating and creative ideas comes in. In every age there is a distribution of power. There are the people who matter and the people who do not. There are the people who represent what is coming, the new, and the people who represent what is dying away, the old. In the Middle Ages feudal lords represented the principle of progress because they defended the peasants, who were then the producers of the goods that were needed by humanity. They protected them against interruption of their work, and in general did their best to enhance that particular order. Soldiers were needed by the order too, and priests. Christianity in its day was an immense progressive force, and so long as it was a progressive force the priests who taught it were progressive men, people who taught something more adjusted to the needs of their time than the Roman religion or the Greek religion or the Jewish religion would have been. But they became obsolete, they have given way to quite a different set of men.

Today it is not priests, it is not soldiers, it is not feudal lords who matter, it is quite a different class of men: scientists, industrialists, bankers, experts – people, ultimately, who represent science and industry. Science and industry have come to stay, but the only way in which we can organise a world in which human beings can satisfy their wishes is by applying science in the most productive manner, that is to say in the manner that will develop the great new disciplines which are at last rising in the world – commerce, industry, and above all credit banking.

Saint-Simon is extraordinarily obsessed by the importance of bankers, because he is so committed to the game of playing historical analogies, so deeply affected by the notion of history, by the notion of development and evolution, by the fact that nothing stands still and that everything in one age may correspond to something (which is never identical) in any other age. He often asks who corresponds in his own age to the people who were responsible for unity and centralisation in the Middle Ages, say, or in the Roman Empire. The Romans were great because they reigned over almost all mankind and their laws were universal. The Middle Ages were great because the Church disciplined the whole world, civilised it, and therefore prevented strife, prevented provincialism, prevented the waste which is for Saint-Simon the worst of all crimes – the flooding away, the complete destruction of human resources in isolated, private, individual directions. Who is like that now? Banks, he says: credit is the great octopus, the great universal force which holds everybody together, and people who slight it, people who defy it, people who think they can do without it are destroyed by it. The greatest power in the world is the interconnection of international finance. But far from attacking it, far from being against it as an oppressive system which sucks the blood out of the people (as for example Cobbett or even Sismondi were apt to do at about that time), he welcomed it as a great riveting, centralising, connecting force, because unity to him is everything.

The only way in which humanity can develop is by the rational concentration of its resources, so that every single object which is possessed, every single art, every single gift, every single aspiration which people have, shall not be wasted but used in the best way, directed to its best possible use. Anything which unifies is better than anything which disintegrates. It is bad enough to have to obey stupid rulers, but chaos is worse still, and Saint-Simon, like Hobbes after the English revolution in the seventeenth century, is frightened above all of meaningless bloodshed, violence, mobs sweeping through the streets, maddened Jacobins, their heads filled with empty slogans provided by rhetorical lawyers who do not understand the time in which they live – hence his worship of industrialists, bankers, men of business, and his conception of society as an enormous business establishment, something like ICI[1] or General Motors. The State for him is already obsolescent, though needed at one time for the protection of individuals against the power of the encroaching Church. Then he suddenly observes that of course the clergy purported to be scientists; but now that the clergy have been discredited there is no further need for protection against them, and therefore the useful, the creative part of the State, which made possible economic and social and

[1] [Imperial Chemical Industries (1926–2008).]

spiritual development for human beings without the dead hand of the no longer living Church, is gone, and the State itself has become dead, oppressive and unnecessary. Therefore (he says very firmly) what we need is simply a State which has become a kind of industrial enterprise of which we are all members, a kind of enormous limited liability company – or unlimited liability, perhaps, precisely as envisaged by Burke, who was also historically minded. Saint-Simon demands not merely what Burke calls 'a partnership in all science; a partnership in all art; a partnership in every virtue', although he believes in that, of course, passionately, but also a partnership in the most literal sense (in the sense in which Burke's State was decidedly not meant as a partnership), a partnership in trade, in calico – exactly what Burke denied – a partnership in commerce, in industry, in the sale of all that humans need, and in knowledge, without which men cannot get anything done at all.

What are the purposes of society? Well, says Saint-Simon, we are told it is the common good, but that is very vague. The purpose of society is self-development, the purpose of society is 'the best application, in order to satisfy human needs, of knowledge acquired by the sciences, in the arts and crafts, the dissemination of such knowledge, and the development and maximum accumulation of its fruits, that is, in the most useful combination of all separate activities, in the sphere of the sciences, the arts and crafts'. Enough homage to Alexanders, he says: long live the Archimedeses. Enough homage, in other words, to soldiers, priests and kings. These persons are as dead and obsolete as astrologers and athletes. What we need are scientists and industrialists, because theirs is the realm where the knowledge and the needs of today are to be found. These are the people who get things done. These are the people under whose regime we do in fact live, although we do not know it and they do not know it. They themselves stupidly obey feudal relics, which they do not realise they could flick off with their little finger. But why should we suffer this to happen? The whole of history is the tale of the sordid exploitation of human beings by human beings, which is a most dreadful waste. Why should human beings waste their energies on exploiting other human beings, when they might be exploiting nature? When one human being oppresses another, too much energy is lost, both by the oppressor and by the oppressed, who resists. Let the oppressor cease to oppress; let the resister cease to resist; let them both throw themselves into the sacred task of exploiting the wealth of mankind – nature – building, creating, making a material culture. Hence all those paeans of Saint-Simon's to production, to organisation.

As for rights, 'right' is an empty sound: there are only interests. Interests are that which humanity happens to want at any given moment. It is the business of producers to give it to them. Humanity divides into two vast classes, the idle and the industrious, the *oisifs* and the *producteurs*, he calls them sometimes – the indolent and the workers. By 'workers' he does not seem to mean manual workers or the proletariat; he means anybody who works, including managers, captains of industry, bankers, industrialists.

Above all, we must have professionals and not amateurs. Poverty is always due to incompetence, and we must replace the appalling waste of competition by concerted planning: what we want is a centralised industrial plan for society. We want association in place of competition, we want labour, which must be compulsory if necessary, because that is the end of man, and we want to take every opportunity for the maximum advance of research – and of the arts too, because unless the human imagination is kindled, by artists, by people who work upon the emotions, nothing will occur at all. The arts have their part to play also in this vast human advance, which will consist of the harnessing and conditioning of human emotions, human passions, human energies, towards that which the present age makes so attainable, namely a kind of vast self-effecting industrial system in which everybody will have enough, nobody will be miserable, and all human ills will disappear. In order to conduct the system, we must have elites, because the people have certainly been too busy to create it – here he talks like an eighteenth-century Encyclopedist – and to run it themselves.

Of whom shall these elites consist? Saint-Simon's view changed through his long life. First he thinks it ought to be scientists, then he alters his view and thinks it ought to be bankers and industrialists. In early life he has mysterious bodies called the Councils of Newton – these are a kind of international co-operative or scientific academy, administered by public subscription and a mysterious system of voting, in which artists and industrialists and mathematicians combine in some inscrutable manner. By the end he has a parliament consisting of three parts. First of all there is the Chamber of Invention, which is populated by engineers and artists – painters, poets and so forth – men who produce, men with ideas, men who, whether in the arts or the sciences, are the first to have flashes of genius. The second chamber sifts and checks: it consists of mathematicians, physicists, physiologists and the like. The final chamber consists of executives – industrialists, bankers, people who really know how to get things done because they understand the nature of the time in which they live and because the sheer struggle for survival, the sheer necessity of competition, has taught them what can be done, and what cannot.

He has various other plans which always come to the same thing – we must produce. We must produce, we must invent. Creativity is the great cry. Every man must realise himself in as many directions as possible. That great medieval notion according to which the flesh was martyred and the human ideal consisted in some kind of self-subjugation, in some kind of self-refusal, in escaping to some inner life from temptations of the flesh and the devils of the outer world – let that be buried for ever. The Christian doctrine that rewards shall be laid up for us in another world, while here the flesh is subordinate to the spirit, must be abolished; harmony between the flesh and the spirit must be introduced. The spirit cannot work without a great material development; no material development can occur without a great spiritual awakening, without the ideas of genius after genius, without general human advance in all possible directions. It is a picture rather like Tintoretto's notion of Paradise – a vast happy conglomeration of humanity holding hands, circling in an endless dance of gaiety and joy in which all their faculties, all their desires, all their inclinations are richly – over-richly – satisfied in the great cornucopias which only the industrialists and the bankers, now no longer oppressed by ancient institutions and ludicrous laws which hem them in, can produce.

About the elite he sounds a very modern note, when he says that they must practise two moralities. What was so wonderful about the priests of Egypt, for example, who were a very early and original elite, was that they believed one thing and fed the population with another. That is good, that is exactly how things should be conducted, because the people cannot be expected to face the truth at once, but must be gradually educated. Consequently we must have a small body of industrialists and bankers and artists who gradually wean mankind, who gradually condition them to take their proper part in the industrial order. That is a familiar kind of neo-feudalism. The great phrase, indeed, on which Communism is built – 'From everyone according to his capacity [...]' – comes from Saint-Simon and the Saint-Simonians. Again, when Stalin said that artists – novelists, for example – are 'engineers of human souls', that their business is applied, not pure, that the end of art is not itself, but the moulding and the conditioning of human beings – that is a Saint-Simonian idea. Everybody, then, must be an engineer, whether of unanimated stuff or of human souls. But if this is to be done we cannot have a lot of outworn unintelligible metaphysical beliefs obstructing us. Therefore Saint-Simon devised anti-democracy, for example, because nothing could be achieved by democracy; no great plan can be achieved except by intelligent men who understand the time in which they live, who have power concentrated in their hands and who do things as experts, because only experts can get things done. Only experts ever have got anything done, and experts will never be overthrown, as by the French Revolution, whose result was bloodshed, chaos and terrible human retrogression.

Similarly, liberty is a ludicrous slogan. Liberty is always disorganising; liberty is always something negative, against oppression from outside. But in an advanced regime where everything is progressive there is no oppression, there is nothing to resist, there is no need to use a battering ram. Liberty is always a kind of dynamite which will blow things up, but in a constructive era, in a creative era as against a destructive one, dynamite is not to be used – not for that kind of purpose at any rate. Hence all his cries that individual liberty is dangerous and must be suppressed.

He deals similarly with laissez-faire. At one period he believed in laissez-faire, being a disciple of the man whom he calls 'the divine Smith'; but laissez-faire, again, leads to absolute chaos; it is quite impossible to get anything done unless we plan things, direct things from the centre. Consequently we have the terrifying notion of the great neo-feudal hierarchy, with bankers at the top, industrialists somewhat below them, engineers and technicians below them, then artists and painters and writers. Every imaginative human being who has something to offer is somewhere in this hierarchy, this great new feudal regime in which everything is arranged in a rigid order. This is the way in which advance can be achieved, this is the way in which an army marches, and we are an army, the whole of history is an army, for Saint-Simon – he more or less calls it that.

Similarly, he is violently against equality, which he regards as an idiotic cry on the part of the oppressed masses, which should have nothing to do with a world ordered by rational government. We must have the administration, not of persons, but of things. The administration of things means leading us towards a proper goal, which is the satisfaction of wishes by the best – most efficient – methods possible. If that is to be the human goal, then the great cry is not equality, not liberty, but fraternity – for all men certainly are brothers.

This brings us to the last phase of Saint-Simon's thought, his *nouveau christianisme* – his new Christianity. He felt towards the end of his life that a cult was needed, that something must be done, because we do not know by technology alone; that the beliefs of men must be fixed upon something. He says: Consider the age of Cicero; the Romans' religion was dying, although the temples were still visited, and Cicero believed in preserving the outer husk of the Roman religion, although he himself no longer believed in its inner essence. This cannot be done. There are plenty of people now who do not believe in the God of Christianity or in Christ or in any of the *dogmata*, but who have a good deal of use for the Church because they think it curbs the evil instincts of men. But it is no use when the belief is worn away, the Church will collapse. The shell cannot continue without the yolk. We must therefore create a new religion, a new faith which will respond to the needs of the time. The golden age is before us: it is a blind tradition which places it behind us; we are marching towards it with rapid step. Our children will arrive there; it is for us, he says, to trace the path.

How are we to trace the path? He is not very clear about that. Above all, by association and by love. If human beings understand each others' needs, identify themselves with them, then their creative imaginations will pour themselves out in the direction of the greatest and most harmonious production of those goods which will go to everyone according to his need. Enfantin, the leader of Saint-Simon's sect after he died, said: 'You are an aspect of me, and I am an aspect of you.' Indeed when the sect – for it became a religious sect – went to live in the outskirts of Paris, a special tunic was designed which could be buckled on only from behind, so that every member of the little

Félicien David in Saint-Simonian Attire by Raymond Bonheur

Saint-Simonian sect was dependent upon someone else. This was a symbol of co-operation rather than competition, and there is an exquisite picture by Raymond Bonheur of the composer Félicien David wearing one of these Saint-Simonian tunics with a great 'D' embroidered in front, incorporating strings like those of a harp. Saint-Simonians were in love with medieval pageantry, and wanted to reconstitute the medieval hierarchy in industrial terms: this is really what is original in Saint-Simonism.

It is quite clear in what way Saint-Simonism influences us whenever there is an attempt to construct a coherent society by applying science to the solution of human problems – not as in the eighteenth century, when it is a question of the solution of perennial problems which are always the same, and in terms of principles which are always the same, which never alter, because they are engraved in the human heart, or because they are discovered in nature or by metaphysical insight or by whatever means; but in terms of values which themselves evolve with the times. We ask which invention affects which other invention, which human beings affect which other human beings, and the notion that one must make human society coherent, that one must create some kind of planned single entity out of it, and not allow human beings to freewheel, not allow them to do what they want to do simply because they want to do it, because this might interfere with a state of affairs in which many more of their faculties might be realised, if only they knew – that is the Saint-Simonian idea.

It takes mild and humane forms in the case of, for example, the American New Deal, or the post-war socialist State in England. It takes violent, ruthless, brutal, fanatical forms in the case of directively planned Fascist and Communist societies. In their case the notion of a new secular religion which should be an opiate for the masses, urging them on towards an idea which they may not intellectually be able to understand, has been taken over from Saint-Simon also. So too has the conflation of the notion that we are part of the historical stream going forward – and therefore there are no absolute ideals, and any ideal is to be estimated in terms of its own perfection, the degree to which it satisfies present needs, not the needs of some past or future age – with the notion that history is a history of altering technology, because technology represents the human spirit at its most active, and humanity is to be divided into those who work and those who do nothing, the drones and the producers, the active and the passive, the doers and the done-to.

At the heart of the whole conception is science, or scientism – the belief that unless things are done under a rigorous discipline by people who alone understand the material of which the world is composed, human and non-human, chaos and frustration are the result. This can be achieved only by the elite. The elite cannot but practise a double morality – one for themselves, one for others. Liberty, democracy, laissez-faire individualism, feudalism – all these metaphysical notions, slogans, words which do not mean very much, must go in order to make room for something clearer, bolder, newer: big business, State capitalism, scientific organisation, an organisation of world peace, a world parliament, a world federation. All this is Saint-Simonian.

Saint-Simon did not believe in revolutions, because he had seen one. He believed in powers of persuasion. But revolution need not be the means. The one thing that he cared about most deeply was that humanity itself should at last obtain the satisfaction of its wishes. On his death-bed he said to his disciples, 'There is one thing I wish to say to you: love each other and help one another. My whole life can be summed up in one single thought – to assure all men the freest development of their faculties.' And 'The party of the workers shall be built [by "workers" he meant those who were productive] – the future is with us.' It was, but perhaps not quite in the sense in which Saint-Simon, who was the most liberal, generous, optimistic and ultimately naive man, believed.

In all this talk about fraternity and love and association and organisation with which the dying Saint-Simon adjures his friends and humanity in general, what about liberty? What about liberty, not perhaps in the empty sense in which he says the eighteenth-century lawyers used it, as a battering-ram against the survival of feudalism, but real liberty, civil liberty, the liberty of human beings to do what they wish within a limited sphere? On this point Saint-Simon says something which strikes a chillier note than anything else he said, for he really was against it. He did not care who put forward his ideas, or how oppressively they were put forward, whether by Napoleon or the Holy Alliance or King Louis XVIII, to all of whom he appeals indifferently. He says that the discussions about liberty which so greatly agitate the middle classes have become a matter of indifference to the lower classes, since we know all too well that in the current state of civilisation the arbitrary use of power does not affect them very much. The small men, the lower classes, the largest and poorest class of mankind, without which no reconstruction of humanity can occur – these people do not care about liberty; they are bored by justice, as the Russian left-wing socialist thinker Chernyshevsky was to say later in the century. What the people want is not parliament, liberty and rights. These are the cravings of the bourgeoisie. What they want is boots, and this cry for bread, boots and not a lot of liberty and liberal slogans then becomes the staple refrain of all the hard-boiled left-wing parties up to Lenin and Stalin. This somewhat sinister note may also be traced to the gentle, humanitarian, noble Saint-Simon.

Maistre

JOSEPH DE MAISTRE was a very frightening figure to many of his contemporaries – frightening because of what he wrote rather than because of what he was. Indeed his contemporaries had not very much chance of meeting him, since the most important years of his life were spent in the service of the King of Sardinia, and at the court of St Petersburg, to which he was appointed as diplomatic representative. He was frightening to them because of the violence, the intransigence and the extremely uncompromising and hard-headed dogmatism with which he wished to strike down the doctrines of which he disapproved.

The normal view of him is fairly stated by Émile Faguet, perhaps the most accurate and the fairest-minded critic of Maistre in France in the nineteenth century. He calls Maistre 'a fierce absolutist, a furious theocrat, an intransigent legitimist, apostle of a monstrous trinity composed of Pope, King and Hangman, always and everywhere the champion of the hardest, narrowest and most inflexible dogmatism, a dark figure out of the Middle Ages, part learned doctor, part inquisitor, part executioner'. And again, 'his Christianity is terror, passive obedience and the religion of the State'; his faith is merely 'a slightly touched-up paganism'; he is a 'Praetorian of the Vatican'. An admirer speaks of his 'Christianity of terror'; Edgar Quinet, a Protestant under the influence of the German Romantics, writes of Maistre's 'inexorable God aided by the hangman; the Christ of a permanent Committee of Public Safety'; and in our own day the Spanish philosopher Miguel de Unamuno refers to Maistre's 'slaughter-house'.

This is the usual portrait of him, largely invented by Sainte-Beuve, and perpetuated by various other thinkers in the nineteenth century. Maistre is painted, always, as a fanatical monarchist and a still more fanatical supporter of papal authority; proud, bigoted, inflexible, with a strong will and an unbelievable power of rigid reasoning from dogmatic premisses to extreme and unpalatable conclusions; brilliant, embittered, a medieval doctor born out of his time, vainly seeking to arrest the current of history; a distinguished anomaly, formidable, hostile, solitary and ultimately pathetic; at best a tragic patrician figure, defying and denouncing a shifty and vulgar world, into which he had been incongruously born; at worst an unbending, self-blinded diehard pouring curses upon the marvellous new age whose benefits he was too wilful to see, and too callous to feel.

His works are regarded as interesting and *outré* rather than important – the last despairing effort of feudalism in the dark ages to resist the march of progress. He is described either as a brave but doomed paladin of a lost cause, or as a foolish or odious survival of the older and more heartless generation, according to whatever attitude the nineteenth-century critics happen to take. But both sides, whether for or against him, always assume that his day is done, that his world has no relevance to anything contemporary. This is the point of view which is shared alike by Victor Hugo and Lamennais, by Sainte-Beuve and Faguet, by James Stephen and Morley, and particularly by Harold Laski, who wrote an essay on him in which he took the view that Maistre was to be rejected as a played-out force.

This view, which may have been intelligible in the nineteenth century, seems absurd in the present age. For although Maistre may have spoken the language of the past, the content of what he had to say is the absolute substance of anti-democratic talk of our day; in comparison with his progressive contemporaries he is really ultra-modern, born not so much after as before his time. If his ideas did not have more immediate influence, it is because the soil in his own time was unreceptive. His doctrines, and still more his attitude of mind, had to wait a century before they came – as come they did – into their own.

Maistre's task, in his own eyes, was to destroy everything which the eighteenth century had built up. Let me explain how he came by this state of mind. He was born in 1753 in Chambéry in Savoy, then part of the Kingdom of Piedmont-Sardinia. This kingdom, of which Maistre was a subject all his life, was relatively enlightened in the eighteenth century: it abolished feudalism a good many years before the French did so. Like other liberal aristocrats, Maistre was a mild reformer, not particularly reactionary and not particularly bigoted. He was a grown man when the Revolution finally broke out. He was over thirty, and like others who went through the Revolution – like Saint-Simon, like Schiller, like Hegel – he took most violently against it. The spectacle of the Jacobin Terror was something which he never forgot for the rest of his life, and this is what turned him into an implacable enemy of everything that is liberal, democratic, high-minded, everything connected with intellectuals, critics, scientists, everything which was to do with the kind of forces which created the French Revolution. When he talks about Voltaire he talks about him almost as if he were a personal enemy.

Being a Savoyard, Maistre entered the royal service, and began writing pamphlets, after the French revolutionaries had invaded Savoy, against the Revolution. These pamphlets were very sharp: they had a peculiar freshness, indeed a ferocity, which immediately attracted attention. But the King of Sardinia felt that he was an uncomfortable man to have about the court. The court was very small, very limited, rather provincial, and Maistre was too brilliant, too active, too imaginative and too interesting a man to be altogether comfortable there. But he was obviously very able, and he attracted a great deal of attention by the brilliance of his writings. Consequently it was decided to send him as far away as possible, and he was duly sent away to St Petersburg as a minister of the King of Sardinia, or the equivalent of a minister, from 1803 until he left in 1817.

In St Petersburg he was regarded as a man of particular charm, courtesy, urbanity; he was a brilliant and agreeable conversationalist, delightful company and greatly sought after in society. He enjoyed his life in St Petersburg; he was fascinated by the Russian monarchy, and he got on very well with the immediate circles around Alexander I; indeed, that Emperor used him as a political adviser at various moments during his reign.

After the war against Napoleon was over, for some reason Alexander demanded his recall; it may be that he had converted too many ladies of fashion to the Roman Church. Several of these ladies were destined to play a very large part in Catholic circles in western Europe. Possibly he interfered a little too much in Russian policy, with so strong a personality; at any rate, the King of Sardinia, now restored to his throne, was induced to recall him. Maistre went back to Turin, the capital, was given a sinecure, and died, in considerable honour but with no kind of political power, or indeed any other kind of power, in 1821. His reputation is largely posthumous.

The aim to which Maistre addressed himself most vigorously, as I say, was to destroy the eighteenth century, and the thought of the eighteenth century. It is a mistake to assume that the thought of the eighteenth century was a seamless garment; indeed, some of the eighteenth-century thinkers were divided by deep differences. But there are certain things which are common to them all. They might not all believe in progress; they might not all believe in God; they might not all believe in the immortality of the soul. Some of them believed in intuition; others believed in empiricism. Some believed in spontaneity and simplicity of feeling; others believed in science and sophistication. What they had in common was the belief that men were by nature, if not good, at any rate not bad, potentially benevolent, and that each man was the best expert on his own interests and his own values, when he was not being bamboozled by knaves or fools; that on the whole men were prone to follow the rules of conduct which their own understanding provided. Most thinkers of the eighteenth century believed that progress was desirable – that is to say, for example, that freedom was better than slavery; that legislation founded on what was called 'the precepts of nature' could right almost every wrong; that nature was only reason in action, and its workings, therefore, could in principle be deduced from a set of axioms like those of a theory in geometry, or like those of physics and chemistry, if only you knew them. They believed that all things that were good and true and virtuous and free were necessarily compatible, and indeed more than that, that they were interconnected.

The more empirically-minded among them were sure that the science of human nature could be developed no less than that of inanimate things, that ethical and political questions, provided they were genuine – and how could they not be so? – could be answered no less certainly than those of mathematics and astronomy, and that a life founded upon these answers would be free, secure, happy and wise. They believed that the millennium could be reached by the use of faculties and the practice of methods which had for over a century, in the spheres both of knowledge and of action, led to triumphs more magnificent than any hitherto attained in human history. That, roughly speaking, is the common belief, the general temper and attitude, of the rational thinkers of the eighteenth century.

All this Maistre set himself to destroy completely. Any characteristic of the eighteenth century of this kind he was determined to root up so that it should stand no more. He took on this enormous task because he believed that the Revolution in which the innocent had suffered was an appalling disaster. He had loved and admired France from outside (he was on the margins of it in Savoy) with the peculiar passion which people on the edges of countries have for those countries when they wish to be identified with them – there are many instances of this in history. With the peculiar indignation born of the desire to demolish a really golden ideal, he determined to discredit the forces which in his opinion were responsible for the destruction of his dream. Therefore, in place of the a priori formulae of this idealistic sociology, he decided to appeal to the empirical facts of history and to observe human behaviour. In place of the ideals of progress, liberty, perfectibility he preached the sacredness of the past, the virtue, and the necessity, indeed, of complete subjection, because of the incurably bad and corrupt nature of man. In place of science he preached the primacy of instinct, superstition, prejudice. In place of optimism, pessimism. In place of eternal harmony and eternal peace, the necessity – for him the divine necessity – of conflict, of suffering, of bloodshed, of war. In the place of peace and social equality, of common interests and the simple nature of the uncorrupted natural man about whom Rousseau had talked, he insisted that what was important was diversity, inequality, conflict of interests – those were the normal conditions of individuals and of nations. He denied all meaning to such abstractions as Nature, Man, Natural Rights. His doctrine of language contradicted everything which Condorcet and Condillac and all the great scientists of the eighteenth century had tried to formulate. He tried to breathe new life into the discredited doctrine of the Divine Right of Kings. He defended the importance of mystery, of darkness, almost of ignorance, and above all of irrationality, as the basis of social and political life. With immense effectiveness and brilliance he denounced every form of lucidity, every form of rationality. Temperamentally Maistre was as ruthless and as extreme as his great enemies, the Jacobins; and he had something of their faith and their integrity.

Alexander Herzen, the Russian revolutionary, remarks that what distinguished the men of 1792 was the wonderful completeness of their rejection of the entire old order. He says that they denounced not merely its vices, but all its virtues too. They wished to leave nothing standing, they wanted to destroy the entire evil system, root and branch, in order to build up something absolutely fresh, entirely pure. They wanted to make no compromise; they wanted to have no debt to that upon whose ruins their new cities would be raised. Maistre was the exact inverse of this. He attacked eighteenth-century rationalism with the intolerance and the passion and the power and the gusto of the great revolutionaries themselves. He wanted to destroy what has so well been called 'the heavenly city of the eighteenth-century philosophers'. He wanted to raze it to the ground, not leaving stone upon stone.

The method which he used, as well as the truths which he preached, although he officially said he derived them from Thomas à Kempis or Thomas Aquinas, or the great preachers of the seventeenth century in France, Bourdaloue or Bossuet, in fact displays very little of the spirit of these great pillars of the Church. They had far more to do with the anti-rationalist approach of someone like Augustine, or with the Freemasons and the illuminists among whom Maistre's youth was spent.

Maistre's fundamental doctrine is this: nature is red in tooth and claw, it is a vast scene of carnage and destruction. The men of the eighteenth century turn to metaphysics, to logic, even to geometry, in order to find out what nature is like. Those are not the sources of our knowledge of nature. If they want to talk about nature, let them be serious. They speak about using observation as a weapon, using our eyes, not accepting a great many dogmatic truths merely because a lot of preachers have spoken to us about them. Very well then, they must be taken at their word. Let us look at what is going on round us, Maistre says, let us not look at books, let us look at nature, at ourselves, let us study history, yes, and zoology. They are the true guides to nature. What do we see if this is where we look? Let me quote what Maistre says:

> In the vast domain of living nature there reigns an open violence, a kind of prescriptive fury which arms all the creatures to their common doom: as soon as you leave the inanimate kingdom, you find the decree of violent death inscribed on the very frontiers of life. You feel it already in the vegetable kingdom: from the vast catalpa to the humblest herb, how many plants *die*, and how many are *killed*! But from the moment you enter the animal kingdom, this law is suddenly in the most dreadful evidence. A violent power, at once hidden and palpable, [...] has, in each major subdivision of the animals, appointed a certain number of species to devour the others. Thus there are insects of prey, reptiles of prey, birds of prey, fishes of prey, quadrupeds of prey. There is no instant of time when one creature is not being devoured by another. Over all these numerous races of animals man is placed, and his destructive hand spares nothing that lives.

The passage which follows is more effective in French. It is a curious litany:

> il tue pour se nourrir, il tue pour se vêtir, il tue pour se parer, il tue pour attaquer, il tue pour se défendre, il tue pour s'instruire, il tue pour s'amuser, il tue pour tuer: roi superbe et terrible, il a besoin de tout, et rien ne lui résiste. [...] à l'agneau [il demande] ses entrailles pour faire résonner une harpe, [...] au loup sa dent la plus meurtrière pour polir les ouvrages légers de l'art, à l'éléphant ses défenses pour façonner le jouet d'un enfant: ses tables sont couvertes de cadavres. [...] Cependant quel être [dans le carnage permanent] exterminera celui qui les extermine tous? Lui. C'est l'homme qui est chargé d'égorger l'homme. [...] Ainsi s'accomplit [...] la grande loi de la destruction violente des êtres vivants. La terre entière, continuellement imbibée de sang, n'est qu'un autel immense où tout ce qui vit doit être immolé sans fin, sans mesure, sans relâche, jusqu'à la consommation des choses, jusqu'à l'extinction du mal, jusqu'à la mort de la mort.

Let me translate this:

> Man kills to obtain food and kills to clothe himself. He kills to adorn himself and he kills in order to attack. He kills in order to defend himself and he kills in order to instruct himself. He kills to amuse himself and he kills in order to kill. Proud and terrible king, he wants everything and nothing can resist him. [...] From the lamb [he demands] its guts to make his harp resound, [...] from the wolf its deadliest tooth to polish his trifling works of art, from the elephant its tusks to make a toy for his child: his tables he covers with corpses. [...] But who [in the general carnage] will exterminate the one who exterminates all the others? He will himself. It is man who is charged with the slaughter of men. [...] Thus is accomplished [...] the great law of the violent destruction of living creatures. The whole earth, perpetually steeped in blood, is nothing but a vast altar upon which all that is living must be sacrificed without end, without measure, without pause, until the consummation of things, until evil is extinct, until the death of death.

And yet, says Maistre, man is born to love. He is tender and gentle and good. Whence comes his divine fury? Is it the earth calling for blood? Why is it, asks Maistre, that troops in battle never, or very seldom, mutiny against the instructions of their commanders, who tell them to exterminate other innocent men? Is there not something paradoxical in the fact that soldiers – innocent, honourable men, whom we receive with the greatest courtesy in private life, and who in ordinary life are gentle, virtuous, God-fearing, polite persons, who would not hurt a fly – go into battle in order to kill other soldiers, as innocent as themselves, without any demur? Whereas the executioner, who is the man, after all, who, under instruction, kills people who on the whole are presumably not innocent – parricides, murderers and other criminals – and kills many fewer of them than the soldiers do, is nevertheless regarded as a social outcast; nobody shakes him by the hand; he is regarded with horror and loathing, not as an ordinary member of society. Is there not something strange in admiring the shedding of innocent blood, and recoiling before the shedding of guilty blood? It must be, says Maistre, because war is in some sense divine in itself, because it is the law of the world. This is a central doctrine in Maistre: that rationalist notions do not work. If you really want to know why people behave as they do, you must seek the answer in the realm of the irrational. This is a mysticism which puts its faith in the other world, not in this one.

Maistre is fascinated by the spectacle of war. Consider, he says, a battlefield. People imagine that a battlefield is a place where things happen in a planned manner. The commander gives orders, the troops march into battle, and battles are won or lost in accordance with the preponderance of troops, or the skilful instructions issued by the generals. Nothing could be less true. Consider an actual battle. Once more, do not look at the textbook, look at life: zoology and history are Maistre's masters. If you find a battlefield, what you will encounter upon it is not at all an orderly procession of events matching the descriptions of eyewitnesses, or even of strategists, of tacticians or historians. What you will find is appalling noise, confusion, slaughter, death, ruin, the shrieks of the wounded, the groans of the dying, the violent firing of firearms. 'Five or six kinds of intoxication' possess people upon the field; a general cannot possibly tell whether he is losing the battle or winning it. Nobody can possibly tell this. Wars are not won by rational calculation, they are won by moral force. They are won by people who feel they are winning them. They are won by some kind of irrational inner certainty. You cannot, in the moment of battle, calculate whether your troops are still more numerous upon the field of battle than the enemy's. It is not like a duel between two human beings, where the strength of one is obviously greater or obviously smaller than the strength of the other. Battles are won psychologically, battles are won by acts of faith. What happens happens as a result of some kind of mysterious inner force which is certainly not rational calculation or the careful application of a textbook set of rules, some kind of elaborate rational calculation or plan which wins or loses battles.

Tolstoy, when describing the Battle of Borodino in *War and Peace*, carefully followed this account of Maistre's. Tolstoy read Maistre because Maistre lived in Petersburg during the period in which he was interested, and he echoes his description of what a real battle is like, describing the experience of people present at the battle rather than giving the orderly, tidied-up account constructed later by eyewitnesses or historians. For both Maistre and Tolstoy, too, life itself is a battle of this sort, and any attempt to describe it in rational terms is a dreadful distortion, a smoothing over, tidying up, ordering of something which is by nature deeply irrational, deeply untidy, and obeys no discoverable laws or rules.

Maistre protests above all against the assumption that reason is the great mistress of things. It is impossible to govern men or achieve anything by means of reason. He says: What do you think reason is to me? Reason is simply a feeble faculty in men for the purpose, now and then, of fitting means to ends. You really think that the great institutions of mankind are rational constructions? Remember that the business of an institution is to be authoritative. The business of government is to govern. Every human society must have a government, and every government must have this sovereignty. Every sovereignty must contain within it a principle of infallibility, and the only thing that is absolutely infallible is the word of God.

Anything which human beings make, human beings can mar. Anything which human beings can construct, human beings can destroy. Suppose you create an artificial institution, a republic or a limited constitutional monarchy, by means of that reason which the eighteenth century recommended – say some utilitarian arrangement for the securing of the greatest happiness or the greatest freedom of the greatest number. Well, clever men construct that in one generation, and still cleverer men in the next generation can puncture it full of holes, can completely destroy it by means of their superior, their still subtler, still cleverer, still more destructive reasoning. Nothing can stand perpetually but what something other than reason builds up, for what reason builds up, reason will pull down.

Man is by nature vicious, wicked, cowardly and bad. What the Roman Church says, what Christianity says, about original guilt, original sin, is the truest psychological insight into human nature. Left alone, human beings will tear each other to pieces. Here Maistre is completely opposed to his time: he regards human beings, unless clamped with iron rings and held down by means of the most rigid discipline, as likely to destroy themselves. He regards human nature as fundamentally self-annihilating, and needing to be curbed and controlled. The only thing which is reliable, the only thing which is dependable, is not man-made; for if it is man-made it can equally be unmade by man.

What did the eighteenth century teach us about this? It taught us that society was founded upon a contract. But this is a logical as well as a historical absurdity. What is a contract? A contract is a promise. So we have a lot of rational persons coming together – says Maistre in a mocking manner – for the purpose of arranging a peaceful life which will give people rather more of worldly goods, or security, or happiness, or liberty, or whatever it is they may happen to want, than they would get in a so-called state of nature. And how do they do this? By constructing a State as one might a bank, or a limited-liability company. But even to do that requires that the promise, the social contract, be enforceable. If somebody breaks it there must be some kind of instrument for the purpose of forcing him back into conformity, or expelling him. But a body of men who already understand such concepts as promises, and the enforcement of promises, is a completely mature, sophisticated human society.

The notion that barbarous creatures, wild aborigines from the woods, coming together for the first time in history in order to construct something called a social contract, are already furnished with such elaborate and sophisticated social notions as promises towards each other, obligation, duty, enforcement of promises, that they have all this ready to put into the intellectual pool, is a grotesque logical absurdity. People who are armed with the notion of a promise, the notion of respecting each other's will, the notion of punishment, the notion of reward, do not need a society, they are in it already. Quite clearly, therefore, society is presupposed by the notion of a contract. Furthermore, it was not created by man, for if it had been created by man it would not have stood up to the ravages of centuries. It lies in the deep darkness of antiquity; and for Maistre (here he is deeply influenced by Burke) anything which goes back to the mists of antiquity was made by God and not by man.

Similarly with language. M. Rousseau, he says, tells us that he wants to know about the origins of language. Well, of course M. Condillac, who can answer all questions, can answer this question too. How was language constructed? Why, of course, by the division of labour. A lot of rationalist persons, seeking their own personal advantage, cosily gathered together and proceeded to invent language, says Maistre. The first generation of men, presumably, said BA and the next generation of men said BE. The Assyrians invented the nominative, and the Medes invented the genitive. That is how grammar was made.

This kind of bitter irony is very appropriate. Maistre was one of the first to perceive that the whole eighteenth-century notion that human institutions are constructed by rational men for limited and intelligible purposes is totally untrue to human nature. Herder had had some such ideas already, and of course the German Romantics had them too. Maistre employed a particularly biting and mordant irony for the purpose of dismantling the rickety structures of eighteenth-century theories about the origins of society, especially their peculiarly unhistorical approach.

But his most savage onslaughts are directed against the notion of nature. M. Rousseau, he says, tells us that it is strange that man, who was born free, should be everywhere in chains: 'What does he mean? [...] This mad pronouncement, *Man is born free*, is the opposite of the truth.' Faguet encapsulates Maistre's response to Rousseau in a brilliant epigram: Rousseau's claim, he says, is as if one were to say how strange it is that sheep, who were born carnivorous, should nevertheless everywhere be nibbling grass. Maistre mocks at the all-providing, all-explaining entity which is dignified by the name of Nature by the Encyclopedists. Who is this lady, he says, of whom one hears so much? Nature, so far from being the beneficent provider of all good things, the source of all life and knowledge and happiness, is to him an eternal mystery; savage in her methods, the principal source of cruelty, pain, chaos; no doubt serving God's inscrutable purpose, but seldom the source of comfort or enlightenment.

Rousseau had preached a return to the simple virtues of the noble savage. What noble savage? Savages are, according to Maistre, not noble at all but subhuman, cruel, dissident and brutal. Anyone who has lived among them can testify that they are the refuse of mankind. So far from being the great uncorrupted prototypes, early exemplars of natural taste and natural morality, virtuous, high-minded, truthful, from which civilisation has perverted the nations of the West, they are merely the failures of God's creative process. It is true that Christian missionaries who have been sent among the Indians of America, for example, speak about them with kindness, but that is because they are good priests who cannot bring themselves to attribute to any of God's creatures the squalor and the vices in which all these people were in fact sunk. It does not follow from their testimony that the Indians are models for us to follow. The language of savages is not something with primitive strength, with the beauty of a beginning; it has only the confusion and the ugliness of decay.

As for the state of nature, which – for the thinkers of the

eighteenth century – acts as a repository of the so-called rights of man which primitive man is supposed to be recognising, in whose name do these eighteenth-century speakers affect to speak? In the name of nature? There is no such lady, says Maistre, otherwise why have we never met her? What are these rights? Inherent in what men? No metaphysical magic eye will detect abstract entities called rights, not derived from either human or divine authority. As for the famous abstract Man in whose name the great revolution was started, in whose name the cruellest massacres were organised, in the name of whom innocents were slaughtered: 'In the course of my life', says Maistre, 'I have seen Frenchmen, Italians, Russians etc.; I know, too, thanks to Montesquieu, *that one can be a Persian*. But as for *man*, I declare that I have never met him in my life; if he exists, he is unknown to me.'

In our day, says Maistre, what has happened as a result of faith in completely empty words and empty formulae is that 'the two anchors of society – religion and slavery – having failed at one and the same moment, the ship was carried away by the storm, and was wrecked'. That is why, in his advice to the Russian Emperor, he was always saying: There are only two anchors upon which society rests, by which wicked man can be confined, protected from his blindly self-destructive impulses. One is the Church and the other is slavery. The Christian Church abolished slavery because it was powerful enough to keep man in fetters by herself, but if you in Russia, where the Orthodox Church is not very highly regarded by the populace, let serfdom go, if you, as your advisers tell you, liberate the serfs, why then your country will be plunged into the most vicious revolution. It will go from barbarism into anarchy. Nobody can want as violently as the Russians want, and once you allow all these 'Pugachevs of the University',[1] as he calls them, all these intellectual rebels, all

[1] Emel′yan Ivanovich Pugachev (*c.*1742–1775) was the leader of a peasant and Cossack rebellion crushed in the reign of Catherine the Great.

these economists and scientists and sophisters and magicians, to dominate you, then your kingdom – which rests upon authority as all kingdoms must rest, upon faith in blind authority – will collapse.

What is the principal notion of the eighteenth century? That society is founded upon recognition of reciprocal interests by people who want to live together as happily and as freely as possible. This is denied forcefully and passionately by Maistre. He says society is not founded upon this at all. Society is founded upon self-immolation. Why do soldiers march to battle? They do not know. If a king wishes to introduce something as harmless as a census or the alteration of a calendar, there are mutinies and riots among the population. But if there is a war, in which many innocent men will be slaughtered, and in which many hundreds of thousands will not come back to their wives and children, then people peacefully obey. Why, we cannot tell; it is irrational.

Maistre really makes two points here. One is that the cause of things cannot be fathomed by the mere feeble contrivance of men; the other, that the only things which last are irrational. For example, he says, take the institution of hereditary monarchy: what could be more irrational? Why should a wise king have an equally wise son, or indeed a son who is wise at all? Here is an institution of a patently idiotic nature, for which no good reason can be given, and yet it lasts. It has lasted for many centuries, and upon it the foundations of the Western world are built. But far more rational, far more logical and reasonable, would be to abolish such a monarchy and see what happens. What happened to the unhereditary, elected monarchy in Poland? There chaos and ruin followed almost immediately. Why? Because a rational system had been adopted. Take the institution of marriage. What could be more irrational than that two human beings, merely because they happen to love each other at one stage of their lives, should be together with each other for the rest of their lives, for no better reason than that this happened in the past? But nothing is more short-lived, nothing more destructive, nothing becomes so hateful as the regime of free love. So he goes on, from institution to institution, paradoxically asserting that whatever is irrational lasts, and that whatever is rational collapses; it collapses because anything which is constructed by reason can be pulverised by reason; anything which was built by the self-critical faculties cannot stand up to attack by them. The only thing which can ever dominate men is impenetrable mystery.

The eighteenth century thinks – and the seventeenth century thought, too – that there are certain social and political questions which can be answered in a certain fashion. Some think they can be answered by metaphysicians, others by scientists; some by the word of conscience, by looking into the heart, and others by reading the books of specific experts on these matters. Maistre says: Once you allow such a question to be put, the answer will demand the next question. The answer will never stand up, and people will question the answer, and the answer to that question in turn, and will go on asking for the why of the why of the why. The only way to get people to live in societies at all is to stop them from questioning, and the only way in which you can stop them from questioning is by terror. Only if the heart of things is dark and mysterious, impenetrable, will people obey. Once they have penetrated the heart of things, and once it is rational, once it is something which they can understand, they will not be afraid of it. They will not be in awe of it, they will not revere it, and so it will collapse. What we need, therefore, is something dark and unintelligible.

Take the problem of language, says Maistre. Language is identical with thought. The eighteenth century, which thought that language was a human invention, was mistaken on this point. In order to invent you have to think, and in order to think you have to employ symbols; to say that language can be constructed is an absolute absurdity. M. Condorcet wants to have a scientific language which will be clear and intelligible, which can be spread among all the nations – a kind of scientific Esperanto. Nothing would be more disastrous. It would be disastrous precisely because it was clear, precisely because it was intelligible. Clarity, intelligibility must be put out of court, must be stopped, because it is they which create unrest, criticism, questioning, which end in the overturning of ancient institutions, in injustice, blood, revolutions and chaos.

Latin is the language which we must teach our children. Why? Because it is unclear. People argue against prejudice, against superstition. What is prejudice? It is merely the beliefs of the centuries, tested by experience. History is, after all, the only teacher we have, and politics is only experimental history. Here Maistre talks rather like Burke, who defended prejudice in exactly the same way. Prejudice is simply the skin which humanity has acquired in the course of centuries, traditionally, which has been tested against many diverse situations, and to throw it away is to remain trembling and naked before the destructive forces of life. Latin is a language of an irregular kind. Latin is a language whose grammar is not rational. It embodies all kinds of prejudices, all kinds of ancient superstitions, blind faith, unconscious experience, everything which science is against. That is why it is the language to which we must cling, for there are only two things which are ever good in the world – one is antiquity, and the other is irrationality. Only the combination of these two creates a force sufficiently powerful to resist the corrosive influence of the critics, the askers of questions, the scientists.

Against whom are we trying to preserve the social order? The enemies of the social order, whom Maistre calls 'la secte', are a very interesting collection of men. They are, for him, Jansenists and Calvinists, and all Protestants in general; lawyers, metaphysicians, journalists, writers, Jews, American revolutionaries, intellectuals, scientists, critics; in short, the intelligentsia, and everything which belongs to it. This list – of liberals, of all kinds of critics, of all kinds of people who believe in some sort of abstract truth, of people who do not accept the dogmatic premisses of society – was compiled almost for the first time by Maistre, and by now it is familiar. It has been the stock-in-trade of every violently reactionary, Fascist movement of our day.

But of all these Maistre hates scientists the most. They are the people who have the least capacity for understanding life, and for government, and he warned the Tsar of Russia, in extremely solemn tones, not to commit the fatal blunder of allowing the arts and the sciences to dominate the country. He says: Take the greatest nation that ever was, at any rate the greatest in the art of government, the Romans. They knew very well that they would merely make fools of themselves as scientists. They hired Greeks because they knew they would merely be undignified if they tried to do the job themselves. No great statesman, he says, from Suger to Richelieu, was ever a scientist, or knew anything about science. There is something about science, about its dry, abstract, unconcrete nature, something about the fact that it is divorced from the crooked, the chaotic, the irrational texture of life with all its darkness, which makes scientists incapable of adapting themselves to the actual facts, and anyone who listens to them is automatically doomed. He says to the Emperor of Russia: Do not allow all these Lutheran Germans to come and teach in your schools. Who are these people who are pouring in, in endless numbers, into your kingdom? Good men – family men, men who have traditions, faith, religion, respectable morals – do not leave their countries. Only the feckless and the restless and the critical do so. This is the first real sermon against refugees, against freedom of the spirit, against the circulation of humanity – the first, certainly, made in violent and intelligible and, indeed, memorable terms.

What then does society rest upon? Society is part of the vale of tears where we cannot understand the sources of things, where God governs us in an inscrutable way. It rests upon terror; it rests upon obedience, blind obedience to authority. Without it institutions become chaotic and restless, and go down in a welter of disaster. What represents this element of terror? Here Maistre makes a most paradoxical observation, and writes the most famous page in all his writings. He says that the person who stands in the centre of it all is none other than that hated figure, the executioner. Let me quote the famous passage in which he speaks of him:

> Who is this inexplicable being? […] He is like a world in himself. […] Hardly has he been assigned to his proper dwelling-place […] when others remove their homes elsewhere […]. In the midst of this desolation […] he lives alone with his mate and his young, who acquaint him with the sound of the human voice. But for them he would hear nothing but shrieks of agony … One of the lowest menials of justice knocks at his door and tells him that his services are wanted. He goes. He arrives in a public square where people are crowded together with faces of expectancy. A prisoner, a parricide, a man who has committed a sacrilege is flung to his feet. He seizes the man, stretches him, ties him to a cross which is lying on the ground, raises his arms, and there is a terrible silence. It is broken only by the sound of the crushing of bones under the blows of the iron mace, and the screams of the victim. He unbinds the man, he carries him to the wheel; the broken limbs are twined round the spokes and the head hangs down; the hair stands on end and from the mouth – open like the door of a glowing furnace – there come at intervals only a few broken syllables of entreaty for death. The executioner has finished his task; his heart is beating, but it is with pleasure; he is satisfied with his work. He says in his heart, 'No man breaks on the wheel better than I.' He comes down from the scaffold and holds out his bloody hand, into which, from a distance, an official flings a few gold pieces. The executioner carries them off between two rows of human beings who shrink from him with horror. He sits down to table and eats, he goes to bed and sleeps, but when

> he awakes next morning his thoughts run on everything but his occupation of the day before. Is he a man? Yes, God allows him to enter his shrines and accepts his prayers. He is no criminal, and yet no human language dares to calls him, for instance, virtuous, honourable or estimable [...]. Nevertheless all greatness, all power, all social order depends upon the executioner; he is the terror of human society and the tie that holds it together. Take away this incomprehensible force from the world, and at that very moment order is superseded by chaos, thrones fall, society disappears. God, who is the source of the power of the ruler, is also the source of punishment. He has suspended our world upon these two poles, 'for the Lord is the lord of the twin poles, and round them he sets the world revolving'.

This is not a mere sadistic meditation about crime and punishment. Lamennais said of Maistre that it is strange how a man who is so noble should have only two realities in his whole life: crime and punishment. 'It is as if all his works were written from the scaffold.' But my quotation from Maistre is not merely cruel. It is the expression of a genuine conviction, coherent with all the rest of Maistre's passionate but very lucid thought, that men can be saved only by being hemmed in by the terror of authority. They must be reminded at every instant of their lives of the frightening mystery that lies at the heart of creation; must be purged by perpetual suffering, must be humbled by being made conscious of their stupidity, malice, helplessness at every turn. War, torture, suffering are the inescapable human lot.

Man is a fool; man is a child; man is a lunatic; man is an absentee landlord; life is – ought to be – a kind of penal settlement with guardians to look after this creature. He must be controlled by appointed masters – people who are imbued with a duty which has been laid upon them by their maker, who made nature a hierarchy – by the ruthless imposition of rules, and the ruthless extermination of the enemy. The enemy, as we have seen, is 'la secte', the disturbers, the subverters, the secular reformers, the intellectuals, the idealists, the lawyers, the perfectibilians, the people who believe in conscience, or equality, or the rational organisation of society, the liberators, the revolutionaries – these are the people who must be rooted out.

There is something very extraordinary about a man who, in the most lucid possible manner, speaking a language which is certainly as clear and as beautiful as that used by anybody in the eighteenth century, says things which are the precise opposite of the general tenor of that century. Yet Maistre is also in a sense a child of the century, precisely because of the extraordinary contrariety with which he meets every single thing that the century says. Saint-Simon believed that there was something in common between Maistre and the people whom he most particularly disliked, the followers of Voltaire – indeed, even Voltaire himself. Voltaire was the enemy, and Maistre talks with immense hatred about the perpetual hideous grin of this dreadful monster. Yet Saint-Simon says that perhaps the future of human society lies in the combination of Maistre and Voltaire.

At first this is a wild paradox. How can there be such a combination? Voltaire stands for individual liberty and Maistre for chains. Voltaire cries for more light and Maistre for more darkness. Voltaire hated the Church so violently he denied it even the minimum of virtue; Maistre liked even its vices and regarded Voltaire as the Devil incarnate. Yet there is something in what Saint-Simon says, very odd as it may seem, because, although they are polar opposites, both Voltaire and Maistre belong to the hard, cold, dry, lucid, tough-minded tradition of French thought. Their ideas may appear strictly to contradict one another, but the quality of mind is often exceedingly similar. Neither is guilty of any degree of softness or vagueness or self-indulgence, nor do they tolerate these qualities in others. They stand for the dry against the moist; they are implacably opposed to everything which is turbid and misty, romantic, gushing, impressionistic.

Both of them are equally opposed to the spirit of Rousseau, Chateaubriand, Victor Hugo, Michelet, Renan, Bergson. They are ruthless and deflationary writers; they are heartless and, at times, genuinely cynical. Beside this cold, clear, glossy surface even Stendhal's prose – and Stendhal borrowed a great deal from Maistre – seems romantic. Marx, Tolstoy, Sorel, Lenin – they are their true successors.

This tendency to cast a cold look upon the political scene, to deflate and to dehydrate, to submit politics and history to a genuinely ruthless as opposed to a merely shocking analysis – this is what has entered modern political techniques to a great degree, and it has entered them equally from just such ideas as those of Voltaire and of Maistre. The violently deflationary atmosphere of Voltaire was responsible for the exposure of sentimental popular values. Maistre stresses historicism and political pragmatism, and has a low estimate of the human capacity for goodness, plus a belief that the essence of life is the craving for suffering and sacrifice and surrender. If you add to this Maistre's belief that government is impossible without repression of the weak majority by a minority of dedicated rulers, hardened against all temptation to indulge in any kind of humanitarianism, we are gradually approaching modern totalitarianism. Voltaire can be made to strip away the liberal delusion, Maistre to provide the nostrum by which the bleak, bare world which results can be subdued. True, Voltaire did not like either despotism or deception; and Maistre recognised the need for both. 'The principle of the sovereignty of the people', says Maistre, 'is so dangerous that, even if it were true, it would be necessary to conceal it.' So what Saint-Simon said was not so paradoxical after all. The combination of the two leads to the ruthless totalitarianism, whether of the right or of the left, of the twentieth century.

What really fascinates Maistre is power. Power, for him, is divine. It is the source of all life, of all action. It is the paramount factor in the development of mankind, and whoever knows how to wield it acquires the right to use it; it is by that token the instrument chosen by God, at that particular moment, to work his mysterious purpose. To recognise power where it truly lies – in ancient, established, socially created institutions, not made by the hand of man – is political and moral insight and wisdom. All usurpation must fail in the end, because it flouts the divine laws of the universe. Permanent power, therefore, resides only in him who is the instrument of such laws. To resist power is criminal childishness and folly, directed against the human future.

Maistre preached the doctrine that all events must be studied empirically if we are to understand the workings of the divine will. His stoicism and relativism, his interest in nature and the distribution of power over human beings – these constitute Maistre's deeply considered view, and that is why, strangely, he approved of the Jacobins, which did not make him any more popular in émigré circles. Maistre said: When there is a vacuum, somebody must enter it. The King failed dismally. King Louis XVI and his miserable liberal advisers, and still more miserable Girondin reformers, were simply human dust, weak, optimistic, reformist, with no understanding of human nature, obviously the ruiners and subverters of society. Then, at a moment of vacuum, the Jacobins did at least do something. At least they killed somebody. They set up guillotines; they performed executions; they let blood flow. That Maistre approved of, because it was an exercise of power, because it held society together, because it made things cohere. He believed in sovereignty. Of course the Jacobins were the scourge of God, sent to punish a godless generation for betraying the faith of their fathers. But still, it is better to do what the Jacobins did and hold France together and make it a powerful kingdom and resist the enemy and crush the opposition of the feeble Prussians or the feeble Austrians – better that than a lot of intellectual jabbering. That is the Fascist note in Maistre.

Similarly, Napoleon was the Corsican monster; he was a fearful usurper, and one must not recognise him. Yet he was a powerful monarch, and power always comes from God, and certainly his title to his throne is no worse than that of Elizabeth of England or William of Orange or the House of Hanover. Maistre was fascinated by Napoleon, just as Napoleon was rather fascinated by Maistre, and each wished to meet the other, except that the King of Sardinia was horrified by any such idea. He was a pensionary of both England and Russia and a victim of Napoleon, and the thought of one of his diplomats meeting the destroyer of mankind plunged the court of Sardinia into absolute terror. Maistre replied with distinct sadness, saying that of course he would not meet Napoleon if the King did not wish him to, but nevertheless he thought this a wrong and shortsighted policy. He said: I see that you regard my proposal as very surprising. Well, I shall serve you to the end of my days, for I believe that the throne is more important than its occupant. As for not surprising you – I cannot promise that.

Maistre stresses tradition, the past, the unconscious, dark forces, not the amiable imaginary attributes of the folk soul, as did its enthusiastic champions – the German Romantics – or the champions of the simple life (which he too always praised). On the contrary, he stresses the stability, the permanence and the impregnability of the authority that belongs to the dark mass of half-conscious memories and traditions and loyalties, and the power of institutions in exacting obedience, especially in regard to the supernatural. He lays great emphasis on the fact that absolute rule succeeds only when it is terrifying, and he fears and detests science, precisely because it pours too much light, and so dissolves the mystery, the darkness, which alone resists sceptical enquiry.

In a sense, then, Maistre is a kind of precursor and early preacher of Fascism, and that is what makes him so interesting. Behind the classical mask, behind the classical façade, behind the air of the Grand Seigneur, behind the orthodox Thomism, behind the official complete subservience to the monarchy of his day, which was nothing very splendid or impressive, there is in Maistre something much wilder, much more romantic, much more terrifying. He reminds one of someone like d'Annunzio or Nietzsche – not to seek for later examples. In that way he resembled Rousseau. Just as Rousseau imposed a Calvinist logical straitjacket upon what was really a burning private lunacy, so Maistre imposes an official legitimist Catholic framework upon what is really a deeply violent, deeply revolutionary, ultimately Fascist inner passion.

What made Maistre so fascinating to those of his own generation was that he forced them to look at the seamy side of things. He forced them out of bland optimism; out of mechanical psychology; out of all the smooth ideals of the eighteenth century, which had suffered such a crushing disaster in the French Revolution. At the end of positivist, optimistic periods of human construction, in which men rise up and say they are about to cure all the world's ills by some economic or social solution, which then does not work, there is always a penchant for reaction on the part of ordinary people, satiated by so much false optimism, so much pragmatism, so much positive idealism, which become discredited by the sheer pricking of the bubble, by the fact that all the slogans turn out to be meaningless and weak when the wolf really comes to the door. Always, after this, people want to look at the seamy side of things, and in our day the more terrifying sides of psychoanalysis, the more brutal and violent aspects of Marxism, are due to this human craving for the seamy side – something more astringent, more real, more genuine, meeting people's needs in some more effective fashion than the rosy, over-mechanical, over-schematised faiths of the past. This is what Maistre provides for his own generation, too. Men cannot live by the ideals he opposed, and Maistre's contribution is a violent antidote to the overblown, over-optimistic and altogether too superficial social doctrines of the eighteenth century. Maistre earns our gratitude as a prophet of the most violent, the most destructive forces which have threatened and still threaten the liberty and the ideals of normal human beings.

Men may be divided into those who are in favour of life and those who are against it. Among those who are against it there are sensitive and wise and penetrating people who are too offended and discouraged by the shapelessness of spontaneity, by the lack of order among human beings who wish to live their own lives, not in obedience to any common pattern. Among such was Maistre. On the whole he has no positive doctrine, and if he has to choose between liberty and death he rejects liberty. He has his disciples in the twentieth century – Charles Maurras, for example, and Ezra Pound – and although we may disagree with such persons, let us remember that liberty needs its critics as well as its supporters. After all, as in Goethe's *Faust*, Mephistopheles, who criticised the ways of God, is not left altogether without an answer.

APPENDIX TO THE SECOND EDITION

'Two Concepts of Liberty': Early Texts

Editorial Note

Blot out, correct, insert, refine,
Enlarge, diminish, interline.

Jonathan Swift[1]

Isaiah Berlin's inaugural lecture as Oxford's Chichele Professor of Social and Political Theory, 'Two Concepts of Liberty', has its proximate origins in a long typescript prepared by Berlin in the early 1950s, the surviving part of which was published in 2006 as *Political Ideas in the Romantic Age*.[2] Berlin also drew on this material in 1952 when he gave the BBC lectures printed in the present volume, which therefore claim joint paternity of the inaugural.

'Two Concepts of Liberty' was delivered and published[3] in 1958, and ever since it appeared it has been the most discussed and the most contested of his texts. Parts of it have given rise to widely differing interpretations, and parts of it (sometimes the same ones) have been found unconvincing, ambiguous, inconsistent, equivocal or otherwise unclear, despite the undoubted clarity of Berlin's prose.

Fortunately several drafts of the lecture survive. As often

[1] *On Poetry: A Rapsody* (Dublin, 1733), 8 (lines 87–8).
[2] 27/2.
[3] By the Clarendon Press in Oxford.

happens in the case of texts that have been reworked a number of times before publication (especially if, as here, they began life in dictated form), earlier drafts, if at times cruder and less elegant, can throw useful light on the meaning of later ones, since the ideas they contain are sometimes expressed more simply and directly, and are less set about with qualifications, defences and digressions. Seen through the prism of a previous version, a later one can yield more meaning than when read in isolation – or even a different meaning. This is especially true of a philosophical pointillist like Berlin, an intellectual impressionist who, in his later work, tends to communicate his thoughts with a cumulative, often repetitive, rhetorical scatter-gun rather than by providing a plain, sober, rigorous exposition, step by explicit step.

It is certainly true in the case of this lecture, which is why I am including much of the draft material as an appendix to this volume, and have posted most of the rest of it in the Isaiah Berlin Virtual Library. My hope and belief is that the preparatory drafts, as well as being of considerable interest in their own right, will at times provide illumination for interpreters of Berlin's classic portrait of his pluralist liberalism.

The surviving drafts include not only a series of typescripts, the first of which is heavily corrected in manuscript, but also several 'Dictabelts', the now obsolete sound carrier (manufactured by Dictaphone) that Berlin used for dictation at the time.

I use the following code to refer to the successive drafts:

A Original text (continuous text plus 5 additional passages)
B A amended in manuscript
C Revised version of B
D Revised version of C
E Revised version of D, submitted to the Clarendon Press
F Shortened version of E, used for delivery of the lecture
G Alterations marked in proofs of E
H BBC talk on 'The Search for Status'[1]
J Additions marked in published text of E for *Four Essays on Liberty*

[1] In 1959 Berlin gave four talks, based on his lecture, on the BBC's European

These letters are inserted into the text in square brackets to show which version is used at which point: the text following an inserted letter is taken from the draft in question, until another letter appears. In footnotes the scope of an inserted letter ends with the note.

The Dictabelts provide the whole of A and the last part of C. The sound they preserve was transferred to analogue tape by the National Sound Archive over twenty years ago, as part of a wider rescue operation that made it possible to complete the fragmentary surviving typescript of Berlin's long essay on J. G. Hamann, dictated in the 1960s.[1] The taped sound has now been digitised by Phil Nixon of Wolfson College, Oxford, and I have checked the result against the transcripts (where available) made in 1958 by Mrs Olive Sheldon, a freelance typist who worked for Berlin at the time. These include a complete transcript of A, which forms the principal ingredient of the text printed below.

In the course of dictating A, when he reached the end of the section on negative liberty, Berlin broke off and dictated five separate passages, which I number A1–A5. Transcripts by Mrs Sheldon of all of these except A4 were inserted into the main text of A in their proper places, A3 and A5 into the part of the text Berlin had already dictated, and A1 into the part he then went on to dictate. A2 is a revised version of a sentence he had already dictated. If A4 was transcribed at the time, the transcript is lost. Did Mrs Sheldon overlook it, or did Berlin discard it? He does indicate in B where it is to be inserted, which seems to imply that he had it before him and wanted to include it. On the

---

Service, in the series 'London Calling Europe: As I See It'. The last talk, 'The Search for Status', broadcast on 20 July 1959, survives as a BBC transcript in Berlin's papers, and was published in Berlin's *The Power of Ideas* (xiv/1). For its bespoke ending see 229. The other talks are lost.

[1] 'The Magus of the North: J. G. Hamann and the Origins of Modern Irrationalism', first published as a book with that title in 1990, now included in *Three Critics of the Enlightenment: Vico, Hamann, Herder*, ed. Henry Hardy (London and Princeton, 2000; 2nd ed., Princeton, 2013). See 306 in the second edition for an account of the rescue process.

other hand, it has no successor in later drafts or in the published version.

Berlin corrected A heavily in manuscript – between the lines, in the margins, on the backs of pages, on separate sheets – much of the time rewriting it wholesale. This yielded a characteristic palimpsest (B), from which he seems to have dictated C, revising further as he read from his script. The Dictabelts provide what appears to be the last half (roughly speaking) of C, starting with the equivalent of the new paragraph on p. 192 of *Liberty*.[1] No contemporary transcript survives of this lengthy passage: it has now been transcribed, and is printed below (246–61).

There are no more surviving recordings, but we do have Mrs Sheldon's transcript of a still further revised version of the whole lecture (D), presumably based on C. We therefore have, by the stage at which D was dictated, four versions of the last half of the lecture – A, B, C and D – but only three versions of its first half – A, B and D.

Both B and D contain a number of new passages of varying length. In the case of B, these are sometimes very hard (once or twice impossible) to decipher, though consultation of C (where available) or D often helps. Further additional passages in D are not represented in the earlier texts we have, though at least some of them were probably drafted by hand on the lost contemporary transcript of C.

The most heavily reworked passage in the early drafts is the lecture's famous peroration, the last paragraph of which is altogether absent from A. In B this passage is so heavily corrected and amplified that I have included its version separately in full (242–5). D's version of the important last sentence of the lecture resolves a significant ambiguity in other drafts, and in the published text, as I explain in my postscript.

[1] *Liberty*, ed Henry Hardy (Oxford and New York, 2002), is referred to hereafter as L. Page references are given in the form 'L 192'; 'L 123/1' means note 1 on p. 123 of L.

E is the text delivered to the Clarendon Press for publication, and is for the most part a copy of D lightly amended by hand, though the opening pages have been revised and retyped. F is a shortened version of E, only half its length, freshly typed and marked up with stresses (underlinings or accents) for delivery.[1]

I have posted transcripts of B, D and E in the Isaiah Berlin Virtual Library – see <http://berlin.wolf.ox.ac.uk/published_works/tcl/> – for those who wish to compare the drafts in detail. F appears as an appendix to the second edition of *Political Ideas in the Romantic Age*. Reading this alongside E will show what changes were made to reduce the text to deliverable length: not all of these changes are mere abbreviations.

Berlin did not usually follow his manuscript corrections exactly when he was dictating from them. I have not recorded below all the minor differences between B and the drafts that precede or follow it, but these can be deduced from comparisons with the online text of B. Comparison of E with the text published in 1958 will reveal what further changes were made in the proofs (G);[2] and comparison of the latter text with that included in *Liberty* (an informative exercise)[3] shows what Berlin altered for

[1] Three pages have been interpolated into F, marked as footnotes. This makes no sense in a text intended for delivery. Did Berlin at one time intend to publish the shorter text? Was he simply using the wrong text by mistake? The passages from F below are taken from these intercalated pages.

[2] 'You have certainly had a field day with the proofs' (Colin Roberts of Oxford University Press to Berlin, 6 November 1958). The lecture had to be completely reset, and the proofs, which survive (see 175), show why.

[3] Cf. Anthony Arblaster's notorious attack on Berlin, 'Vision and Revision: A Note on the Text of Isaiah Berlin's Four Essays on Liberty', *Political Studies* 19 no. 1 (1971), 81–6, which implies that Berlin was disingenuous when he stated in his introduction to the book that he had not made substantive alterations to the texts of the component essays. In particular he mocks IB's alterations in his lists of names, citing an example from 'Historical Inevitability': 'In the earlier version the list [which in the later version (L 130) begins "From Zeno to Spinoza, from the Gnostics to Leibniz, from Thomas Hobbes to Lenin and Freud"] began with "From Plato to Lucretius", continued with the Gnostics

the latter incarnation of the lecture (J), first published in 1969 in *Four Essays on Liberty*. The arabic numbers in square brackets in the text below indicate (sometimes necessarily roughly) where the pages of the text published in *Liberty* begin.

I have inserted the more substantial of the passages added in B–J in the text below, using the earliest available version, so that the composite text published below as 'First Drafts' provides the earliest surviving version of most of the material in the final text. (The distinction between new and revised matter is at times somewhat penumbral and subjective. This is one reason why I have made all the drafts available in full, so that readers can if they wish trace the evolution of the text in more minute detail than it is practicable to exhibit here.) Short insertions from later versions have been used where the recording is corrupt – old Dictabelts are sometimes brittle, and the stylus can jump, as on a scratched vinyl recording – or the manuscript defective.

Where Berlin corrected himself in the course of dictation, the text silently follows his correction. Where his dictated text is ungrammatical (strikingly rarely), I have preserved what he dictated, sometimes amending it in square brackets where it seemed helpful to do so. I have introduced paragraph breaks where these are present in *Liberty*, to facilitate comparison of the differences between texts; I have also retained one or two dictated paragraph breaks that do not appear in *Liberty*, and introduced further breaks in some long paragraphs to give additional relief to the reader. I have inserted section numbers and titles from the final text as further useful signposting. I have corrected Berlin's direct quotations where I can: fidelity to his drafts seemed in this case misleading rather than illuminating. Where the same quotations appear in *Liberty*, I have not repeated the references provided there, but I have added references for other quotations.

---

and Leibniz, but had Thomas Aquinas, instead of Thomas Hobbes, almost as if it had to be Thomas somebody' (85).

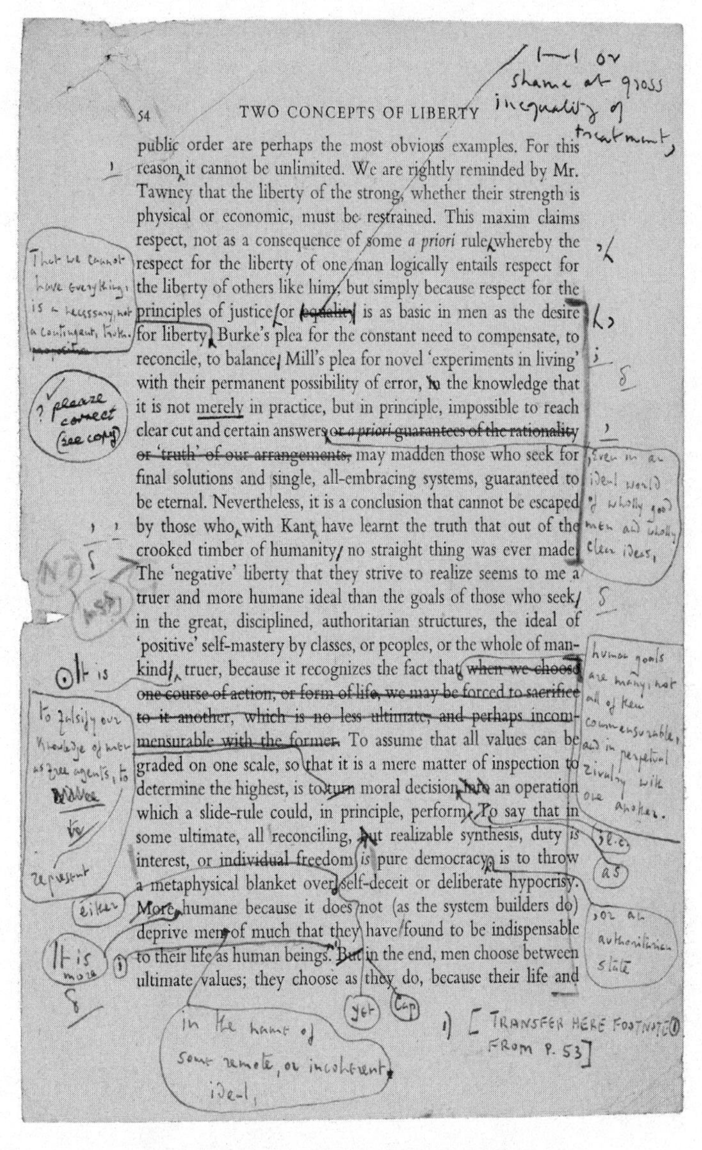

54 TWO CONCEPTS OF LIBERTY

public order are perhaps the most obvious examples. For this reason it cannot be unlimited. We are rightly reminded by Mr. Tawney that the liberty of the strong, whether their strength is physical or economic, must be restrained. This maxim claims respect, not as a consequence of some *a priori* rule whereby the respect for the liberty of one man logically entails respect for the liberty of others like him, but simply because respect for the principles of justice or equality is as basic in men as the desire for liberty. Burke's plea for the constant need to compensate, to reconcile, to balance; Mill's plea for novel 'experiments in living' with their permanent possibility of error, in the knowledge that it is not merely in practice, but in principle, impossible to reach clear cut and certain answers or *a priori* guarantees of the rationality or 'truth' of our arrangements, may madden those who seek for final solutions and single, all-embracing systems, guaranteed to be eternal. Nevertheless, it is a conclusion that cannot be escaped by those who with Kant have learnt the truth that out of the crooked timber of humanity no straight thing was ever made. The 'negative' liberty that they strive to realize seems to me a truer and more humane ideal than the goals of those who seek in the great, disciplined, authoritarian structures, the ideal of 'positive' self-mastery by classes, or peoples, or the whole of mankind; truer, because it recognizes the fact that when we choose one course of action, or form of life, we may be forced to sacrifice to it another, which is no less ultimate, and perhaps incommensurable with the former. To assume that all values can be graded on one scale, so that it is a mere matter of inspection to determine the highest, is to turn moral decision into an operation which a slide-rule could, in principle, perform. To say that in some ultimate, all reconciling, but realizable synthesis, duty *is* interest, or individual freedom *is* pure democracy, is to throw a metaphysical blanket over self-deceit or deliberate hypocrisy. More humane because it does not (as the system builders do) deprive men of much that they have found to be indispensable to their life as human beings. But in the end, men choose between ultimate values; they choose as they do, because their life and

A page from the proofs of *Two Concepts of Liberty*[1]

[1] Oxford, Bodleian Library, MS. Berlin 450, fol. 111: scan © Bodleian Library 2014.

As will be seen, the history of this central text is somewhat tortuous; but study of its development is rewarding. To spell out the results of such study is a task for another time, and probably another student.

I am grateful to George Crowder and Martin Liddy for helpful comments on a draft of the appendix.

First Drafts

[A] INAUGURAL LECTURE
[166] TWO CONCEPTS OF LIBERTY[1]

Mr Vice-Chancellor: The subject to which my chair is dedicated – social and political thought – has fallen upon evil days in this country. It is a melancholy reflection that in the land which has made a great, perhaps the greatest, contribution to political thought, among a people which still feels a legitimate pride in the names of Hobbes, Locke, Hume, Mill, Green, Bradley, so few men [B] gifted with a [A] capacity for theoretical thought should today wish to deal with social or political ideas. Whatever the cause of this phenomenon, whether it is because the decline in power, wealth and influence of England has led to a preoccupation with sheer survival on the part of all political parties and institutions, and so diminished attention to the ultimate ends of life, and in particular to disagreement about them, without which politics cannot live; or whether it is because our philosophers, intoxicated by their magnificent successes in more abstract realms, have no time [for] or interest in a field in which radical discoveries are less likely to be made, and gifts of minute analysis less likely to be rewarded[2] – whatever the cause, political thought as an academic subject is at present a backwater in English-speaking countries.

[167] And yet this is in a sense both strange and dangerous. Strange, because there has perhaps been no time in modern history when so large a number of human beings, both in the

[1] [Berlin first dictated 'Liberty' as 'Freedom'.]

[2] [B adds here:] It may be that the relative stability and mild climate of our social life – compared with the storms that sweep over our neighbours – is [sc. are] not propitious to the raising of fundamental social or political issues.

East and the West, have had their notions and indeed their lives altered, and in some cases most violently upset, by social and political doctrines which have cast their spell upon them or their rulers. And dangerous, because when ideas are neglected by those who ought to attend to them – that is to say, intellectuals, persons trained to think – they acquire a momentum and a power over great multitudes of men too great and violent to be altered by rational criticism. Over a hundred years ago the German poet Heine warned the French not to underestimate the power of ideas: philosophical concepts nurtured in the stillness of a professor's study could destroy a civilisation. He thought that the *Critique of Pure Reason* was the sword with which the old religion and the old metaphysics had been beheaded; and the works of Rousseau the bloodstained weapon which in the hands of Robespierre – like the analogous doctrine of Fichte in the hands of fanatical German philosophers – would one day destroy liberal culture in the West. [B] Who shall say that he was mistaken? Yet if professors can wield this fatal power, it may be that other professors [J], or, at least, other thinkers (and not governments or congressional committees), [B] can disarm them.

[A] It is a very vulgar historical materialism that denies the overwhelming power of ideas, and says that ideas are mere material interests in thin disguise. It may be that, without the pressure behind them of social or economic forces, ideas often remain impotent; what is certain is that these social and economic forces – which, after all, are no more than men working, feeling, striving with and against other men and inanimate nature – achieve their effect through the medium of ideas, and most of all social and political ideas. Ideas are of interest solely so far as they constitute problems or answers to problems which arise in the course of men's reflection about their place and their purpose in the world, and the nature of that world, and their own relationship with it. Political theory, even in its most active aspect, as a political doctrine or faith which finds issue in action, is nevertheless part of this general self-consciousness which commonly goes by the name of philosophy. Despite every effort to separate them, guided by a blind scholastic pedantry, politics has remained indissolubly intertwined with ethics and with every form of thought which enquires about the ends of life and the hierarchies of human values. To neglect it on the grounds of its necessarily imprecise subject matter or the proportion in it of empirical content in comparison, say, with logic or the philosophy of the sciences or of our knowledge of the external world is merely to allow oneself to remain at the mercy of primitive and uncriticised beliefs in one of the great realms of human experience.[1]

[168] Political philosophy is a branch of moral philosophy and consists in the application of moral ideas to the sphere of social relations. It seems to me that unless this truth is grasped the present condition of our world is unlikely to be understood. [B] I do not mean, as I think Hegel may have meant, that all historical movements or conflicts between human beings are reducible to movements or conflicts of ideas or spiritual forces. But I do mean that to understand such movements and conflicts must, in the first place, be to understand the clashing ideas or complete attitudes that alone make them a part of human history and experience, and not mere natural events.

[A] The world is today divided between two great outlooks which, although they show certain common assumptions, are split, it seems to me, most of all by the difference in their conceptions of the deepest and most central of all political problems, that of obedience. Why should I (or anyone) obey anyone else? Why should I not do as I wish? This seems to me the central problem of all political theory, for if it were not necessary or desirable that some men should obey the orders of others, or

[1] [Here, as in *Liberty*, I have omitted a dutiful encomium of Berlin's predecessor in his chair, G. D. H. Cole.]

yield to the superior force or authority of these others – whatever form the obedience takes – all men could do as they wished, and in the total absence of friction between men the problems that give rise to political speculation could scarcely have arisen.

[D] At this point someone may declare that even a wholly harmonious society – a perfect monastic community or a society of saintly anarchists, where no conflicts about ends arise – will still be faced with political problems: questions of which of several possible policies with regard, for instance, to legislation or administration the society is to adopt. But this seems to me a radical mistake. Where ends are agreed, and clashes of ultimate direction – whether on the part of individuals or groups (or classes) – are *ex hypothesi* non-existent, all questions must be those of means. And problems of means are not political but technical – of how best to bring about the agreed purpose – and always capable of being settled in terms of accepted criteria of what is and what is not feasible (as in arguments between experts – engineers or doctors or lawyers). Problems of behaviour become political (or moral) only when there is some collision of purposes or attitudes which cannot be settled by specialists, or the application of technical rules. That is why those who believe that political problems can be totally solved by some device – the moral re-education of mankind; or the triumph of reason, or of enlightened elites; the destruction of capitalism by the proletariat – also hold that the real life of humanity will begin only after that, when all human problems will be soluble by technological means, that is to say, the application of scientific methods. This is the doctrine of Condorcet and Saint-Simon, Marx and Lenin, and is the meaning of the celebrated formula about 'replacing the government of persons by the administration of things'. This outlook is called utopian by those who think there is something absurd in conceiving a world in which differences between men about ultimate social issues – and therefore political problems – will wholly disappear.

[A] The central problem of political theory seems to me to be that of coercion. Nobody will deny that upon the answer to it diametrically opposed views are held in large areas of the world today, and [sc. or] that the opposition of these views, if not the cause, is at any rate the most articulate expression of the great systems embattled against each other at this moment. It seems to me therefore that no problem is more worthy of examination.

[I]

Coercion is the deprivation of freedom. And what is freedom, at least in its political sense? [B] Almost every moralist in human history has praised it: like happiness and goodness, its meaning is so vague that there is little it has not been used to mean. [A] We know that more than two hundred definitions of this word have cast a dark cloud upon the subject. Yet there are at least two senses of the word which few would deny to be central, or at least two criteria which determine whether a man or a nation or a group is free or not. [169] The first, which I shall call the negative sense or criterion, is the answer to the question 'What is the area within which the subject – a person or group of persons – is left to do what [he or] they like without control by other persons?' The second is the answer to the question 'What is the source of control, when it exists, which can prevent someone from doing what he wishes?' To say that there is only one sense of the word 'freedom', but two criteria for its determination, seems to me merely a confusion; for the two questions seem genuinely different, even though the answers to them may overlap. Let us take them one by one.

1. The negative concept

I am said to be free to the degree to which no human being interferes with my activity. This is the classical sense of liberty in which the great English philosophers, Hobbes, Locke, Bentham,

Paine, and indeed Mill, used it.[1] Political freedom was simply the area within which a man could do what he liked. If I was prevented by other persons from doing what I liked, I was to that degree unfree; and if the area within which I could do what I wished was legally contracted beyond a certain minimum, I could be described as being enslaved.

'Slavery' was not the term that covered every form of inability. If I say that I am unable to jump more than ten feet in the air, or cannot see because I am blind, or cannot understand the more esoteric pages of Hegel, it would be eccentric to say that I was to that degree enslaved or coerced. Coercion implies the deliberate interference of other human beings within the area in which I wish to act. If someone is described as a slave to his passions, for instance, there is a feeling, which is quite correct, that the word is being used in a somewhat metaphorical sense. Certainly there is a sense in which he is not free; and this sense is of the greatest importance, as will, I hope, presently be made clear. But it is not primarily a political sense: a man who is a slave to his passions is certainly a slave in some sense different from that in which Uncle Tom was a slave to Simon Legree. Uncle Tom was a slave because he was coerced by another human being in the relevant respects. To be prevented from attaining what you or (in the case of the slave to his passions) in your rational moments you desire is certainly to be, to that degree, not free.[2] But you lack political freedom only if some other person deliberately prevents you from attaining your goal. [B] Mere incapacity for attaining our goal is not lack of political freedom.[3]

[1] [B] 'A free man', said Hobbes, 'is he that [...] is not hindered to do what he has a will to.' Law is always a 'fetter' [*De cive*, chapter 14], even if it protects you from being bound in chains that are heavier than the law's – arbitrary despotism or chaos. Bentham says the same. [The sentence to which this note is attached is deleted in G.]

[2] [Previous five sentences deleted in G.]

[3] Helvétius made this point very clearly: 'The free man is the man who is not in irons, not imprisoned in a gaol, nor terrorised like a slave by the fear of

[A] This is brought out best by the expression 'economic slavery' and its counterpart, 'economic freedom'. It is argued, very plausibly, that men who are too poor to purchase something upon which there is no legal ban are as little free to acquire it as they would be if it were [170] legally forbidden, i.e. if they were threatened with legal coercion if they attempted to do so. If it were the case that my poverty was like a disease – that I could not buy a house as I cannot see if I am blind – this would not naturally be described as a lack of freedom. It is only because it is suspected or believed that my inability to purchase the house is due to the fact that other human beings have made arrangements whereby I am prevented from having enough money with which to buy the house that I begin to speak of slavery. [B] In other words, it is due to a particular socio-economic theory about the causes of my poverty. [A] If my poverty is due to bad luck or accident, or the unintentional effect of social or political institutions, then I simply speak of lacking economic freedom. If I believe that I am being prevented from acquiring the objects that I desire by a deliberate plan on the part of certain other human beings, which they desire to implement but to which I am hostile, I speak of oppression. [B] The nature of things does not madden us, only ill will does, said Rousseau.[1] [A] In all these cases the criterion of whether I am justified in speaking of myself as deprived of liberty is the part played by other human beings in frustrating my wishes. I am then in a position to say that by freedom I mean a situation in which others do not interfere with my actions. The wider the area of non-interference the wider my freedom.

This is certainly what Hobbes and Bentham and J. S. Mill

punishment.' It is not lack of freedom not to fly like an eagle or swim like a whale or be a king or a pope or an emperor.

[1] ['[I]l est dans la nature de l'homme d'endurer patiemment la nécessité des choses, mais non la mauvaise volonté d'autrui': Émile, book 2; *Oeuvres complètes*, ed. Bernard Gagnebin, Marcel Raymond and others (Paris, 1959–95), iv 320.]

meant when they used this word.[1] They disagreed about how wide this area could or should be; they all admitted that it could not be unlimited, because, if it were, then all men could interfere without limit with all other men, and their minimum needs – without which men cannot survive – could not be satisfied in the condition of lawless anarchy which would prevail; or at least the needs of the weaker majority would have little chance against the force employed by the stronger minority; [171] which at any rate justified some limits upon the freedom of individuals, with a view to letting all of them, or a great majority, attain, not indeed to as much as they would wish, but to more than they would succeed in getting under any other system.

But it was not denied that this minimum of social organisation entailed the curtailment of the area of liberty. If liberty were the only goal which men pursued, this would be a frustration of it; as it is, it is an attempt to compromise between their desire for liberty and their need for a minimum of food, shelter, security and whatever other basic needs men have which cannot be secured without some interdependence, entailing some loss of individual liberty. Nevertheless it was assumed by these thinkers, especially by such liberals as Locke and Mill, and by such even more eloquent defenders of it as Constant and Tocqueville in France, that although the area of men's free action must needs be limited by law, there was a certain minimum which must on no account be violated; for if it was overstepped, the individual would find himself in an area too narrow for the minimum development of his natural faculties, which alone made life worth living, and alone conferred such value as they possessed upon the various ends which men held good or right or sacred. A frontier must be drawn between the area of private life and that of public authority. Where it is to be drawn is a matter of argument, indeed of haggling. [B] Men are largely interdependent

[1] [182/1 moved to this position in G.]

and no man's activity is so private as literally never to affect – and potentially interfere with – the lives of others in any way. The liberty of the weak depends on restraint of the strong.

[F *as footnote*] 'Freedom for an Oxford don', others have been known to say, 'is a very different thing from freedom for an Egyptian peasant.'

This proposition derives its force from something that is both true and important, but the phrase itself remains a piece of rhetorical nonsense. It is true that to offer political rights or safeguards against intervention by the State to men who are half-naked, illiterate, underfed and diseased is to mock their condition; they need medical help or education before they can understand, or make use of an increase in their freedom. [J] What is freedom to those who cannot make use of it? Without adequate conditions for the use of freedom, what is the value of freedom? [F] First things come first: in their situation, as a nineteenth-century writer declared, boots are superior to the works of Shakespeare. In other words, freedom is not everyone's primary need. Freedom is not the mere absence of frustration of whatever kind; this would [172] inflate the meaning of the word until it meant too much or too little. The Egyptian peasant needs clothes or medicine before, and more than, personal freedom, but the minimum freedom that he needs today, and the greater degree of freedom that he may need tomorrow, [is not] some species of freedom peculiar to him, but identical with that of dons or colonels or millionaires.

[G] What troubles the consciences of Western liberals is not, I think, the belief that the freedom that men seek differs according to their social or economic conditions, but that the minority who possess it have gained it by exploiting, or, at least, averting their gaze from, the vast majority who do not. They believe, with good reason, that if individual liberty is an ultimate end for human beings, none should be deprived of it by others; least of all that some should enjoy it at the expense of others. Equality of liberty;

not to treat others as I should not wish them to treat me; repayment of my debt to those who alone have made possible my liberty or prosperity or enlightenment; justice in its simplest and most universal sense – these are the foundations of liberal morality.

Liberty is not the only goal of men. I can, like the Russian critic Belinsky, say [F] 'If my freedom depends on the slavery of others, I reject it! Why should I be free, while my brothers are sunk in poverty and squalor?'[1] These are cries not for freedom but for *equality* or for *justice*. We abhor glaring inequalities; or we wish to pay back to others for what they have done for us; or we cannot bear [to] be happy alone. These may be ineradicable feelings, and the values to which they are directed may be as fundamental as the desire for liberty: but they are not identical with it. [*end of footnote in* F] [G] To avoid glaring inequality or widespread misery I am ready to sacrifice some, or all, of my freedom: I may do so willingly and freely; but it is freedom that I am giving up for the sake of justice or equality or the love of my fellow men. I should be guilt-stricken, and rightly so, if I were not, in some circumstances, ready to make this sacrifice. But a sacrifice is not an increase in what is being sacrificed, namely freedom, however great the moral need or compensation. Everything is what it is: liberty is liberty, not equality or fairness or justice or human happiness, or a quiet conscience. If the liberty of myself or my class or nation depends on the misery of a vast number of other human beings, the system which promotes this is unjust and immoral. But if lose my freedom in order to lessen the shame of such inequality, and do not thereby materially increase the individual liberty of others,[2] an absolute loss of liberty occurs.

[1] [Paraphrase of a passage in a letter to V. P. Botkin, 8 September 1841: V. G. Belinsky, *Polnoe sobranie sochinenii* (Moscow, 1953–9), xii 69. For a fuller, more literal version see Berlin's *Russian Thinkers*, ed. Henry Hardy and Aileen Kelly, 2nd ed. (London etc., 2008), 194.]

[2] [Here 'or increase it by less than I lose myself, there then is' is crossed out.]

This may be compensated for by a gain in justice or in happiness or in peace, but the loss remains, and it is a confusion of values to say that although my 'liberal', individual freedom may go by the board, some other kind [173] of freedom – 'social' or 'economic' – is increased. But it remains true that the freedom of some must at times be curtailed to secure the freedom of others. Upon what principle should this be done? If freedom is a sacred, untouchable value, there can be no such principle. [J] One or other of these conflicting rules or principles must, at any rate in practice, yield: not always for reasons which can be clearly stated, let alone generalised into rules or universal maxims. [B] Still, a practical solution must and can be found.

[A] Philosophers with an optimistic view of human nature and a belief in the harmonisation of human interests, such as Locke or Adam Smith or, in some of his moods, Mill, believed in a large area of private life, that is to say, in a large extension of liberty which the State or other authority must not be allowed to overstep. Hobbes and those who agreed with him, especially conservative or reactionary thinkers in the nineteenth and twentieth century, argued that if men were to be prevented from cutting each other's throats and making social life a chaos and a wilderness, far greater safeguards must be instituted to keep them in their places, and wished correspondingly to increase the area of State control, and decrease that of the individual. But both sides agreed that some portion of human existence must remain independent of the sphere of social control. To invade that, however small, was despotism. Thus Constant, who had experienced the full horrors of Jacobin dictatorship, declared that the liberty of religion, opinion, expression, property must be sacrosanct, and guaranteed against arbitrary invasion. Why? Because we cannot sacrifice 'eternal principles of justice and mercy'[1] without 'degrading or denying our nature'. No doubt we

[1] Benjamin Constant, *Principes de politique*, chapter 1, 'De la souveraineté

cannot be absolutely free, and must give up some of our liberty to preserve the rest. But total self-surrender is self-defeating, for then there will be nothing left to preserve.

What then must the minimum be? That which a man cannot give up without offending against the essence of our human nature. 'Nature', it may be objected, is a vague term, and many views have been taken as to what the true nature of man is. To this Constant replies that there are some uses of it which are virtually accepted by all men, with whom we have a common language. If a law is passed according to which children are to be punished for not denouncing parents, or trying to save them from the executioner, then what we do may be illegal (for Robespierre or Napoleon or Louis XI passed just such laws), but nobody will say that it is natural. A law which tells us to condemn the innocent, to betray, to refuse asylum to the weak and persecuted, is felt to be iniquitous in the sense that it tramples on standards in terms of which we judge human beings to be human. Those who reject these standards without a qualm, or do not feel their moral force, are correctly described as 'inhuman', and communication with them is difficult. But whatever may be the principle in terms of which the area of non-interference is to be drawn, whether it is that of natural law or [174] natural rights, or utility in the narrow sense given it by Bentham, [or] the wider sense in which Mill speaks of it as 'grounded on the permanent interests of man as a progressive being',[1] or the pronouncements of the categorical imperative, or the sanctity of the social contract, or many another concept with which human beings have sought to clarify and justify their convictions, 'liberty' means liberty *from*, absence of interference beyond a certain frontier.

---

du peuple': Benjamin Constant, *Écrits politiques*, ed. Marcel Gauchet ([Paris], 1997), 318.

[1] *On Liberty*, chapter 1: *Collected Works of John Stuart Mill*, ed. J. M. Robson and others (Toronto/London, 1963–91), xviii 224.

'The only freedom which deserves the name is that of pursuing our own good in our own way', said Mill, and meant by this liberty of thought, feeling, conscience, opinion, expression, tastes and pursuits, and liberty of combination. Was compulsion ever justified? No doubt it was: in extreme cases, where a society was genuinely endangered and the institutions which themselves preserved freedom were in peril, individual liberty could perhaps be at any rate temporarily curtailed or suspended. Moreover, since all individuals were entitled to this minimum degree of freedom, all other individuals were of necessity to be restrained, if need be by force, from depriving anyone of it. Indeed the whole function of law was the prevention of collisions: the law was what the socialist Lassalle was contemptuously to describe as being that of a nightwatchman or traffic policeman, guarding of a property and preventing collisions, with no positive functions at all.

What made this area of liberty so sacred to Mill? In a famous tract, perhaps the most famous of all essays on the subject, which had so profound an influence upon the thinking of generations of Englishmen and those they governed, he declares that unless men are left to live as they wish, 'in the part [of their conduct] which merely concerns [themselves]', civilisation cannot advance; the truth will not, for lack of a free market in ideas, come to light; spontaneity, energy, character, individuality in all its forms will decline; there will be no scope for genius, for mental vigour, for moral courage. Society will be crushed by the weight of 'collective mediocrity'. Whatever is 'rich, diversified, and animating'[1] will be crushed by the weight of custom, by men's constant tendency to conformity, which breeds only 'withered' capacities, 'pinched and hidebound', 'cramped and dwarfed' human beings. 'Pagan self-assertion' is as worthy as 'Christian self-denial'. 'All errors which [a man] is likely to commit against advice and warning are far outweighed by the evil of allowing

[1] ibid., chapter 3: xviii 266.

others to constrain him to what they deem his good.' Liberty consists in the preservation of an area within which human personality is to have the fullest possible play. Unless a man can pursue ends because they are his ends, make acts of choice which, even if they lead to disaster, are nevertheless felt by him as his acts, the pursuit of goals which are, at any rate for him, absolute in that they are not means to other ends, but that alone which makes all other acts worth doing, which gives his life such value as it has in his own eyes – in short, enough political space to allow him not to suffocate, nor to survive on condition of being an instrument of other peoples' wishes – [175] that is liberty as it has been conceived by liberals in the modern world from the days of Erasmus to our own. Constant and Mill are its noblest and most convincing advocates. Every plea for civil liberty, for individual rights, for the preservation of individual variety and spontaneity against the encroachment of public authority, or the levelling tendency of custom or organised propaganda, stems from this central conception.

Two[1] aspects of it may be noted. [B] The first is that, amongst the defenders of 'negative' liberty – the liberty that is non-interference – Mill, as so often, here confuses two distinct ideals. One is that all coercion, in so far as it frustrates human desires, is bad as such (although it may have to be applied to prevent other, greater, evils), and liberty, which is the opposite of coercion, is good as such (although it is not the only good). The other is that men should seek to develop a certain type of character of which Mill approved – original, imaginative, independent, non-conforming to the [D] point of [B] eccentricity, and such [a] character can be bred only in conditions of liberty.

Both these are noble aims, but they are not identical; and the connection between them is at best empirical. If the thesis used

[1] [D] Three.

by James Stephen in his formidable attack on Mill,[1] that bold independence and fiery individualism grow at least as often in conditions of severe repression – puritan Calvinist[s] in Scotland or America – [as] in the more liberal climate of Scandinavia or modern Switzerland, were accepted, Mill's argument for liberty as a *sine qua non* of human genius would fall to the ground. If his two goals proved incompatible, Mill would be faced with a cruel dilemma, quite apart from the inconsistency of his doctrine with strict utilitarianism, even in his own humane version of it. This is but another illustration of the natural tendency of all but a few thinkers to believe that all things they hold good must be intimately connected or at least compatible with one another. The history of thought, like the history of nations, is strewn with examples of inconsistent, or at least disparate, elements artificially yoked together in some despotic system, or held together by the union against some common enemy. In due course conflicts between them arise which often disrupt the system, sometimes to the great benefit of mankind.

[176] [A] The first is that it[2] is comparatively modern. There is scarcely any consciousness of individual liberty as an ideal in the ancient world. Condorcet had already remarked that the notion of individual rights is absent from the legal and moral conceptions of the Romans and Greeks, still more so of the Hebrews, and of all other ancient civilisations that have since come to light.[3] Nor are the periods in which these notions have been dominant at all frequent even in the history of the Western world. It has seldom if ever formed a rallying cry for the great masses of mankind, as equality or democracy have been. It has remained the ideal of civilised men who wish to be left in peace to pursue their duties or

[1] *Liberty, Equality, Fraternity* (London, 1873).

[2] [D] In the second place the doctrine.

[3] [D] See the very valuable discussion of this in Michel Villey, *Leçons de'histoire de la philosophie du droit*, who traces the embryo of the notion of individual rights and liberty to Occam.

their pleasures or their avocations. The desire not to be impinged upon, not to be dictated to, to be free from the arbitrary deprivation of rights and liberties, has been a mark of high civilisation both on the part of individuals and communities. The desire to be left alone, to live one's life as one chooses, the very sense of privacy, of the area of personal relationships as sacred in its own right; the belief that it is more worthy of a human being to go to the bad in his own way than to the good under the control of a benevolent authority; this, which is almost a defining notion of a large element in Western civilisation, is scarcely older than the Renaissance and the Reformation.[1] Absolute values are not necessarily timeless or eternal, but their death marks the death of an entire civilisation, the end of an entire moral system.

Another[2] characteristic of this 'negative' conception of liberty is that it is compatible with autocracy, or at any rate the absence of self-government. Liberty in this sense is concerned with the area of control, not with its source. Just as a democratic community may in fact deprive the individual citizen of a good many liberties which he might have in some other society, so it is perfectly conceivable that a benevolent despot would allow his subjects a very wide area of personal freedom. Even though in a despotic society the individual would only enjoy such rights and liberties as the despot granted him, it is, at any rate in theory, conceivable that a very liberal-minded despot would grant his subjects wider liberties than they would enjoy under other systems of government.[3] Indeed, it is arguable that in the Prussia of Frederick the Great

[1] [D] Christian (or Jewish) belief in the absolute authority of either divine or natural laws, or in the equality of all men in the sight of God, is very different from belief in freedom to live as one thinks good.

[2] [D] The third.

[3] [A2 *in place of the previous sentence*] The tyrant who leaves us a great area of liberty may be unjust, encourage the wildest inequalities, care little for order or virtue or knowledge; he may be a savage or a lunatic, but provided he does not curb our liberty, he meets with Mill's specification. It seems to me that it is only by conceiving an extreme and perhaps improbable situation of this kind that

or the Austria of Joseph II, men of spontaneity, imagination, originality and creative power, whom Mill desired to encourage, were less interfered with and felt the pressure of both institutions and custom far less heavy upon them than they would have done in the Switzerland of that time or many a later democracy.

[177] Freedom in this sense is not, at any rate logically, connected with self-government. Self-government may indeed be a guarantee of its preservation, and has been defended as such by believers in individual liberty. But there is no necessary connection: the question of who governs me is logically distinct from the question how far government interferes with me; and upon this the great contrast between the two concepts fundamentally rests.[1] For the 'positive' sense of liberty is an answer to the

---

the full contrast between individual liberty in Mill's sense and self-government can be made clear.

[1] [A5] Negative liberty is something the extent of which it is difficult to estimate. It might prima facie seem to depend simply on the power to choose between at any rate two alternatives. Nevertheless not all choices are called free. If in a totalitarian State I betray my friend under threat of torture, I can reasonably say that I did not act freely. Nevertheless I did of course make a choice, and could, at any rate in theory, have chosen to be tortured. The mere existence of a minimum of possibilities is not therefore enough to make my choice free in the normal sense of the word. The extent of my freedom depends on: (*a*) how many possibilities are open to me (although the method of counting these can never be more than impressionistic: possibilities of action are not discrete entities like apples which can be exhaustively enumerated); (*b*) how easy or difficult each of these possibilities is; (*c*) how important in my plan of life, given my character and circumstances, these possibilities are when compared with each other; (*d*) how far they are closed or opened by deliberate human acts; (*e*) what value not merely the agent but the general sentiment of the society in which he lives puts on the various possibilities. All these factors must be 'integrated' in the conclusion, necessarily never precise or indisputable, drawn from this process. It may well be that there are many incommensurable degrees of freedom and that they cannot be drawn up on a single scale of magnitude, however conceived. [D] Moreover, in the case of societies we are faced by such (logically absurd) questions as 'Would the arrangement X increase the liberty of Mr A more than it would of Messrs B, C and D between them, taken together?' The same

question: By whom am I governed? Who is to say what I [178] am and what I am not to be or do? And although it seems at first as if there was an intimate connection between individual liberty in the sense of an area free from interference, and democracy in the sense of government not by some outside body but by myself and others like myself with whose interests mine were intertwined, direct government by us of ourselves, or at any rate by our representatives, yet the difference [sc. similarity] is more apparent than real. The desire to be governed by myself, or at any rate to participate in the process whereby my life is to be controlled, is no doubt as basic a wish as that of [sc. for] a free area for action, perhaps more so. But it is not the same; so different, indeed, as to have led in the end to the great clash of ideologies of which I spoke at the beginning. For it is nothing other than the positive conception of liberty which those who believe in the negative concept represent as being at times no better than a disguise for total slavery.[1]

[II]

[2. *The positive concept*]

The positive sense of the word 'liberty' derives from the desire on the part of the individual to be his own master. I wish my

---

difficulties arise in applying utilitarian criteria. [B] Nevertheless, provided we do not demand precise measurement, we can give valid reasons for saying that the average subject of the King of Sweden is, on the whole, a good deal freer than the average citizen of the Republic of Romania today. The total patterns of life can be directly compared as wholes, although the truth of [the] conclusion may be difficult to demonstrate. [D] But the vagueness of the concepts, and the multiplicity of the criteria involved, is an attribute of the subject matter itself, not of our imperfect methods of measurement, or incapacity for precise thought.

[1] [At this point Berlin broke off to dictate A1–A5.]

life and my decisions to depend on myself and not on external forces of whatever kind. I wish to be a subject, not an object; to be moved by reasons, by conscious purposes which are my own, and not by causes which affect me, as it were, from outside. I wish to be somebody, not nobody, self-directed and not directed by external nature or other men as if I were an inanimate object, an animal, a slave incapable of playing a human part, i.e. of conceiving purposes and realising them. This is what I mean when I say that I am rational, and that it is my reason that distinguishes me as a human being from the rest of the world. I wish above all to be conscious of myself as a thinking, willing, active being whose choices are his own, bearing responsibility for his acts, and able to explain them by reference to his own ideas and purposes. I feel free in proportion as I know this to be true, and enslaved in proportion as the facts make me realise that it is not true.

[B] The definitions of freedom as consisting in being one's own master, and as consisting in not being prevented from choosing as I do by other men – the positive and negative notions of freedom respectively – may seem prima facie to be [at] no great logical distance from each other. Yet close as they are at their source, they [179] developed in divergent directions, [J] not always by logically reputable steps, [B] until, in the end, they came into direct conflict with each other.

[D] One way of making this clear is in terms of the independent momentum which the metaphor of self-mastery acquired. 'I am my own master'; 'I am not slave to any man'; but may I not (as, for instance, T. H. Green is always saying) be a slave to nature? Or to my own 'unbridled' passions? Are these not so many species of the identical genus 'slave' – some political or legal, others moral or spiritual? Have not men had the experience of liberating themselves from spiritual slavery, or slavery to nature, and is it not one in which they become aware, on the one hand, of a self which dominates, and, on the other, of something in them which is brought to heel? This dominant self is then variously identified with reason, with my 'higher nature', with the self which calculates and aims at what will satisfy it in the long run, with my 'real' or 'ideal' or 'autonomous' self, or with my self 'at its best', which is then contrasted with irrational impulse, uncontrolled desires, my 'lower' nature, the pursuit of immediate pleasures, my 'empirical' or 'heteronomous' self, swept by every gust of desire and passion, needing to be rigidly disciplined if it is to rise to the full height of its 'real' nature.

Presently the two selves may be divided by an even larger gap: the real self may be conceived as something wider than the individual (as the term is normally understood), a social 'whole' of which the individual is an element or aspect: a tribe, a race, a Church, a State, the great society of the quick and the dead and the yet unborn.[1] This entity is then identified as being the 'true' self, which by imposing its collective, or 'organic', single will upon its recalcitrant 'members', achieves its own, and therefore their, 'higher' freedom.

The perils of using organic metaphors to justify the coercion of some men by others in order to raise them to a 'higher' level of freedom have often been pointed out. But what gives such plausibility as it has to this kind of language is that we recognise that it is possible, and perhaps at times justifiable, to coerce men in the name of some ideal which they would, if they were more enlightened, themselves pursue, but do not, because they are blind or ignorant or corrupt. In other words, it is possible for me to conceive of myself as coercing others for their own sake, perhaps even on their behalf. I am then claiming that I know what they truly need better than they know it themselves. What, at most, this entails is that [180] they would not resist me if they were

[1] [A reference to Edmund Burke's description of society, in *Reflections on the Revolution in France* (1790), as 'a partnership not only between those who are living, but between those who are living, those who are dead, and those who are to be born': *The Writings and Speeches of Edmund Burke*, ed. Paul Langford (Oxford, 1981–), viii, *The French Revolution*, ed. L. G. Mitchell, 147.]

rational, and as wise as I, and understood their interests as I do. But I may go on to claim a good deal more than this, namely that they are actually aiming at what they consciously resist, because there exists within them an occult entity – their latent rational will, or their 'true' purpose – and that this entity, although it is belied by all that they overtly feel and do and say, is their 'real' self, of which the poor empirical self in space and time may know nothing, or little; and that this inner spirit is the only self that deserves to have its wishes taken into account.[1]

Once I take this view, I am in a position to ignore the actual wishes of men or societies, to bully, oppress, torture them in the name of their 'real' selves, in the secure knowledge that whatever is the true goal of man (happiness, fulfilment of duty, wisdom, a just society, self-fulfilment) must be identical with his freedom – the free choice of his 'true', albeit submerged and inarticulate, self.

But this is a paradox which has been often exposed. It is one thing to say that I know, while he himself does not, what is good for X; and even to ignore his wishes for its – and his – sake; and a very different one to say that he has *eo ipso* chosen it, not indeed consciously, not as he is in everyday life, but in his role as a rational self of which the empirical self may not know – a self which discerns the good, and cannot help choosing it when he sees it. This monstrous impersonation, which consists in equating what X would choose if he were something he is not,

[1] [J] '[T]he ideal of true freedom is the maximum of power for all members of human society alike to make the best of themselves', said T. H. Green in 1881 ['Lecture on "Liberal Legislation and Freedom of Contract"', in *Lectures on the Principles of Political Obligation and Other Writings*, ed. Paul Harris and John Morrow (Cambridge etc., 1986), 200]. Apart from the confusion of freedom with equality, this entails that if a man chose some immediate pleasure – which (in whose view?) would not enable him to make the best of himself (what self?) – what he was exercising was not 'true' freedom; and, if deprived of it, [he] would not lose anything that mattered. Green was a genuine liberal: but many a tyrant could use this formula to justify his worst [acts of] oppression.

or not yet, with what X in fact seeks and chooses, is at the heart of all political theories of self-realisation. It is one thing to say that I may be coerced for my own good, which I am too blind to see; [J] this may, on occasion, be for my benefit; indeed it may enlarge the scope of my liberty; [D] and another that if it is my good, I am not being coerced, for I have willed it whether I know this or not, and am free even while my poor earthly body or foolish mind bitterly rejects it, and struggles [181] against those who seek to impose it, with the greatest desperation.

This magical transformation (for which William James so justly mocked the Hegelians) can no doubt be perpetrated just as easily with the 'negative' concept of freedom, where the self that must not be interfered with is no longer the individual with his actual wishes and needs as they are normally conceived, but the 'real' man within, identified with the pursuit of some ideal purpose which his empirical self may never have conceived; and as in the case of the 'positively' free self, may grow into some superpersonal entity – a State, a class, a nation or the march of history itself – regarded as a more 'real' subject of attributes than the empirical self. But the 'positive' conception of freedom as self-mastery, with its suggestion of the self divided against itself, lends[1] itself more easily to this splitting of personality into two: the transcendent, dominant controller, and the empirical bundle of desires and passions to be disciplined and brought to heel. This demonstrates (if demonstration of so obvious a truth is needed) that the conception of freedom directly derives from the view that is taken of what constitutes a self, a person, a man. Enough manipulation with the definitions of this last, and freedom can be made to mean whatever the manipulator wishes. Recent history makes it only too clear that the issue is far from being merely academic.

[1] [J reads: 'has in fact, and as a matter of history, of doctrine and of practice, lent'.]

[A] This desire to be self-directed has, historically, taken two major forms: the first, that of self-denial to attain independence; the second, that of conquest of obstacles in my path to attain the same end.

[III The Retreat to the Inner Citadel]

1. I am the possessor of reason and will. I conceive ends and I desire to pursue them. But if I am prevented from attaining them, I no longer feel master of the situation. I may be prevented by the laws [182] of nature – physical or physiological or psychological – or by chance or accident, or the malice of men, or the power, sometimes undesigned, of human institutions. These forces may be too much for me: what am I to do to escape from being crushed by them? I liberate myself from unfulfillable desires. I wish to be master of my kingdom, but my frontiers are too vulnerable; therefore I contract the frontiers in order to reduce the area of vulnerability. I desire happiness, but I cannot command it; I wish to strive after nothing that I cannot be sure to obtain; therefore, instead of vainly striving for happiness which may elude me, I eliminate from myself all desire for it. I withdraw into my inner self. Physical and biological laws make it impossible for me to attain goals – health or success – which I should have had if I had been differently built. I determine myself not to desire these unattainable ends. The tyrant threatens me with destruction of my property, with physical imprisonment, with the exile or death of those whom I love, but if I do not feel attached to property, do not care if I am in prison or outside it, and have killed within myself my natural affections, he cannot touch me. It is as if I were to perform a strategic retreat into an inner citadel – my reason, my soul – which, do what he might, neither external blind force nor human beings can touch. There and there alone I am safe; there and there alone I am master of all that I possess.

It is as if I were to say 'I have a wound in my leg; if the process of curing it is too precarious and uncertain, then I can get rid of the wound by cutting off my leg, and by teaching myself not to want anything for which my leg might have provided an opportunity.' This is the traditional self-emancipation of quietists, not only individual sages – Stoics, Buddhists, Jews, Christians, and indeed individuals dedicated to no religion: men who liberate themselves from the yoke of society or public opinion by a process of self-transformation which makes them care nothing for its values, and remain isolated and independent on its edges, no longer vulnerable to its weapons.[1] Every form of isolationism, monasticism, autarky – every form of autonomy, in short – has some element of this in it. I eliminate the obstacles on my path by abandoning the path. I retreat into the only territory of which I can be fully certain – my own inner spirit, or, in the case of groups, my own sect, my own planned economy, my own isolated territory, where no voices from outside need be listened to, [183] and no external forces can effectively reach. This is a form of the search for security, but it is also legitimately called inner freedom.

[A] Kant, who was perhaps the most profound secular defender of this point of view, built his concept of freedom upon it. I am free because I am autonomous: I obey laws which I have invented for myself. Freedom is obedience, 'obedience to a law which we prescribe to ourselves' [Rousseau]. Heteronomy is dependence on outside factors, being a plaything of circumstances, which include such psychological causes as desires, affections – everything, in short, which I cannot fully control, everything therefore which belongs to the outside world beyond the frontier of my personality – which must *ex hypothesi* be lifted above the empirical world of causality. This is not the place in which to discuss the validity of this point of view, but the notion

[1] [B] 'A wise man, though he be a slave, is at liberty, and from this it follows that though a fool rule, he is in slavery', said St Ambrose. It might equally well have been said by Epictetus or Kant.

of freedom as autonomy in this sense has been central in politics also.

If men must be treated in the first place as authors of values, of ends in themselves, whose ultimate authority consists precisely in the fact that they are willed by men not themselves dependent upon outside factors, then the greatest crime of all is to treat them as if they were not this, but in some sense dependent upon nature or other men, as if they were incapable of choices and must be chosen for, not allowed to choose for themselves: for that is to treat them as if they were not men. 'Nobody can compel me to be happy in his own way', said Kant; and paternalism is 'the greatest *despotism* imaginable'. Why? Because it is to treat men as if they were stuff for me, the reformer, however benevolently disposed, to mould in accordance with my, not their, rational purpose.

This [184] is what the Utilitarians recommended. Helvétius (and Bentham) did not object to dangling rewards and punishments before men – the acutest form of heteronomy – if by this means they might be made happier. But to manipulate men in this sense, to propel them towards goals which you see but they may not, is to deny their human essence, to degrade them.[1] That is why to lie to men or to deceive them is in effect to treat them as slaves, to behave as if other men's ends are less absolute and sacred than my own. This is false and leads to the humiliation of other men, which is the ultimate sin. There is only one source of ends for the sake of which everything is worth doing, and that is the individual who creates values, who creates these ends. In the name of what could I force them to do that which they do not will? In the name of something higher than themselves. But there is nothing higher than themselves if all values are the

[1] [D] 'Proletarian coercion, in all its forms, from executions to forced labour, is, paradoxical as it may sound, the method of moulding communist humanity out of the human material of the capitalist period.' These lines by the Bolshevik leader Nikolay Bukharin, written in 1920, especially the term 'human material', convey this attitude well.

creations of the human spirit. Therefore I am compelling men in the name of something lower than themselves – expediency, reasons of State, convenience, my own selfish desires. This is a contradiction of what I know myself to be. Exploitation, degradation, humiliation, because they deny what makes men men – their inner autonomy – is the worst crime committable by a human being. For if this is done, then no absolute ends will be left for the sake of which that which is done is to be done; and that would mean that rational self-mastery disappears and men are reduced to mere things; to behave as if those ultimate ends for the sake of which alone life is worth living or sacrificing do not exist. All forms of tampering with human beings, getting at them, shaping them against their will in your own form, brainwashing and conditioning,[1] is therefore the deprivation of men of that freedom in virtue of which alone they are men.

[185] This is the heart of the humanism, both moral and political, deeply influenced by Kant in the eighteenth century. It is a form of secularised Protestant individualism in which the place of God and the individual soul which strains towards union with him is taken by the abstract conception of the rational life, and the reason of the individual who strains after total rationality, to be governed by reason and by reason alone, not to depend upon anything that he does not understand or whereby he is affected or deluded. Autonomy, not heteronomy: to act and not to be acted upon. Deeply different though their metaphysical doctrines were, the Stoic sage, the self-directed rational man of Spinoza, the rational will that can will only what is right and can attain what it wills, for what it cannot attain it cannot will: these are different approaches to a very similar ideal – the man

[1] [G] Kant's psychology, and that of the Stoics and Christians too, assumed that some element in man – the 'inner fastness of his mind' – could be made secure against conditioning. The development of the techniques of hypnosis, 'brainwashing', subliminal suggestion and the like has made this a priori assumption, at least as an empirical hypothesis, less plausible.

who has made himself independent of chance and causality, and the malice and stupidity of men, by withdrawing, rising above it, making himself unassailable, impermeable, as it were, to anything that might deflect him.

The notion of slavery to the passions is now no longer a metaphor; to rid myself of fear or love or the desire to conform is to liberate myself from the slavery to something which I cannot control. Cephalus,[1] whom Plato reports as saying that old age alone has liberated him from passion – the yoke of a terrible master – is speaking as literally as those who speak of freedom from a flesh-and-blood tyrant or slave-owner. The psychological experience of observing myself yielding to some 'lower' impulse, and doing something which, at the very moment of doing it, I abhor, and reflecting later that I was not 'myself' when I did it; the distinction of the true self – inner, rational, pure, master of its resources – as opposed to the less real attributes, physical or emotional, which are the play of external forces; belong to this way of thinking and speaking. I am identified with my critical, rational faculty: the external results cannot matter, for they are not in my control, only motives are. Provided my motive is rational, I can ignore or even defy the outer world, and take refuge in my own integrity and independence. This is the creed of the solitary thinker, the successful rebel who has emancipated himself from the chains of things.[2]

[187] [B][3] If the pursuit of freedom by self-abnegation leads to self-annihilation, the pursuit of it by the removal of obstacles leads to wholly different results. Faced with obstacles to my will, I can yield before them and alter the direction of my will; but I can also transform them by using them as means to my ends. How can I achieve this? Those who are wedded to the 'negative'

[1] [In fact in Plato's *Republic* (book 1, 329c) Cephalus reports Sophocles to this effect. Corrected in later versions.]

[2] [B inserts here the passage identified at 208/1.]

[3] [B starts the section on self-realisation here.]

conception of freedom may perhaps be forgiven if they think that the only method of overcoming obstacles is by removing them: in the case of non-human objects, by physical action – if I am obstructed by men, by force of persuasion, as when I induce someone to make room for me in his carriage, or conquer a country which threatens the interests of my own. This may be unjust – it may involve violence, cruelty or enslavement of others – but it can scarcely be denied that the increase of freedom of the agent does take place. But these negative aims and empirical methods are rejected by the philosophical and, later, political adherents of the 'positive' conception of freedom.[1] It is their view that dominates half our world: if for no other reason, its metaphysical basis must be examined seriously.

[IV Self-Realisation]

[2.] The only true method of attaining freedom is by[2] [A] the use of critical reason, by understanding what is necessary and what is contingent. If I am a schoolboy, the difficult truths of mathematics present themselves as an obstacle, as theorems whose necessity I do not understand, but which are asserted to be true by some external authority, and which I must therefore mechanically learn; but when I [188] understand the function of the symbols, the axioms, the transformation rules, the logic whereby the conclusions are obtained – and that these things cannot be otherwise, either because they are given as part of the structure of the rational mind, or because I have invented them for myself as a game or convention which I play in accordance with rules which I myself have imposed – then it no longer

[1] [This sentence is replaced in G by: 'It is an irony of history that this truth is repudiated by some of those who practise it most forcibly, men who, even while they conquer power and freedom of action, reject the 'negative' concept of it in favour of its 'positive' counterpart.]

[2] [A] How am I to achieve this condition? By.

presents itself to me as an external obstacle which I must accept whether I will it or not, but as something which I freely move in. To the mathematician, the rules of mathematics are part of the free exercise of his natural logical capacity; to the musician, because he has assimilated the pattern of the composer's score and has made the composer's ends his own, the playing of the music is a free exercise; he does not feel bound to the score as an ox to his plough or the factory worker to his machine. He has absorbed the score into his own system, has appropriated it; and to appropriate something, to identify it with one's self, is to transform it from an obstacle into one's own texture, from an impediment to free activity into an element in that activity itself.

What applies to music or to mathematics must in principle apply to all other problems which present themselves as lumps of external stuff blocking free self-development. That is the programme of rationalism. 'Sapere aude', said Kant: 'Dare to know.' What you know, that of which you understand the necessity – the rational necessity, that is – you cannot, while remaining rational, want to be otherwise; for wanting it to be otherwise is to be pro tanto irrational. Ignorance, passion, fear, neuroses come from ignorance [*sic*]. Myths and illusions, whether they spring from the wilful activity of wicked men, who invent them in order to keep us in chains – as religion was declared to be the opium of the masses – or from the influence of psychological causes, or the unintended results of social institutions, are all forms of heteronomy, or being acted upon by the outside factors in a direction not willed by the agent. The eighteenth-century enlightened radicals thought that the study of mathematics, physics and other natural sciences, and of society on the model of the natural sciences, would make the operation of such causes transparent, and thus enable individuals to [189] choose whether to be acted upon by them (for if they so choose they are no longer acted upon but have made them their own instruments by willing them to be their own), or alter or destroy them.

Later thinkers in the same tradition, no matter how radically they disagreed about what true knowledge consisted in, fundamentally accepted this programme – the programme of self-knowledge. Herder and Hegel believed that earlier thinkers had not understood the part played by change in what made human beings human. To understand, it is not enough to understand mathematics or physics, one must also understand history, that is, the laws of continuous growth of individuals and groups in their interplay with each other and with nature. Not to understand this is to fall into a particular kind of delusion, namely a belief in a static nature and the possibility of creating a utopia on the assumption that men's needs are unaltering, and that the wise, wholly rational man in all ages and countries will always will the same unaltering ends. Hegel believed that his contemporaries (and indeed all his predecessors) misunderstood the nature of institutions because they did not understand the laws – the rational laws, since they spring from the operation of the human spirit – that create institutions and change human character and human action. Marx maintained that human beings were enslaved by external factors which they could not control, in the form of institutions which they had, not always consciously, created for certain purposes, but whose functioning, owing to the working of certain social and economic laws which they could not escape, they misunderstood systematically, and believed to be independent forces which must needs be obeyed as slaves obey a master (e.g. the laws of supply and demand, or property as an unaltering human category, or the division of society into rich and poor, or owners and workers), [190] simply because they did not understand that these laws and institutions were themselves the work of human minds and hands whose origins had been forgotten, whose function was misunderstood, and which were therefore falsely regarded as inexorable, external powers which it was idle to try and alter.

And Freud maintained that fears and obsessions and other curbs to the fully rational life were due to psychological causes, and that understanding these hitherto uninvestigated causal processes would put men in a position of either losing – discarding – their effects if they felt their freedom curtailed thereby, or of freely incorporating them in their purposive deliberate activity.

Nothing can be shaken off if it is not understood. [B] We are imprisoned by masters – institutions or beliefs or neuroses – which can be removed only by being analysed and understood. We are enslaved by evil spirits which we ourselves have – albeit not consciously – created, and can, by becoming conscious, and acting accordingly,[1] exorcise. [A] Freedom is to plan my life in accordance with my own will. Plans entail rules; a rule does not oppress me or enslave me if I impose it on myself or accept it freely, having understood it, even if it was invented by others. [D] To accept such necessities is to understand why things must be as they must be. [G] Knowledge liberates, [J] as Epictetus taught long ago, [G] not by offering us more open possibilities amongst which we can make our choice, but by preserving us from the frustration of attempting the impossible. [D] To want necessary laws to be other than they are is to be prey to an irrational desire – a desire that what must be X should also be not-X. To believe these laws to be other than they necessarily are is to be insane. [A] That is the heart of rationalism. And the notion of liberty contained in it [is] not that of the earlier 'negative' notion of a field without obstacles – the removal of impediments, a vacuum in which I can do as I please – but the notion of self-direction or self-control: I can do what I will with my own, I am rational. Whatever I can demonstrate to myself as being necessary, in the sense of incapable of being otherwise in a rational world – in a world directed by rational minds – towards goals such as a rational being might have, I do not wish to sweep out of the way. I assimilate it into my substance as I do the laws

[1] [J reads 'and can exorcise them only by becoming conscious and acting appropriately: indeed, for Marx understanding is appropriate action'.]

of mathematics, of art, of whatever I understand the purpose of, and therefore cannot want otherwise.

A socialised form of this belief has taken many contemporary forms: nationalism, Marxism, Hegelianism, authoritarianism of various types, as well as what has been called totalitarian democracy. To this I shall come in a moment.

[185][1] Meanwhile it is perhaps worth remarking that in its individualistic form the concept of the rational sage impervious to the slings and arrows of the world – the withdrawal in depth, the escape into the inner citadel of my true self, my rational being – has historically arisen, almost always, when the external world has proved too tyrannical and unjust. 'He is truly free', said Rousseau, 'who desires what he can perform, and does what he desires.' In a world where a man seeking virtue or justice or freedom (in whatever sense) finds that he can perform little, [186] the temptation to withdraw into himself can become irresistible. It was so in Greece, where the Stoic ideal cannot be wholly unconnected with the disappearance of the free democracies and the imposition of the Macedonian despotism. It was so for analogous reasons in early Rome.[2] It was so among the Eastern sages during the great autocracies at periods when human beings were apt to be humiliated, or at any rate ignored, taken for granted, ruthlessly managed by those who possessed the instruments of physical coercion. And it was so in Germany in the eighteenth century, the period of the deepest national degradation of the small German States, in the most part small and governed by petty despots, when the external world offered little asylum to those who prized the dignity of human life. For the doctrine

[1] [In B the passage from here to 'not the only way out' at 210 is moved to follow 'chains of things' at 203.]

[2] [D] It is not perhaps far-fetched to assume that the quietism of the Eastern sages was a response to the despotism of the great autocracies, and flourished most at periods when individuals were apt to be humiliated, or at any rate ignored or ruthlessly managed, by those possessed of the instruments of physical coercion.

which maintains that what I cannot have I must teach myself not to want, for to want the impossible is to be frustrated – to be a slave to my unfulfillable desires – is, despite the noble moral consequences which the Stoics or Kant and his followers drew from it, in the end a sublime form of the doctrine of sour grapes. [B] What I cannot have I cannot truly want. I only imagine that I want it, and can cure myself of this delusion.

[J] This makes it clear why the definition of negative liberty as the ability to do what one wishes – which is, in effect, the definition adopted by Mill – will not do. If I find that I am able to do little or nothing of what I wish, I need only contract or extinguish my wishes, and I am made free. If the tyrant (or 'hidden persuader') manages to condition his subjects (or customers) into losing their original wishes and embrace ('internalise') [sc. embracing ('internalising')] the form of life he has invented for them, he will, on this definition, have succeeded in liberating them. He will, no doubt, have made them *feel* free – as Epictetus feels freer than his master (and the proverbial good man is said to feel happy on the rack). But what he has created is the very antithesis of political freedom.

[B] It is difficult to see how ascetic self-denial, a policy of abandonment and retreat for the sake of the security of the little that is left, can be called the enlargement of liberty. I may save myself by retreating and locking every door and crevice before my adversary. I may remain freer than if I had been captured, but I am not freer than if I had defeated and captured him. And if I go too far, contract myself into too small a space, I shall suffocate and die. The logical culmination of the process of destroying everything through which I could possibly be wounded is suicide. While I exist in the natural [187] world I can never be wholly secure. Total liberation (as Schopenhauer perceived correctly) can come only in death.[1]

[1] [J] It is worth remarking that those who demanded – and fought for –

[A] Those who demanded liberty for the individual or for the nation in France never fell into this attitude, perhaps because, despite the despotism of the French monarchy, and the arrogance and irrationality of privileged groups in the French State, France was a proud and powerful nation where the reality of political power was attainable to men of talent, and where the withdrawal from battle into the untroubled heaven above it, whence it could be surveyed dispassionately by the self-sufficient philosopher, was not the only way out.

[190] I have said that the socialised [191] form of this doctrine is at the heart of the freedom that is discussed or fought for in many quarters today. This is not the place to trace the historical evolution of this situation. Let me give two familiar illustrations.

[V The Temple of Sarastro]

[191] Those who believed in freedom as self-direction were doubtless bound to consider, sooner or later, how this was to be applied, not merely to the individual's inner life, but to his relations to other members of his society. Even the most individualist among them – and Rousseau, Kant and Fichte certainly started as individualists – were bound to ask themselves whether and how, not merely a rational life for the individual, but a rational life for society, was possible. I wish to be free to live as my rational

---

liberty for the individual or for the nation in France during this period of German quietism did not fall into this attitude. Might this not be precisely because, despite the despotism of the French monarchy and the arrogance and arbitrary behaviour of privileged groups in the French State, France was a proud and powerful nation, where the reality of political power was not beyond the grasp of men of talent, so that withdrawal from battle into some untroubled heaven above it, whence it could be surveyed dispassionately by the self-sufficient philosopher, was not the only way out? The same holds for England in the nineteenth century and well after it, and for the United States today.

will wills; but so must others be. How am I to avoid collisions? Where is the frontier between my rights and the identical rights of others (for if I am rational, I cannot deny that what I deserve, others who are rational like me deserve for similar reasons)? A rational State would be a State the laws of which would be such that all rational men would accept them, i.e. such laws as they would themselves have promulgated had they been in a position to do so; the frontier would be such as we should all agree, as rational men, was the right frontier for rational beings.

But who in fact is to decide this? On the assumption which all these thinkers made (and their use of the word 'reason' led them to it), that moral and political problems, like problems in mathematics or physics or any other sphere, were in principle soluble – i.e. that there was one true solution to any problem, as opposed to the many false ones, and that the truth could be discovered by a rational thinker, and demonstrated so clearly that all other rational men could not but accept it (as is the case in, say, the natural sciences) – on that assumption political problems were soluble by [192] establishing a just order which would give to each man all the freedom that a rational being is entitled to. The rational solution of one problem cannot collide with the rational solution of another, for two true solutions cannot be incompatible. Therefore such an order must in principle exist – the ideal state of affairs, sometimes imagined as the paradise before the flood, in which all men lived happily in a state of blessedness together, sometimes as a golden age still before us, in which all men, having become rational, would no longer have desires, passions or habits which could in principle collide with that which other similarly perfect men could ever demand.

In existing societies justice and equality are ideals which it is necessary to obtain with some measure of coercion, because freedom from social controls might lead to the oppression of the weaker by the stronger, of the stupider by the more energetic or unscrupulous. But it is only irrationality on the part of men (according to this doctrine) which leads them to wish to oppress or exploit or humiliate one another. Rational men will respect the principle of reason in each other and lack all desire to fight one another or seek to dominate one another. The desire to dominate is itself irrational and can be explained by rational methods. Hegel explains it in one way, Marx in another, Freud in yet a third way: some of these can perhaps supplement each other; others are not combinable. But be that as it may, in a society of perfectly rational beings the lust for power will be absent, and a rational society will not possess in it anyone desiring to oppress anyone else. The existence of oppression will be the first symptom that the true solution to the social problems (and it must be remembered that there is one, otherwise the problem is no problem, for all true problems must have solutions, whether they have been discovered or not) has not been reached.[1]

[B] This can be put in another way. Freedom is self-mastery, the elimination of obstacles to my will, whatever these obstacles may be – the resistance of nature, of my own ungoverned passions, of irrational institutions, of the opposing wills of others. Nature I can mould by technical means, and impose my will upon it: but how am I to treat recalcitrant human beings? I must, if I can, impose my will on them too, 'mould' them to my pattern, cast parts for them in my play. But this will this not mean that I am free, while they are slaves? They are if my plan has nothing to do with their desires and values, [193] only with my own. All true solutions to all genuine problems must be compatible; more than this, they must coincide; for that is what is meant by calling them all rational. Each man has a specific character, abilities, aspirations, ends: if I grasp what these ends and natures are, I can, at least in principle, if I have the knowledge and the strength, satisfy them all. Rationality is to know things and people for what

[1] [From this point the Dictabelts provide a revised text (C), intermediate between B and D; C's version appears at 246–61.]

they are: I must not use stones to make violins, nor try to make born violin-players play the flute. If the universe is governed by reason – that is, if a pattern is discoverable in which everything and everyone plays the part it is meant to play by its own inner nature – there will be no need for coercion. A planned life for all will coincide with full freedom – the freedom of rational self-direction – for all: provided, that is, that the plan is the true plan, the one unique pattern which alone fulfils the claims of reason. Laws then are the rules which reason prescribes: they will only seem irksome to those whose reason is dormant – who do not understand their own 'true' needs. If each player plays the part which his reason – which understands his true nature and discerns his true ends – sets him, there can be [no] conflict. Each is a liberated, self-directed actor in the cosmic drama.

When Spinoza says that children, although they are coerced, are not slaves, because they obey orders given in their own interests, and the subject of a true commonwealth is no slave because a common interest must include his own; or when Locke says, 'Where there is no law there is no freedom', because rational laws are directions to his proper interests or 'general good', and what 'hedges us from bogs and precipices' 'ill deserves the name of confinement', and calls any desire outside this irrational – 'license' or 'brutish' etc.; when Montesquieu, forgetting his 'negative' moments, speaks of political liberty as 'the power of doing what we [194] ought to will', and Kant comes near to echoing this;[1] they assume that the rational ends of our 'true', i.e. rational, natures coincide, and to make them coincide, against all the violent resistance of our poor empirical selves, is no tyranny but liberation.[2]

[1] [D] Burke proclaims the individual's 'right' to be restrained in his own interests because 'the presumed consent of every rational creature is in unison with the predisposed order of things'. [New paragraph begins here in L.]

[2] [B] On this Bentham seems to me to have said the last word: 'The liberty of doing evil, is it not liberty? If it is not liberty, what is it then? [...] Do we not

[A] This is, in effect, what eighteenth-century thinkers say. Rousseau tells me that, if I freely surrender all the parts of my life to society, I create an entity which, having been built by an equality of sacrifice of all its members, cannot wish to hurt any one of them; it can in such a society be in nobody's interest to damage anyone else. In giving myself to all I give myself to no one, and I get back as much as I lose, together with enough force to preserve my new gains. Kant tells me that when the 'individual has entirely abandoned his wild, lawless freedom to find it again unimpaired in a state of dependence according to law', that is true freedom, 'for this dependence is the work of his own will, acting as lawgiver'. Liberty, so far from being incompatible with equality, cannot be made actual without it; hence the Declaration of the Rights of Man and Citizen in [195] 1789 and again in 1793 both speak of the fact that liberty consists 'in doing anything which does not conflict with the rights of one's neighbour', for 'the exercise of the natural rights of each individual has no bounds except those which are necessary to ensure the enjoyment of the same rights to the other members of the society'.[1] These bounds can be established by any rational man, for any rational man can in principle discover the true solution to any problem, but it takes a society of wholly rational men freely to accept this solution as the truth, for only rational men can tell the truth when they meet it. The rule of such a State is that what one man can do, all men can do; thus, if anyone infringes this rule, all men are damaged thereby.

If the assumption were correct – if a solution to social

---

say that liberty should be taken away from fools, and wicked persons, because they abuse it?' [E] Compare with this a typical statement of Jacobin doctrine of the same period: 'no man is free in doing evil. To prevent him is to free him.' [Crane Brinton, 'Political Ideas in the Jacobin Clubs', *Political Science Quarterly* 43 (1928), 257.] [J] This view is echoed in almost identical terms by British idealists at the end of the following century.

[1] [The latter wording does not appear in the 1793 Declaration.]

problems were like a solution to those of the natural sciences, and if a society of wholly rational men could be conceived – this would no doubt be a true conclusion. Liberty would coincide with law. Autonomy would coincide with authority. Men would be wholly equal and wholly free, wholly rational and wholly just. This is the ideal of anarchism. [B] But all liberal rationalism holds less or more watered-down versions of this ideal.

[A] The thinkers who bent their energies to the solution of the problem were presently faced with the question of how men were to be made rational in this way. Clearly they must be educated, for only the uneducated are irrational, heteronomous, and may need to be coerced to make life possible for the rational, if they are to live in the same society with them, and not withdraw to some Olympian height. Education, says Fichte quite consistently, works in such a way that 'You will later recognise the reasons for what I am doing now.' Children cannot be expected to understand why they are compelled to go to school, nor the uneducated – i.e. the majority of mankind – why they are made to obey laws which will presently make them rational and so retrospectively justify such coercion as they may have suffered. This is the task for the State. 'Compulsion is also a kind of education.' [B] If you [196] do not understand your own interests as a rational being, I cannot be expected to consult you or abide by your wishes in the course of making you a rational being. [A] I force you to be protected against smallpox though you may not wish it. Even Mill is prepared to say that a man may be forcibly prevented from crossing a bridge if there is not time to warn him that it is about to collapse, for he cannot wish to fall into the water. I, the sage, know your wishes better than you can know them yourself, for you are the victim of your passions, a slave living the heteronomous life, purblind, unable to understand your best interest. You want to be a human being: it is the aim of the State to procure this right for you. 'Compulsion is justified by education for future insight.'

Here the fatal analogies begin. Just as reason within me, if it is to triumph, must eliminate and suppress my 'lower' instincts, my passions and desires, which render me a slave, so the higher elements in society – the better educated, the more rational, those who 'possess the highest insight of their time and people' – can exercise compulsion to rationalise the irrational sections of society; for by obeying the rational man we obey ourselves – not indeed as we are, sunk in our ignorance and our passions, children afflicted by disease that needs a healer, wards who need a guardian – but as we potentially are, as we could be if we were rational, as we are now if only we would listen to the rational element which is *ex hypothesi* within every human being deserving of the name.

[D] The Hegelian philosophers, from the tough, rigidly centralised, 'organic' state of Fichte, to the mild liberalism of T. H. Green, certainly supposed themselves to be fulfilling, and not resisting, the rational demands which, however inchoate, were to be found in the breast of every sentient being. [C] And, pursuing the same line of reasoning, if I break away from the teleological schema of the Hegelians towards some more voluntarist philosophy, may I not conceive the idea of imposing on my society – always for its own betterment – a plan of my own which in my rational wisdom I have elaborated, which unless I act on my own, and perhaps against its wishes, [197] may never come to fruition at all? Or, abandoning the concept of reason altogether, I may conceive myself as an inspired artist who moulds men into patterns in the light of his unique vision, as painters combine colours or composers sounds. Humanity is the raw material on which I impose my creative will; even though men suffer and die in the process, they are lifted by it to a height to which they could never have risen without my coercive but creative violation of their lives.

[A] This is the argument used by every dictator, inquisitor and bully who seeks for moral justification for his conduct. I must do for men what they cannot do for themselves, and I cannot ask for their permission or consent because they are in no condition to know what is best for them, and what they will permit and consent to may mean their suicide. [C] The hero may be a rationalist sage, or Napoleon, or a romantic authoritarian who believes in the possibility of creating a race of supermen, as some Fascist leaders claim to do. [B] I quote from Fichte again: [A] 'No one has [...] rights against reason.' 'Man is afraid of subordinating his subjectivity to the laws of reason: he prefers tradition or arbitrariness.' Nevertheless, subordinated he must be, for that is the purpose of man on earth and the only path to true freedom.[1]

It is consistent with this to ask, as Auguste Comte once did, why, if we do not allow free thinking in chemistry or biology, we should allow it in morals or politics. [B] Why indeed? If it makes sense to speak of political truths – in the sense of the true social ends which all rational men would agree to be such when they are discovered – and if scientific methods can reveal them, there is no case for freedom for its own sake, either for men or groups, or for any conduct unauthorised by scientific experts. Comte put bluntly what had been implicit in the rationalist theory of politics from its ancient Greek beginnings: there can, in principle, be only one correct way of life; the wise lead it spontaneously, else they would not be [198] wise; the unwise must be dragged towards it by all the social means in the power of the wise, for why should demonstrable error be tolerated? The immature and untutored must be made to say to themselves: [A] 'Only the truth liberates, and the only way in which I can learn the truth is by doing blindly today what you who know it order me to do, in the conviction that only thus will I rise to your clear vision, and be free like you.'

We have come full circle, for this argument, employed by

[1] [G] 'To compel men to adopt the right form of government, to impose Right on them by force, is not only the right, but the sacred duty, of every man who has both the insight and the power to do so.' *Johann Gottlieb Fichte's sämmtliche Werke*, ed. I. H. Fichte (Berlin, 1845–6), iv 436.

Fichte and Hegel and all other defenders of authority, is what the Stoic and Kantian ethic protests against most bitterly in the name of the reason of the unoppressed individual, following his own light as best he can. The rationalist approach, on the assumption of the single true solution which the experts alone can determine, leads therefore to a Platonic authoritarian State, obedient to the directives of the sages.

[C] What can have led to so strange a reversal, the transformation of Kant's individualism into something close to a pure totalitarian doctrine? This question is not of mere historical interest, for many contemporary liberals have gone through the same peculiar evolution. It is true that Kant insisted, following Rousseau, that all men possessed a capacity for rational self-direction, that there could be no experts in moral matters, for it was not a matter of knowledge, as the Utilitarians maintained, but of the correct use of an inborn faculty; and that what made men free was not acting in certain self-improving ways – which they could be coerced to do – but knowing why they ought to do so, which nobody could do for or on behalf of anyone else. But even Kant, when he came to deal with political issues, said that no law, provided it was such that I should if I were asked approve it as a rational being, could possibly deprive me of my liberty.

With this the door is opened wide to the rule of experts. I can't consult all men about all enactments all the time. The government cannot be a continuous plebiscite. Moreover some men are not as well attuned to the voice [199] of their own reason as others: some are singularly deaf. If I am a legislator or a ruler, I must assume that, if the law I impose is rational, and I can only consult my own reason, it will automatically be approved by all the members of my society qua rational beings. If they disapprove they must pro tanto be irrational, and therefore need to be repressed by reason, whether their own or mine can't matter greatly, for the pronouncements of reason must be the same in all minds.

I issue my orders and, if you resist, take it on myself to repress the irrational element in you which opposes reason. My task would be easier if you repressed it in yourself. I try to educate you to do so. But I am responsible for public welfare, and I cannot wait until all men are wholly rational. Kant may protest that the essence of the subject's freedom is that he and he alone has given himself the order to obey, but this is a counsel of perfection. If you fail to discipline yourself, I must do so for you and you can't complain of lack of freedom, for the fact that you've had to be coerced is merely evidence that you haven't listened to your own inner reason, that you are like a child or a savage, not ripe for self-direction;[1]

[1] [E] Kant came nearest to asserting the 'negative' ideal of liberty in one of his political treatises when he declared that 'The greatest problem of the human race, to the solution of which it is compelled by nature, is the establishment of a civil society universally administering right according to law. It is only in a society which possesses the greatest liberty [...] – and also the most exact determination and guarantee of the limits of [the] liberty [of each individual] in order that it may co-exist with the liberty of others – that the highest purpose of nature, which is the development of all her capacities, can be attained in the case of mankind.' Without the teleological implications, this does not at first appear very different from some of Mill's liberal doctrines. The crucial point, however, is the criterion for the 'exact determination and guarantee of the limits' of individual liberty. Mill and liberals in general want a situation in which as many individuals as possible can realise as many of their ends as possible, without presuming to criticise those end's themselves, so that the frontiers between individuals [are drawn] with the view solely to prevent collisions, so far as possible, between human activities, without being permitted to enquire into their direction as such. Whereas the limits of [positive?] liberty are determined by applying the rules of 'reason', which is the same in and for all men, and in its name nothing [sc. anything] that is non-rational may be condemned – the various personal aims which their individual imaginations and idiosyncrasies may lead men to pursue may be ruthlessly suppressed to make way for reason. The tyranny of reason is identified with freedom on the assumption that only rational ends can be the true objects of man's desire.

I have never understood the meaning of 'reason' in this context, and merely wish to point out that the priori assumptions of this rationalist psychology are not compatible with any doctrine founded on normal experience of what men are and seek.

and [200][1] if this leads to despotism of the best or the wisest, which is then identified with freedom, can it be that there is something gravely amiss in the premisses of the argument? [B] Can it be that some at least of the basic assumptions – that all men as such have one purpose, rational self-direction; that all their goals must harmonise in one universal harmonious pattern; that all conflict is due to [the] clash of reason with the irrational or insufficiently rational; that when everybody has been made rational, at last it is [possible] at once to obey [the] law and be free, for they are one – can it be that some at least of these assumptions are somehow at fault?

[VI The Search for Status]

[A] There is another approach, legitimate enough in itself, which [201] can be made to yield a very similar conclusion. Ever since the middle of the eighteenth century it has been persistently, and with increasing effect, asked: What is meant by an 'individual'? In so far as I live in society, everything that I do inevitably affects and is affected by what others do. Even Mill's distinction between the sphere of private life and that wherein I affect others breaks down under examination. Everything that I do may have effects which deeply affect other human beings, and vice versa. Besides, I am social in a deeper sense than mere interaction, for am I not what I am, to some degree, in virtue of what others think that I am?

When I ask myself what I am, and answer 'An Englishman', 'A Frenchman', 'A Chinese', 'A carpenter', 'A respected member of society', 'A criminal', I find upon analysis that to be an Englishman or a Chinese or a criminal involves me in being recognised as belonging to a particular group or class by other

[1] [New paragraph begins in L.]

persons in the society in which I live and that this recognition by them is part of the meaning of the terms in which I describe what appear to be my most personal, most permanent attributes. I am not disembodied reason; nor am I Robinson Crusoe alone upon an island; it is not only that my material life depends upon interaction with other men, but that my ideas about myself are intelligible only in terms of the social network in which I am an element.

The freedom that a man demands is as often as not the desire for recognition: I may be seeking not for what Mill would wish me to seek, namely freedom from coercion, from arrest, from tyranny, from the deprivation of certain liberties, for a vacuum free from human obstruction of this type; what I may seek to be saved from is – from being taken for granted, from being ignored, patronised, despised; in short, from not being treated as a full human being, from having my existence unrecognised, from being classed as a member of some featureless amalgam, a statistical unit without identifiable unique human features of my own. This is the degradation that I am fighting against, not equality of legal rights, not liberty to do as I wish (although I may want these too), but for a condition in which I can feel [202] a responsible agent as a full human being, even if I am attacked and persecuted for being as I am.[1]

This is a hankering after status: for recognition. I desire to be understood, to be recognised, even if to be unpopular and disliked, and the only people who can so recognise me, and give me the sense of being fully human which recognition alone will give, are the members of the society with which I feel bound up. [B] This has [an] obvious affinity with the Kantian doctrine of human freedom; but it is a socialised and empirical version of it, and therefore almost its opposite. Kant's free man needs

[1] [B] This is vividly brought out in the celebrated words of the leveller Rainborow in 1647: 'The poorest he that is in England hath a life to live as the greatest he.'

no public recognition for his inner freedom. If he is treated as a means to some external purpose, that is wrong on the part of his exploiters, but his own 'noumenal' status is untouched; and he is fully free and fully a man in isolation. The need of which I speak here is bound up wholly with my relation to others: I am nothing if I am unrecognised; I cannot ignore the attitude of others with Byronic disdain, fully conscious of my own intrinsic worth and vocation, or escape into my inner life. I am in my own eyes as others see me: I identify myself with the point of view of my milieu. I feel myself to be somebody or nobody in terms of my position and function in the social whole; it is the most heteronomous condition imaginable.

[A] [There is no need to use such similes as those of organism or growth, or other biological language, in order to convey that in large part what I am is what I see myself as, or feel [myself] to be, and that this is literally something which only other people can give me by having certain attitudes towards me, in terms of which I then think of myself as having this or that position in society.][1] My individual self is not something which I can detach or abstract from my relationships with others, or from those attributes of myself which consist in their attitude towards me. Consequently, when I demand liberation from the status of dependency, what I demand is alteration of status.

[J] And what is true of the individual is true of groups, social, political, economic, religious, that is, of men conscious of needs and purposes which they have as members of such groups. [A] The sense in which the members of oppressed classes or nationalities demand what they perfectly correctly describe as their liberty is not in the first place simply liberty of action, nor equality of opportunity, but recognition of myself (or my class or my nation, or my colour or my race) as an [203] independent source of action, something entitled to direct itself as it wishes, and not

[1] [Deleted in B.]

to be ruled, educated, guided, with however light a hand, as not quite fully human, and therefore not quite fully free.

This is why paternalism is 'the greatest *despotism* imaginable', not because it oppresses more than naked, brutal, unenlightened tyranny, but because it is an insult to my conception of myself as a human being entitled to make my own life in accordance with my own purposes, and above all to be recognised as such by others; for if I am not so recognised then I cannot recognise it fully in myself, for part of what I am is determined by what I feel and think, and what I feel and think is determined by the feeling and thought prevailing in the society to which I belong, of which, in Burke's sense, I form, not an isolable atomic unit, but an ingredient in what may, without danger of misleading metaphor, be called a social pattern. I may feel unfree in the sense of not being recognised as a self-governing human being, as an individual; but I may feel it also as a member of a class or a nation. And then I desire the emancipation of my entire class or nation or profession. But since the other members of my nation – while we are all oppressed – recognise me as a full member of themselves, even as I am recognised as a full member of the slave class by the other slaves, I may prefer to be bullied and ordered about by another slave, or another member of my oppressed nation, to being well and wisely treated by someone who belongs to another class or another nation, because I prefer recognition by my brother human being, even if I am misgoverned by him, to non-recognition by someone whom I do not feel to be a brother, but a being from another sphere, even if he governs me well.

This is the heart of the demand for recognition on the part of individuals and groups, professions and classes, nations and races. Those to whom I look for it may be the representatives of my class or my profession or my nation; I may not get 'negative' liberty at their hands, and may be harried from pillar to post by them, but they are members of my own group, they understand me and I understand them, and this understanding creates within me the sense of being somebody, and not nobody or half a nobody, in the world. It is this that leads the most authoritarian democracies to be preferred by its [sc. their] members to the most enlightened oligarchies, or causes a member of some [204] newly liberated Asian or African State to complain less if he is unjustly imprisoned by members of his own race or nation than if he were ever so lightly displaced by some cautious, benevolent, infinitely well-meaning administrator from outside. [B] Unless this phenomenon is grasped, the ideals and the behaviour of entire peoples who, in Mill's sense, suffer deprivation of elementary human rights, and who, with every appearance of sincerity, speak of enjoying greater liberty than when they possessed a wider measure of these rights, becomes an unintelligible paradox.

[A] [Perhaps the proper term for this is not 'liberty' but 'fraternity', but as words are used it is liberty that such individuals and groups demand. This is liberty in the positive sense of self-direction, and the perversions of the meaning of the word which occur when fallacious analogies are made between reason, which directs the lower emotions in the individual, and the governing elite, which has a similar right to despotic rule over the 'lower' members of a society – these very fallacies are intelligible only on the assumption that one of the central meanings of the word 'liberty' is self-direction, whether by a man over himself or by a group over its members. This alone makes it possible for men to call for leaders and claim that this in some sense liberates them.][1]

[B] And yet it is not liberty, in either the 'negative' or the 'positive' sense of the word, that those who demand status and recognition are fighting for: it is something no less passionately desired, an equally profound necessity for human beings – [D] something akin to, but not itself freedom; [J] although it entails negative freedom for the entire group, it is more closely related

[1] [This paragraph is deleted in B, whose next paragraph appears to signal a change of mind, or at least of emphasis.]

to [B] solidarity, fraternity, mutual understanding, need for association on equal terms, which is sometimes – but misleadingly – called social freedom. Social and political terms are necessarily vague: to attempt to make its vocabulary too precise may render it useless; [but] it is no service to the truth to loosen usage beyond necessity. The desire for liberty is the desire for freedom from something or someone – other men – or one's own obsessions, fears, neuroses. The desire for recognition is a desire for the very opposite: for union, closer understanding, amalgamation of interests, a life of mutual dependence and mutual sacrifice.

Enough has been written on the glaring fallacy of speaking of social groups as being literally persons or selves whose control and disciplining of their members is no more than self-discipline, voluntary self-control which leaves the individual agent free. Perhaps no more need here be said than that if I have voluntarily refrained from doing what I might, I have not therefore grown less free: but if I [have] restrained you from doing so, no juggling with words can show that your freedom has not been curtailed. But it is perhaps more important to note that the analogy between individual and group has been so successful a source of fallacies, and in its consequences so disastrous, precisely because solidarity and fraternity are basic human cravings, and, when they are satisfied, lead to patterns of collective behaviour and feeling which lend themselves easily to analogy with the feelings and thoughts of individuals. The collective desire for the liberation of my social group [from] the yoke of some outside body is, at the very least, similar enough to the individual's wish to rid himself of controls for the word 'liberty' to be used for both phenomena: and the collective desire of a community to assert itself as an independent source of power is sufficiently analogous to that of the individual seeking 'positive' freedom to make the same word as applied to both shed at least as much light as darkness on the situation it seeks to denote.

[D] But even on the 'organic' view, would it be natural or desirable to call the demand for recognition and status a demand for liberty in some third sense? It is true that the group from which recognition is sought [205] must itself have a sufficient measure of 'negative' freedom – otherwise recognition by it will not give the claimant the status he seeks. But the struggle for higher status – the wish to escape from an inferior position – is this to be called a struggle for liberty? Is it mere pedantry to confine this word to the main senses discussed above, or are we, as I suspect, in danger of calling any adjustment of his social situation favoured by a human being an increase of his liberty, and will this not make this term too vague and all-embracing to be useful? And yet we cannot simply dismiss this case as a mere confusion of the notion of freedom with those of status, or solidarity, or fraternity, or equality, or some combination of these. For the craving for status is in certain respects very close to the desire to be an independent agent.

[A] It is a shallow view that assumes that the analogies between a person and a nation, or organic metaphors, or several senses of the word 'liberty' are simply fallacies, either of comparing entities which are in relevant respects unlike, or of simple semantical confusion. What men who are prepared to barter liberty of individual action for the status of their group, and their own status within the group, want is not to surrender liberty for security, or for some assured place in a harmonious hierarchy, as they conceive it, in which every man and every class knows its place and is prepared to surrender the painful necessity of choosing, 'the burden of freedom', for the peace and comfort and mindlessness of an authoritarian or totalitarian structure. No doubt there are such, and no doubt such surrenders of liberty can occur and have occurred; but it is a profound misunderstanding of the temper of our times to assume that this is what makes nationalism or Marxism attractive to nations which have been ruled by foreign masters, or classes whose lives were directed by other classes in some feudal or otherwise hierarchical regime. What they desire is what Mill called 'Pagan self-assertion'. Indeed much of what he says, with excellent insight, about what it is that makes men desire liberty – the craving for non-conformity, for the assertion of their own values in the face of the prevailing opinion, for bold self-reliant personalities, for liberation from the leading-strings of the official [206] lawgivers and instructors of society – has little enough to do with his conception of freedom as mere non-interference, but a great deal with the desire of men not to have their personalities set at too low a value, assumed to be incapable of autonomous, original, 'authentic' (to use a fashionable modern existentialist term) behaviour, even if such behaviour is to be met with social restrictions or inhibitive legislation.

This kind of liberty is the answer to the question, not 'What is to be the area of authority?' but 'Who is to govern me?' – govern well or badly, liberally or oppressively, but the question being 'Who?' And such answers as 'My representatives elected by my untrammelled choice', or 'All of us gathered together in regular assemblies', or 'The best', or 'The wisest', or 'The nation as embodied in this or that person or institution', or 'The divine leader', or whatever it may be, are answers logically – and often politically and socially – independent of what extent of 'negative' liberty I demand for my own personal activities. Provided the answer to 'Who shall govern me?' is somebody or something which I can represent as 'my own', as something which belongs to me or to which I belong, I can in the other sense of the word 'freedom' claim this to be some kind of free life. [B] And indeed more than this: I can sacrifice to it my 'negative' Millian freedom, and claim to be 'liberated' in the other, confused but ardently felt, sense by the process. [A] 'Whose service is perfect freedom' can be secularised, and the State or the nation or the race, or an assembly or a dictator, or the family or I myself substituted for the Deity without thereby rendering the word 'freedom' meaningless.[1]

[1] [D] This argument should be distinguished from the traditional approach of some of the disciples of Burke or Hegel, who say that I am made what I am by society or history, and that to escape from them is impossible, and to attempt

[207] [A1] No doubt every interpretation of the word 'liberty', however unusual, must include the minimum of what I have called 'negative' liberty, that is, an area within which my wishes are not frustrated; for a being who is literally prevented by others from doing anything that he wishes to do is not a moral agent at all, and could not either legally or morally be regarded as a human being in the full sense, even if in a physiological or biological or even psychological sense he is to be included within the human species. But Mill and Constant want more than the minimum: they demand the maximum degree of non-interference compatible with the minimum demands of social life.

It is not clear that this demand for liberty has ever been made by any but a small minority of highly civilised and self-conscious human beings. The bulk of humanity has certainly at most times been prepared to sacrifice this to other goals: security, prosperity, power, virtue, rewards in the next world or indeed justice, equality and many other values which appear wholly or in part incompatible with the attainment of the greatest degree of individual liberty and certainly do not need it as a precondition of their own realisation. [A3] It is not the demand for individual *Lebensraum* which has stimulated the rebellions and wars of liberation for which men were ready to die in the past, or for that matter in the present. Men who have fought for freedom or fought wars of liberation have commonly fought for the right

---

it irrational. No doubt I cannot leap out of my skin, or breathe outside my proper element; it is a mere tautology to say that I am what I am, and cannot want to be liberated from my essential characteristics, some of which are social. But it does not follow from this that all my attributes are intrinsic and inalienable, and that I cannot seek to alter my status within the 'social network' or 'cosmic web' which determine[s] my nature; if this were the case no meaning could be attached to such words as 'choice' or 'decision' or 'activity'. If they are to mean anything, attempts to protect myself against authority or escape from 'my station and its duties' cannot be excluded as somehow irrational or suicidal. ['My Station and Its Duties' is the title of an essay by F. H. Bradley in his *Ethical Studies* (London, 1876), 145–92.]

to be governed by themselves or their representatives – harshly governed if need be, tyrannously and without much individual liberty, but in a manner which allowed them to participate, or at any rate to think they participated, in the legislation and administration of their collective lives. [B] And men who have made revolutions have as often as not meant by liberty no more than the establishment of the rights of a given group of believers in a doctrine, thereby frustrating their opponents; sometimes a [208] claim to the universality of their ideals as those which the 'real selves' of those who resist them also seek, although, unaware of their origin in their own deeper natures, they may be unaware of it. It has little to do with Mill's liberty as the opportunity to do what I wish provided it does not affect others.

[A] It is the non-recognition of this fact which perhaps blinds some contemporary liberals to the world in which they live. [B] Their plea is clear, their case is just: but they do not allow for the variety of human wishes [H], for the different, quite incompatible, kinds of life for which men are ready to fight and, if need be, die. Nor do such good and rational men allow for the terrible ingenuity with which men can prove to their own satisfaction that the road to one ideal also leads somehow to its contrary. Men want too much: they want what is logically impossible. That is why such sacred symbols as 'liberty' and 'democracy' and self-governmental 'rights' cover such a multitude of ideals which conflict with one another. It is as well to realise this. Things are what they are: status is one thing, liberty another; recognition is not the same as non-interference. In the end we all pay too dearly for our wish to avert our gaze from such truths, for ignoring such distinctions in our attempts to coin words to cover *all* that we long for, in short for our desire to be deceived.

[VII Liberty and Sovereignty]

[A] The French Revolution was just such an eruption of the desire for self-government, even if it restricted individual liberty. Rousseau had spoken of the fact that the laws of liberty might prove to be more austere than the yoke of tyranny, for his liberty does not in the first place refer to the freedom of the individual to do as he pleases within a delimited area, but to what Constant had called the liberty of the Ancients, where liberty means the sharing of public power by everyone in the society, but where this public power can interfere with every aspect of every citizen's life. The liberals of the first half of the nineteenth century must be given the credit for foreseeing that liberty in this sense could easily destroy all liberty in the sense in which they desired it, the space within which a man might live his life as he pleased, without control, interference, social pressure.

They pointed out quite correctly that the sovereignty of the people can destroy that of individuals. [B] Laws might be necessary to secure happiness or equality or power or sheer survival; but their function was to restrict freedom: thus was not identical with freedom; but its precise opposite.

[A] Mill had explained patiently and unanswerably that those who govern are not necessarily the same 'people' as those who are governed – that self-government is not the government 'of each by himself' but 'of each by all the [209] rest'. For him coercion was an evil in itself (unlike the seekers after 'positive' liberty, who would admit coercion within the community if it improved its status vis-à-vis other communities, or if it was an inevitable means to the rational State, as Communists and other believers in 'democratic centralism' maintain). He spoke of the 'tyranny of the majority' and the tyranny of 'the prevailing opinion and feeling', and saw no difference between that and any other kind of tyranny which interferes with men's lives beyond the unalterable limits of private life.

[A4] Constant makes this contrast exceedingly clear. In his celebrated essay on the conception of liberty by the 'Ancients' and the 'Moderns' he declares that for modern man liberty means the right not to be arrested, detained, killed, maltreated by the arbitrary will of one or several individuals; the right to express one's opinion, choose one's profession and exercise it; to dispose of one's property, even to abuse it as one pleases; to go and come without having to account for one's motives or moods, or having to ask permission beforehand; the right to unite with others in the pursuit of one's interests, to profess whatever faith one wishes with one's associates, to fill one's days and hours in accordance with one's own inclinations, one's own fancies; finally the right to influence administration by nominating officials, by presenting petitions and demands of which the authorities are obliged more or less to take notice. Liberty in this sense is the security of the enjoyment of the function of private life, and liberty in this sense is something which is guaranteed by institutions which exist for this purpose. This is what modern men mean by liberty and it is not primarily political in content.

For the ancient world, on the other hand, liberty meant the exercise, collectively but directly, of a large portion of sovereignty. It meant the right to deliberate publicly, to decide upon war and peace, treaties with foreign powers, to vote laws, sit in judgement, scrutinise the accounts and acts of public officials, the right to force them to present themselves before the sovereign assembly, to accuse them, condemn them, acquit them. But each man in this system is totally subject to authority. All private acts are in principle to be open to the surveillance of public officials. Nothing is to be left to the independent judgement of individuals, above all the choice of religion – to invent or practise a private religion would have appeared blasphemous. Terpander could not add a string to his lyre without offending the State. A young Spartiate could not visit his wife freely. In Rome, censors could enquire into the most intimate details of private life. Morals were controlled by the law, and since everything is affected by morals, everything was subject to law. The individual, sovereign in public affairs, was a slave in his private life; the all-powerful judge, inquisitor, legislator who condemned men to death and sent them into exile was wholly repressed in private. Liberty meant the sharing of public power.

The danger to the modern conception of liberty is that, while absorbed in private life, we let our political rights – without which our private liberties may slip away – go too cheaply and be captured by adventurers. The danger to the liberty of the Ancients is that in pursuit of political control they allowed their private freedom to go almost completely. The two types of freedom are plainly not compatible with each other, and if I barter my private freedom for the right to take part in collective decisions which may interfere vastly with my private desires, am I more or less free? The ambiguity of the word 'freedom' – or one of its many ambiguities – could hardly be brought out more vividly.

[A] Constant rightly pointed out that mere shifting of unlimited authority (sovereignty) from one set of hands to another does not increase liberty but merely alters the burden of slavery. What care I whether I am crushed by popular government or a monarch? Or even a set of laws? He quite correctly perceived that the problem for those who desire individual freedom is not who wields the authority – for anyone who wields it may become oppressive – but how much authority is to be placed in any set of hands, for unlimited authority in anybody's grasp will crush somebody. Usually men protest against this or that set of governors as unjust, but it is not that that is the cause of oppression, it is the mere mass of power centralised anywhere: it is the very notion of absolute sovereignty itself. 'It is not against the arm that one must rail,' Constant observes, 'but against the weapon. Some weights are too heavy for the human hand.' Democracy may disarm a given oligarchic class, a given privileged individual or set of individuals, but it can still crush individuals as much as any previous ruler. Equality of oppression[1] is not equivalent to liberty. Nor does universal consent to interference cease to make it interference; if I consent to be oppressed, am I the less oppressed? If I sell myself into slavery, am I the less a slave? If I commit suicide, am I the less dead because I have taken my life freely myself?

'Popular government is a spasmodic tyranny, monarchy a more centralised despotism.' Rousseau's thesis, that by giving myself to all [210] I give myself to no one, is founded on the assumption that the sovereign is literally everybody. Even so, this 'everybody' may oppress one of its members; I may prefer to be deprived of my liberties by an assembly in which I am a perpetual minority; it may give me an opportunity, one day, of persuading others to do for me that to which I feel I am entitled; but to be deprived of my liberty at the hands of everyone save myself deprives me of it just as effectively. But of course in practice it is not 'everybody' who rules, but its agent, i.e. a power which can rob you of all you have left. Rousseau knew this, hence the protests against delegation and representation. What he wanted was a continuous plebiscite. Hobbes was at any rate more honest. He does not pretend that a sovereign does not enslave. He justifies this slavery but does not call it freedom.

Throughout the nineteenth century liberal thinkers correctly maintained the doctrine that if by liberty was meant a limit upon the powers of anyone else to force me to do what I did not wish to do, whether in the name of reason or State, my own good or the good of unborn generations, or in the name of God or man, history or class, or the rights of a man of genius to mould inferior beings to his pattern (for thus they too shall

[1] [Added for J in place of the previous three words but not included there: 'In an essay comparing the liberty of the Moderns with that of the Ancients he said that an equal right'.]

share in his free creative activity and be raised to a higher level), absolute sovereignty must be declared to be a tyrannical doctrine in itself. If I wish to preserve my liberty, it is certainly not enough to say that it must not be violated unless someone or other – a sovereign, or the popular assembly, or the king in parliament, or the judges, or all these persons together, or even the laws (for they may themselves be oppressive) – authorise this. I must establish a society in which there must be some interferences which nobody should ever be able to authorise. I may call such frontiers natural rights; I may found them upon what philosophy I please, I may call them the word of God or the demands of the 'deepest interests of man'; I may believe in their validity a priori, or simply declare them to be subjective ends, but sufficiently widely believed and grounded in empirical human nature as it has developed through history to be part of the definition of what a human being is, so that those who do not recognise it are rightly regarded by me as having so different a view of what men are as to be justly called abnormal, morally deficient, deranged; but however I view it, unless some such stand is taken, individual liberty will not remain inviolable, self-government will not be sufficient. In theory, no doubt, in a democracy the majority of its citizens govern themselves, but historically no government has found much diffi[211]culty in forcing its subjects to generate the will that the government wants. The triumph of despotism is to force the slaves to declare themselves free.[1]

How is this to be prevented? Many devices have been suggested, but the principal safeguard of a democracy resides in retaining political rights with which to protect individual rights,

[1] [This sentence was placed in quotation marks by Berlin, but I have not yet been able to find a published source for it. It might possibly derive from Goethe's 'Niemand ist mehr Sklave als der sich für frey hält ohne es zu sein' ('No one is more enslaved than he who believes that he is free without being so'). *Die Wahlverwandtschaften* (Tübingen, 1809) ii 202 (part 2, chapter 5, 'From Ottilie's Diary'). I am indebted to Jaap Engelsman for this hypothesis.]

in an exercise of these rights, and in the preservation of an enlightened public opinion. If it is believed widely enough and repeated often enough that no powers can be absolute – only a right can be that, in the sense that I have an absolute right to refuse to behave inhumanly – that 'natural' frontiers exist in the sense that there are some principles so widely accepted that they have entered into the definition of what it is to be a human being; rights and corresponding laws of which it would be absurd to say that they could be abrogated by some formal procedure of some absolute sovereign; if this is sufficiently often repeated, it is difficult for the worst governments to proceed publicly against it. That is the status, for instance, of the punishment of men not proved guilty even by some semblance of a trial, or indiscriminate destruction of lives and liberties by the arbitrary will of a despot. This causes horror even in this hardened day; and this horror of despotism is precisely this implicit recognition of the existence of barriers to interference. [B] The freedom of a society or a class or group, in this sense of freedom, is measured by the strength of these barriers, and the number and importance of the paths which they keep open before each of their members. [D] In Great Britain such legal power is of course vested in the absolute sovereign – the king in Parliament. [C] What makes a country free is not necessarily that the sovereign is restrained by formal rules, legal or moral or constitutional. It is clear, for instance, that England is free despite the existence in it, at least in theory, of a sovereign. The reason for this is that this omnipotent entity is restrained by custom or opinion. What matters is not the form of the restraint, but its effectiveness.[1] [A] If public opinion does not operate, the tyrants find it only too easy to pay homage to the power of the people, and speak for it even while muzzling it, and crush it in its own name.

[212] What liberals demand, therefore, is the limitation of

[1] [D] See also 193/1.

sovereignty as such; what believers in 'positive' liberty demand is the placing of it in their own and not in others' hands. These views are ultimately not reconcilable.[1] But it is a profound lack of social and moral understanding not to recognise the absolute claims for [sc. of] each of these types of liberty as being among 'the deepest interests of mankind'.

[VIII The One and the Many]

In the end, what is responsible for despotism and the crushing of individuals in the names of ideals – distant ends such as ultimate felicity or their own 'real' selves, of which they may not be aware, or the claims of such embodiments of themselves as the destiny to which they are called, their historical mission, or their 'self-transcendence' in a 'higher' level – nation, race, class, tradition, Church, humanity, progress, liberty itself, all the great altars upon which human sacrifices have been brought – is the belief that somewhere in the past or the future, in divine revelation or the mind of the individual thinker, in the pronouncements of history or science, or the simple heart of an uncorrupt good man, there is a final solution. It is an ancient belief founded upon the assumption that all positive values in which men have believed must in principle be compatible, and perhaps even entail one another. 'Nature binds truth, happiness and virtue together by an indissoluble chain', said Condorcet, perhaps the most enlightened representative of this view.[2]

[1] [B *in place of thr previous sentence*] These are not two different applications or interpretations of a single concept – but two profoundly different and irreconcilable attitudes to the ends of life.

[2] [D] Condorcet, from whose Esquisse these words are quoted, declares that the task of social science is to show 'by what bonds nature has united the progress of enlightenment with that of liberty, virtue and respect for the natural rights of man; how these ideals, which alone are truly good, yet so

[213] But is this true? We know that equality is not compatible with individual liberty, with unrestricted laissez-faire, as things are; that always to tell the truth will not necessarily conduce to universal happiness; that rigorous justice is not compatible with generosity or unrestricted liberty. But somewhere, we shall be told, somehow, a state of affairs must exist in which these virtues can coexist, otherwise the universe is not a cosmos, not a harmony: the conflict of values – tragedy – is an intrinsic part of it.

No situation is conceivable even in principle, let alone realisable in practice, in which men are wholly wise, good, just, free, happy. The very notion of a rational ideal, the total harmony of all values and all interests, is seen to involve incompatibilities. This is a mortal blow to the very nature of a reasonable universe.

There are two things to be said about this. The first is that [C] every rationalist metaphysician from Plato to the last disciples of Hegel or Marx has maintained or implied that to allow this is crude empiricism, surrender to the forces of darkness, abdication before brute facts, the recognition of things as they are without demanding a rational justification – a conclusion that reason must indignantly reject. And yet it seems no less clear that some positive values are not compatible, that no situation seems conceivable in which truth and happiness, or kindness and justice, or liberty and equality can be guaranteed a priori not to conflict. [D] The very notion of a total harmony of all actual values and all interests, like the notions of the unity of all positive attributes, or the reducibility of all values to one, involves incompatibilities.

[A] Unless we are armed with some a priori guarantee, as the

---

often separated from each other that they are even believed to be incompatible, should, on the contrary, become inseparable, as soon as enlightenment has reached a certain level simultaneously among a large number of nations'. He goes on to say that 'Men still preserve the errors of their childhood, of their country and of their age long after having recognised all the truths needed for destroying them.' Perhaps, ironically enough, the belief of this most learned, noble, intelligent man in the need and possibility of uniting all good things was just such an error.

philosophers of antiquity thought that they were, that a total harmony is possible, and that tragedy is mere error, misunderstanding of ends or the choosing of the wrong means towards them, which omniscience could eliminate, we are left with the ordinary resources of empirical observation and ordinary human knowledge, and this certainly gives us no warrant for supposing that all good things (or all bad things for that matter) are compatible. They exhibit the world as a field in which agonising choices must occasionally be made between ends [214] one of which must perforce be sacrificed. Indeed, it is because this is the situation that men place such immense and justified value upon liberty to choose; [B] for if we had assurance that in some perfect state, realisable by men on earth, the ends pursued by men would no longer be in conflict, the need for choice and for freedom of choice, in either of the two senses of the word, would in this state no longer arise; freedom, on this view, ceases to be an end in itself; any method of bringing the final state nearer would be justified by its purpose – no matter how much freedom it sacrificed in its advance. [A] [But] in whichever senses of the word 'liberty', there is certainly no a priori reason for supposing that painful choices are avoidable or that goals will not for ever be many and conflicting.

Secondly, whether it is true or false – and I have no doubt of the answer – it is the monistic view of life, whereby all problems are regarded as at any rate in principle being capable of reduction to some one central issue which can be settled one way or the other by some one final infallible method, that is responsible for the deep, serene, assured conviction in the minds of some of the world's most savage and effective despots and persecutors that what they did was fully justified by its purpose.[1]

[1] [E] Bentham once again seems to me to have stated the truth in this matter: 'Individual interests are the only real interests. [...] Can it be conceived that there are men so absurd as to [...] prefer the man who is not, to him who is; to torment the living, under pretence of promoting the happiness of those who

I do not say that the positive ideal of human freedom which consciously animated some of these men, and the movements which they have led, is false, or the result [of] a deliberately fraudulent use of language or confusion of thought, still less of the deliberate or accidental misuse of words. Indeed, I have tried to show that this positive notion of freedom is at the heart of those demands for recognition which animate the great social and political movements of our time; and that not to understand this is to blind oneself to the most vital facts and ideas of our age. But equally it seems to me that the recognition that whatever might be the case in an ideal universe, to believe and act as if there was some single method of reconciling the different ends of different human beings or groups of men – or indeed the ends of the same human beings in differing circumstances and at various times – is to believe something that is conspicuously false, and to be led by this fallacy into action that is often gratuitously brutal and iniquitous. If, as I believe, the ends of men are many and not all of them compatible with each other, the possibility of conflict can never be eliminated from human life, either personal or public. The power of choosing between incompatible, equally absolute alternatives is one of the characteristics that make human beings human. The value of the act of choosing lies in itself, not as a means to something else.

[A][1] The extent of my liberty to choose as I desire must be weighed against the claims of other values – equality or justice, or happiness, or whatever other ends men or societies may have set their hearts upon. Moreover it will be curtailed by the claims of other persons to an equal measure of liberty, which must be

---

are not born, and who may never be born?' [G] This is one of the infrequent occasions when Burke agrees with Bentham; for this passage is at the heart of the empirical, as against the metaphysical, view of politics.

[1] [This is the point (cf. 172–3) at which B starts to be so exceptionally heavily corrected and amplified that it is worth giving its version in full separately: see 242–5.]

respected not because of some logical principle whereby liberty for one man necessarily entails belief in the liberty of others, but as a claim for justice, or equality of similar claims, a moral end in itself. The need to calculate and weigh and compromise, and adjust and test and experiment, and make mistakes and never reach certain answers or guarantees for rational action, must irritate those who seek for clear and final solutions, and yearn for unity and symmetry, and all-embracing answers. Nevertheless it seems to me the inescapable task of those who, with [216] Kant, believe that 'Out of the crooked timber of humanity no straight thing was ever made' [B], and are doomed to piecemeal operations.[1]

[G] There is little need to stress the fact that monism, and faith in a single criterion, has always proved a deep source of satisfaction both to the intellect and to the emotions. Whether the standard of judgement derives from the vision of some future perfection, as was done by the *philosophes* in the eighteenth century and their technocratic successors in our own day, or is rooted in the past – *la terre et les morts*[2] – as was done by German historicists or French theocrats, or neo-conservatives in English-speaking countries, it is bound, provided it is inflexible enough, to encounter some unforeseen and unforeseeable human development, which it will not fit; and will then be used to justify the a priori barbarities of Procrustes – the vivisection of actual human societies into some fixed pattern dictated by our fallible understanding of a largely imaginary past or a wholly imaginary future.[3]

[1] [D] For the best defence of this point of view see the works of B[enjamin] Constant passim, and Dr Karl Popper's well-known treatise [*The Open Society and Its Enemies*].

[2] 'The land and the dead.' For the use of this phrase by Maurice Barrès see *The Roots of Romanticism* (277), 2nd ed., 187.

[3] [G continues] To preserve our absolute categories or ideals at the expense of human lives offends equally against the principles of science and of history; it is an attitude found in equal measure on the right and left wings in our days,

[A] The liberty that they [sc. those who agree with Kant about 'the crooked timber of humanity'] seek to realise, and the world as they conceive it, seems to me, in comparison with that of the absolutists, more rational, more humane and more nearly realisable, because they alone are [sc. it alone is] compatible [217] with what most human beings have found the facts to be. [B] But in the end one chooses as one chooses, because one's life and thought are determined by fundamental moral categories and concepts that are, [J] at any rate over large stretches of time and space, [B] as much part of one's being and one's world as one's most essential natural characteristics; and one would lose one's identity if they were altered.

It may be that the need for personal liberty is historically conditioned: at remote times or in more primitive societies men untouched by capitalist culture do not know it – and that our posterity will look upon it as a passing phase. This may be so, but [we are] who we are, made as we are: principles are no less sacred because their duration cannot be guaranteed – the very search for eternal guarantees is a return to childish illusions. I can only quote the words of one of the best and most enlightened social critics of our time: 'To realise the relative validity of one's convictions and yet stand for them unflinchingly is what distinguishes a civilised man from a barbarian.' I see no reason to wish to go further. [C] To ask for more is perhaps a deep metaphysical need, but to build tactical conclusions on it is a sign of a no less profound moral immaturity.

---

and is not reconcilable with the principles accepted by those who respect the facts.

Second Draft (conclusion)

B's revised text of the closing passage of the lecture follows.[1] *From 'But in the end one chooses' in the second paragraph, where manuscript takes over entirely from typescript (as the illustration shows), curly brackets – { } – indicate passages that have been crossed out wholesale, and ~~strikethrough~~ records more local deletions. Illegible words are shown as '??', and '[?]' indicates a doubtful reading. I have preserved deleted matter in the later part of this section of B, exceptionally, because it shows Berlin struggling to find the best expression of his concluding thoughts, which were evidently both very important to him, and hard to capture in words. These thoughts may be important to his readers too, and showing the route he took on his way to formulating them may help to clarify nuances of meaning. (I note in passing that this kind of evidence is mostly lost in the era of electronic editing.) The online transcript of B and the closing paragraph on the previous page omit what Berlin deleted.*

[215] The extent of a man's or a people's liberty to choose as they desire must be weighed against the claims of many other values – equality or justice, or happiness, or security or public order, or whatever other ends men or societies may have set their hearts upon. Moreover it will be curtailed much or little, according to the circumstances, by the rights of other persons or groups to an equal, or at any rate not too unequal, measure of liberty. 'Freedom for the pike is death for the minnows.'[2] We are rightly reminded by Prof. Tawney that the liberty of the strong is oppression for the weak, whether their strength is physical or economic, and must be retrained. This maxim must be respected

[1] [See 239/1.]

[2] [F] And it must not be forgotten that freedom for the minnows – enough freedom for enough minnows – may even mean the death of the vigorous and imaginative pike, which Mill would rightly deplore.

not because of some Kantian maxim whereby the respect [for] liberty for one logically entails respect for the liberty of others, but, like him, because respect for the principles of justice or equality is as basic in men as we know them as the desire for liberty. [G] That we cannot have everything is a necessary, not a contingent, truth. [B] Burke's plea for the need to calculate and weigh, compromise, balance and adjust conflicting claims, Mill's plea for experiments in living, with its trials and errors, in the knowledge that we will never reach wholly clear or wholly certain answers or a priori guarantees of rationality or truth, [G] even in an ideal world of wholly good and rational men and wholly clear ideas, [B] must madden all those who seek for clear and final solutions, and yearn for unity and symmetry and single, all-embracing systems guaranteed to be eternal. Nevertheless, that is the inescapable lot of those who, with [216] Kant, have learnt the lesson that 'Out of the crooked timber of humanity no straight thing was ever made' and are doomed to piecemeal operations.

The 'negative' liberty that they seek to realise seems to me [a] [E] truer and [B] more humane ideal than that of those who seek for the great disciplined authoritarian structures that incarnate 'positive' self-mastery by classes or peoples or mankind. [E] Truer, because it recognises the fact that when we choose our course of action, or form of life, we may be forced to sacrifice to it another, which is no less ultimate, and perhaps incommensurable with the former.[1] To assume that all values can be graded on one scale, so that it is a mere matter of inspection to determine the highest, is to turn moral decision into an operation which a slide-rule could, in principle, perform. To say that in some ultimate, all-reconciling but realisable synthesis duty *is* interest, or individual freedom *is* pure democracy, is to throw a metaphysical blanket over self-deceit or deliberate hypocrisy. More humane

[1] [After 'that fact that' this sentence in G reads 'human goals are many, not all of them commensurable, and in perpetual rivalry with one another'.]

32.

incompatible, equally absolute authorities, is one of the characteristics that make human beings human. The value of the act of choosing lies in itself, not as a means to something else. The extent of my liberty to choose as I desire must be weighed against the claims of other values - equality or justice, or happiness, or whatever other ends men or societies may have set their hearts upon. Moreover, it will be curtailed by the claims of other persons to an equal measure of liberty, which must be respected not because of some logical principle whereby liberty for one man necessarily entails belief in the liberty of others, but as a claim for justice or equality of similar claims, a moral end in itself. The need to calculate and weigh and compromise and adjust, and test and experiment and make mistakes, and never reach certain answers or guarantees for rational action, must irritate those who seek for clear and final solutions, and yearn for unity and symmetry and all-embracing answers. Nevertheless, it seems to me the inescapable task of those who, as Kant, believe that out of the crooked timber of humanity no straight thing was ever made. The liberty that they seek to realise, and the mixture world as they conceive it seems to me, in comparison with that of the absolutists, more rational, more humane and more nearly realisable, because they alone are compatible with what most human beings have meant by liberty and humanity, and with what most human beings have found the facts to be.

The last page of B[1]

[1] Oxford, Bodleian Library, MS. Berlin 449, fol. 95: scan © Bodleian Library 2014.

[B] because [it] destroy[s] far less of what most men, sometimes by bitter experience, discover to be indispensable [217] to them as human beings. But in the end one chooses as one chooses, because ~~this is what one believes~~ one's life and thought are determined by ~~a scale of values of which some elements are too~~ fundamental moral categories and concepts that are ~~too~~ as much part of one's being ~~??~~ and ~~and of that of one's society~~ one's world, and[?] to be as one's ~~essential physical or mental~~ most essential natural characteristics; and one ~~cannot~~ would lose one's identity if they were altered.

It may be that the need for personal liberty is historically conditioned: ~~that the[?] ancient Greeks or~~ at remote times or in more primitive societies men untouched by capitalis~~m~~t culture do not ~~feel~~ know it – and that the ~~future society of the~~ ~~our~~ our ~~descendants~~ posterity will look upon it as a passing phase. This may be so, but [we are] who we are, ~~we must~~ made as we are: principles are no less sacred because their duration cannot be guaranteed – the very search for eternal guarantees is a ~~child-ish~~ return to childish illusions. {No doubt ~~such [an] empirical outlook~~ so tentative and ~~relativistic~~ empirical a prospect will ~~not satisfy~~ disappoint those who ~~look for~~ search for absolute values that are guaranteed ~~to last~~ ~~for ever~~ ~~eternally~~ to last for ever. In reply to this I can only quote the words of one of the ~~most enlightened men of our time~~ ~~greatest authors~~ great ~~economists~~ best social thinkers of our time: who said} I can only quote the words of one of the best and most enlightened social critics of our time: 'To realise the relative validity of one's convictions and yet stand for them unflinchingly is what distinguishes a civilised man from a barbarian.' I see no reason to go further. {~~This is the~~ No better words in defence of liberal beliefs were ever uttered.} [C] To ask for more is perhaps a deep metaphysical need, but to build tactical conclusions on it is a sign of a no less profound moral immaturity.

Third Draft (last half)

C's revised text of the last half of the lecture follows.[1] *The opening sentences, very corrupt in the recording, have been repaired with extracts from D.*

[192] [D] This can perhaps be put in another way. Freedom is self-mastery – [C] the elimination of obstacles to my will. If nature resists me, I try to mould her by technical means, and impose [D] my will upon [her]. [C] But how am I to treat [D] recalcitrant human beings? I must, if I can, impose my will on them too, 'mould' them to my pattern, cast parts for them in my play. But [C] will this not mean that I am free while they are slaves? They will be so if my plan has nothing to do with their desires or values, [193] only my own. But if my plan is rational it will allow for the full development of their true natures, the realisation of their rational desires as part of the [D] realisation of their capacities for rational decisions as a part of the realisation of my own. All true solutions to all genuine problems must be compatible; more than this, they must fit into a single whole; for this is what is meant by calling them all rational and the universe harmonious. [C] Each man has his specific character and purposes. If I grasp what these are, how they relate to one another, then I can, at least in principle, satisfy them all, so long as the natures and the purposes are rational. Rationality is knowing things in people for what they are. I must not use stones to make violins, nor try to make born violin players play flutes. If the universe is governed by reason, that is, the discoverable pattern in which everything and everyone plays the part it is meant to play by its own inner nature, then there will be no need for coercion. A correctly planned life for all will coincide with full freedom – the freedom of rational self-direction – for all. So long

[1] See 212/1.

as each player plays the part set him by reason, there will be no conflict. Each man will be a liberated, self-directed actor in the cosmic drama.

When Spinoza says [that] children, though they are coerced, are not slaves, because they obey orders given in their own interests, or [that] the subject of a true commonwealth is no slave, because the common interest must include his own; when Locke says, 'Where there is no law there is no freedom', because rational laws are directions to a man's 'proper interests', and since such [law is] only what 'hedges us in only from bogs and precipices' [it] 'ill deserves the name of confinement', and then speaks of desires to escape from such laws as being forms of 'license', 'brutish' etc.; when Montesquieu, forgetting his liberal moments, speaks of political liberty as 'the power of doing what we ought to will' – what all these thinkers, and many a Jacobin and Communist after them, assume is that the rational ends of our true natures must coincide, or be made to coincide, however violently our poor unreflective desire-ridden passionate empirical selves may protest against this process. Freedom is not freedom to do what is irrational or bad; to force empirical selves into the right pattern is not tyranny but liberation. On this (I may remark in parentheses) Bentham seems to have said the last word: 'The liberty of doing evil, is it not liberty? If it is not liberty, what is it then? [...] Do we not say that liberty should be taken away from fools, and wicked persons, because they abuse it?'

[194] When Rousseau tells me that in giving myself to all, I give myself to none, and I get back as much as I lose, with enough new force to preserve my gains, because an entity built out of the equality of sacrifice of all its members cannot wish to hurt any one of them; when the great declarations of the rights of man and citizen [195] assume that the bounds of human rights can be established by any rational man, for any rational man can in principle discover the true solution to any problem; the assumptions they make are: (1) that solutions to social problems resemble

solutions to the problems of the natural sciences; (2) that reason is what the rationalists said that it is, namely the discerner of true answers to all genuine questions whether of theory or of practice.

If this were true the conclusion would follow. In the ideal case liberty coincides with law, for both are demands of the selfsame reason; autonomy coincides with authority; rational men are wholly free and wholly equal, as well as wise, happy and just. Only one social movement was bold enough to render this assumption quite explicit and accept its consequences, that of the anarchists. But all forms of liberalism founded on rationalist metaphysics are less or more watered-down versions of this creed.

And how are men to be made rational on these lines? They must be educated, by men endowed with reason. But being uneducated, how can they be expected to understand or co-operate with the purposes of their educators? 'Education', says Fichte, [D] must inevitably work in such a way that [C] 'you will later recognise the reasons for what I am doing now.' Children cannot be expected to understand why they are compelled to go to school; in their case, 'Compulsion is also a kind of education.' If you [196] cannot understand your true interests as a rational being, I cannot be expected to consult you or abide by your wishes in the course of making you rational. I force you to be protected against smallpox though you may not wish it. [D] Even Mill is prepared to say that I may forcibly prevent a man from crossing a bridge if there is not time to warn him that it is about to collapse, for whatever his behaviour may indicate, I know that he cannot wish to fall into the water. Fichte knows what I – the uneducated German of his time – wish to be or do better than I can possibly know them for myself. [C] The sage knows you better than you know yourself, for you are the victim of your passions, a slave living a heteronomous life, purblind, unable to understand your goals. You want to be a human being. It is the aim of the State to satisfy your wish. 'Compulsion is justified by education for future insight.'

How am I to educate you? Just as the reason within me, if it is to triumph, must suppress my lower instincts, so (the fatal transition from individual to social concepts is almost imperceptible, yet this is where the crucial argument comes) the higher elements in society, those who 'possess the highest insight of their time and people', must exercise compulsion to rationalise the irrational section of society; for, so Hegel, Bradley, Bosanquet have often assured us, by obeying the rational man we obey ourselves, not indeed as we are in our ignorance and our passions, wards who need a guardian, but as we could be if we listened to the reason within us.

And, pursuing the same line of reasoning, if I break away from the teleological schema of the Hegelians towards some more voluntarist philosophy, may I not conceive the idea of imposing on my society – always for its own betterment – a plan of my own which in my rational wisdom I have elaborated, which unless I act on my own, and perhaps against its wishes, [197] may never come to fruition at all? Or, abandoning the concept of reason altogether, I may conceive myself as an inspired artist who moulds men into patterns in the light of his unique vision, as painters combine colours or composers sounds. Humanity is the raw material on which I impose my creative will; even though men suffer and die in the process, they are lifted by it to a height to which they could never have risen without my coercive but creative violation of their lives.

This is the argument used by every dictator, inquisitor and bully who seeks some moral or even aesthetic justification for his conduct. I must do for men, or with them, what they cannot do for themselves, and I cannot ask their permission or consent because they are in no condition to know what is best for them, and what they will permit and consent to may mean their suicide. The hero may be a rationalist sage, or Napoleon, or a romantic authoritarian who believes in the possibility of creating a race of supermen, as some Fascist leaders claim to do.

Provided that we allow that there is a solution to the social problem, and that they may know it and we do not, then we may with Auguste Comte ask why, if we do not allow free thinking in chemistry or biology, we should allow it in morals or politics. Why indeed? If there is a chosen method which reveals the truth, there is no case for freedom of opinion or action, at least as an end in itself; no case for conduct unauthorised by the relevant experts. [198] The immature and untutored must be made to say to themselves, 'Only the truth liberates, and the only way in which I can learn the truth is by doing blindly today what you who know it order me, or if need be coerce me, to do, in the conviction that only thus will I arrive at your clear vision and be free like you.' For why should demonstrable error be tolerated?

We seem to have wandered far from our liberal beginnings. The authoritarian argument employed by Fichte and Hegel, and after them by other defenders of authority from Marx and the positivists to the latest nationalist or Communist dictator, is precisely what the Stoic and Kantian ethics protests against in the name of the inner reason of the free individual following his own light as best he can. In this way the rationalist argument, with its assumption of the single true solution, leads from an unpolitical doctrine of individual self-perfection to an authoritarian State obedient to the directives of a Platonic elite.

What can have led to so strange a reversal, the transformation of Kant's individualism into something close to a pure totalitarian doctrine? This question is not of mere historical interest, for many contemporary liberals have gone through the same peculiar evolution. It is true that Kant insisted, following Rousseau, that all men possessed a capacity for rational self-direction, that there could be no experts in moral matters, for it was not a matter of knowledge, as the Utilitarians maintained, but of the correct use of an inborn faculty; and that what made men free was not acting in certain self-improving ways – which they could be coerced to do – but knowing why they ought to do so, which nobody could do for or on behalf of anyone else. But even Kant, when he came to deal with political issues, said that no law, provided it was such that I should if I were asked approve it as a rational being, could possibly deprive me of my liberty.

With this the door is opened wide to the rule of experts. I can't consult all men about all enactments all the time. The government cannot be a continuous plebiscite. Moreover some men are not as well attuned to the voice [199] of their own reason as others: some are singularly deaf. If I am a legislator or a ruler, I must assume that, if the law I impose is rational, and I can only consult my own reason, it will automatically be approved by all the members of my society qua rational beings. If they disapprove they must pro tanto be irrational, and therefore need to be repressed by reason, whether their own or mine can't matter greatly, for the pronouncements of reason must be the same in all minds.

I issue my orders and, if you resist, take it on myself to repress the irrational element in you which opposes reason. My task would be easier if you repressed it in yourself. I try to educate you to do so. But I am responsible for public welfare, and I cannot wait until all men are wholly rational. Kant may protest that the essence of the subject's freedom is that he and he alone has given himself the order to obey, but this is a counsel of perfection. If you fail to discipline yourself, I must do so for you and you can't complain of lack of freedom, for the fact that you've had to be coerced is merely evidence that you haven't listened to your own inner reason, that you are like a child or a savage, not ripe for self-direction; and [200] if this leads to despotism of the best or the wisest, which is then identified with freedom, can it be that there is something gravely amiss in the premisses of the argument? Can it be that the basic assumptions are themselves somewhere at fault?

Let me recapitulate them. They are: that all men have one purpose and one only, that of rational self-direction; that the ends of all rational beings must necessarily fit into a single universal harmonious pattern, which the sage discerns more clearly than the ignoramus; that all conflict, and consequently all tragedy, is due solely to the clash of reason with the insufficiently rational, the immature and undeveloped elements in life, and that such clashes are in principle avoidable and for rational beings are quite impossible; so that, when all men have been made rational, they will obey the rational laws of their own rational nature, which is one and the same in them all. Can it be that not one of these basic assumptions is demonstrable or perhaps even true?

[VI The Search for Status]

[207] No doubt every interpretation of the word 'liberty' must include a minimum of what I have called negative liberty, that is, an area within which my wishes are not frustrated. No society literally suppresses all the liberties of all its members. A being who is prevented by others from doing anything at all that he wishes to do is not a moral agent at all and could not either legally or morally be regarded as a human being, even if a physiologist or even a psychologist felt inclined to classify him as a man. But Mill and Constant, the fathers of liberalism, want more than this minimum: they want a maximum degree of non-interference compatible with the minimum demands of social life.

It seems unlikely that this demand has ever been made by any but a small minority of highly civilised human beings. The bulk of humanity has certainly been prepared to sacrifice it to other goals: security, prosperity, power, virtue, rewards in the next world, and indeed justice and equality and fraternity, and many other values that do not appear to need negative liberty as a precondition for their own realisation. It is not a demand for *Lebensraum* for the individual which has stimulated the wars of liberation for which men were ready to die in the past, or indeed in the present. Men who have fought for freedom have commonly fought for the right to be governed by themselves or their representatives, sternly if need be, like the Spartans, with little individual liberty, but in the manner that let them participate, or at least think that they were participating, in the administration of their collective lives – even revolutionaries who have destroyed governments, and done so as a rule in order to establish the rights of a given group of believers in some doctrine, or of a class, or of some other body of men which certainly frustrated those whom they ousted, and sometimes displaced or suppressed vast numbers of human beings. And although such revolutionaries have sometimes argued that the liberty for which they stood [208] was liberty for all, or at least for the 'real selves' of all those who truly understood that liberty was a triumph of their class or order, [this] has little to do with Mill's notion of liberty as limited only by the danger of doing harm to others.

It is the non-recognition of this political fact that has perhaps blinded some contemporary liberals to the world in which they live: their plea is clear, their case is just, but they do not allow for the variety of human wishes, nor yet for the ingenuity with which men can prove to their own satisfaction that the fulfilment of one wish is also the fulfilment of its contrary.

[VII Liberty and Sovereignty]

The French Revolution, at least in its Jacobin form, was just such an eruption of the desire for [the] positive freedom of collective self-direction on the part of a large body of Frenchmen who felt liberated as a nation, even though the result was a severe restriction of individual freedoms. The liberals of the first half of the nineteenth century correctly foresaw that liberty in this positive sense could, especially in its socialised form, easily destroy all liberty in the negative sense, which they held sacred – the protection of the individual from controlled interference and social pressure, to live his life as far as possible as he pleased – and pointed out again and again that sovereignty of the people could easily destroy that of individuals. Mill explained patiently and unanswerably that democratic self-government wasn't in his sense necessarily freedom at all. For those who govern aren't necessarily the same people as those who are governed, and self-government isn't government of each by himself, but at best of each by the [209] rest. He spoke of the tyranny of the majority and of the tyranny of the prevailing feeling and opinion, and saw not much difference between that and any other kind of tyranny which encroaches on men's activities beyond the sacred frontiers of private life.

But no one saw the conflict between the two types of liberty better than Benjamin Constant. He pointed out that transference of unlimited authority, usually called sovereignty, from one set of hands to another doesn't increase liberty but merely shifts the burden of slavery. He asked why a man should care whether he is crushed by a popular government or a monarch, or even by a set of laws. He saw that the problem for those who want negative, that is to say individual, freedom is not who uses this authority but how much authority should be placed in any set of hands. He maintained that usually men protest against this or that set of governors as being oppressive, but that the real cause of oppression lies in the mere fact of the accumulation of power itself, wherever it may happen to be centralised; that liberty is endangered by the mere existence of absolute authority as such. 'It is not against the arm that one must rail, but against the weapon. Some weights are too heavy for the human hand.' Democracy may disarm a given oligarchic class, a given privileged individual, but it can still crush individuals as much as any previous ruler. Equality of the right to oppress is not equivalent to liberty, nor does universal consent to loss of liberty somehow miraculously preserve it merely by being universal or being consent. If I consent to be oppressed, am I the less oppressed? If I sell myself into slavery am I the less a slave? If I commit suicide am I the less dead because I have taken my own life freely?

[210] I may of course prefer to be deprived of my liberties by an assembly in which I am a perpetual minority. It may give me an opportunity one day of persuading others to do for me that to which I feel I am entitled; but to be deprived of my liberty at the hands of a majority deprives me of it just as effectively. Hobbes was at any rate more honest: he didn't pretend that a sovereign doesn't enslave, he justifies slavery, but at least he didn't call it freedom.

Throughout the nineteenth century liberal thinkers repeated over and over again that, if by 'liberty' was meant a limit on the powers of any man to force me to do what I didn't want to do or to refrain from doing what I did wish to do, then whatever the name in which I was being coerced – reason or the State, my own good, the good of unborn generations, God or man, progress or nation, history or class, the rights of a great leader to mould inferior beings to his own pattern and raise him to a higher level of consciousness – whatever the ideal, I was not free, and the doctrine of absolute sovereignty must be declared to be a tyrannical doctrine in itself. If I wish to preserve my liberty it is certainly not enough to say that it must not be violated unless someone or other – the sovereign, or the popular assembly, or the King in parliament, or the judges, or all these persons together, or even the laws themselves (for the laws may be very oppressive) – authorises this. I must establish a society in which there must be some interferences which nobody should ever be permitted to authorise.

I may call such frontiers natural rights, or the word of God, or natural law, or the demands of utility, or the deepest interests of man. I may believe in their validity a priori, or assert them as my own subjective ends, or the ends of my society or civilisation. What would be common to all these cases is that the rules in question are accepted so widely and grounded so deeply in the actual nature of men as to be by now an essential part of what we mean by being human; with the corollary that those who don't in practice take at any rate some of these rules for granted – can break them without a qualm – are so different from me in their view of what men and human relationships are that I look on them as being abnormal, morally deficient, beyond the range of normal human communication. Certainly democracy entails no protection for human rights in that sense, for it is notorious that few governments have found much diffi[211]culty in causing their subjects to generate the will that the government wanted: 'The triumph of despotism is to force the slaves to declare themselves free.'[1] Perhaps the chief value for liberals of political – positive – rights, namely participation in the government, is as a means for protecting what they hold to be ultimate, negative, individual liberty.[2]

[D][3] But if democracies can, without ceasing to be democratic, suppress freedom, at least as liberals have used the word, what would [C] make a society 'negatively' free? For Mill, Constant, Tocqueville and the tradition to which they belong, no society is free unless it is governed by at least two interconnected

[1] See 234/1.

[2] [F] [214] I do not wish to say that individual freedom is, even in the most liberal societies, the sole, or even the dominant, criterion of social action. We compel children to be educated, and we forbid public executions. These are certainly curbs to freedom. We justify them on the ground that ignorance, or a barbarian upbringing, or cruel pleasures and excitements are worse for us than the amount of restraint needed to repress them; and this in turn depends [215] on how we determine good and evil, that is to say, on moral, religious, intellectual, economic and aesthetic values; which are bound [up] in their turn [with] what our conception of man and the basic demands of his nature are. In other words, our solution of such problems is based on the ideal vision, by which we are consciously or unconsciously guided, of what constitutes a fulfilled human life, as against Mill's 'cramped and dwarfed', 'pinched and hidebound' natures. To protest against the laws governing censorship or personal morals in a society as grave infringements of individual freedom presupposes a belief that the activities which such laws forbid are basic needs of men in a good (or any) society; to defend such laws is to hold that these needs are not basic but acquired, or perhaps do not exist at all, or that to satisfy them is to sacrifice other values which come higher in a scale for which some objective status is claimed.

[3] [This and the next insertion replace corrupt sections of the recording.]

principles: first, that no power, but only rights, is absolute, so that all men, whatever power governs them, [D] have an absolute right to refuse to behave inhumanely; and second, that there are frontiers, not artificially drawn, within which men must be inviolable, these frontiers being defined in terms of rules so long and widely accepted that their observance has entered into the very conception of what it is to be a normal human being (and therefore, also, of what it is to act barbarously or inhumanely); rules of which it would be absurd to say, for example, that they could be abrogated by some formal procedure on the part of some court or sovereign body.

It is such rules as these that are broken when a man is punished without being proved guilty; when [C] men are tortured or murdered indiscriminately by the arbitrary will of a despot; when children are compelled to denounce their parents or men to betray one another, or minorities are massacred merely for being minorities. Such acts, even if they are legalised by the sovereign – Robespierre or Lenin or Hitler [or] many a later government – cause horror [D] even in these days, [C] and this springs from the recognition of the moral validity, irrespective of the laws, of some absolute barriers to the imposition of one man's will on another. The freedom of a society or a class or group, in this sense of freedom, is measured by the strength of these barriers, and the number and importance of the paths which they keep open for their members, if not for all, anyhow for a large number of them. [D] In Great Britain such legal power is of course vested in the absolute sovereign – the King in Parliament. [C] What makes a country free is not necessarily that the sovereign is restrained by formal rules, legal or moral or constitutional. It is clear, for instance, that England is free despite the existence in it, at least in theory, of a sovereign. The reason for this is that this omnipotent entity is restrained by custom or opinion. What matters is not the form of the restraint, but its effectiveness.

[212] This is almost at the opposite pole from the purposes of

those who believe in liberty in the positive, self-directive sense. The former want to curb authority as such. The latter want it placed in their own hands. That is the central issue. These are not two different interpretations of a single concept, but two profoundly divergent and irreconcilable attitudes to the ends of life. It is as well to recognise this, even if it is in practice necessary to strike a compromise between them. For each of them makes absolute claims. These claims cannot both be fully satisfied by the same persons in the same place at the same time. But it is a profound lack of social and moral understanding not to recognise that each is an ultimate value which, both historically and morally, has an equal right to be classed among the deepest interests of mankind.

[VIII The One and the Many]

In the end, what is responsible for the crushing of human beings in the name of great ideals such as happiness or justice or progress, or the manifest destiny of a nation or race or class, or the demands of their real selves, of which they may not be aware until awakened by a great leader or some unique national experience, [or] finally liberty itself, which demands the sacrifice of individuals for the freedom of society as a whole – what has sanctified all these great altars on which human sacrifices have been brought is the belief that somewhere, in the past or in the future, in divine revelation or in the mind of the individual thinker, in the pronouncements of history or science, or in the simple heart of the uncorrupted good man, there dwells a final solution. It is an ancient belief founded on the assumption that all positive values in which men have believed must in the end be compatible, or perhaps even entail one another.

[213] But is this true? It is a commonplace that political equality is not compatible with more than so much individual liberty, or that equality of liberty is not the same as maximum liberty.

We have known that to tell the truth in all circumstances doesn't necessarily conduce to universal happiness, that rigorous justice is compatible neither with generosity nor mercy nor unrestricted freedom. But we shall be told that surely somewhere in some way it must be possible for all these values to live together, for unless this is so, the universe is not a cosmos; unless this is so, tragedy must be an intrinsic element in human life. But to say that all conflicts cannot in principle be eliminated is to say that the fulfilment of some of our ideals may in principle make the fulfilment of other ideals impossible; that the notion of total fulfilment is a contradiction, a metaphysical chimera. Every rationalist metaphysician from Plato to the last disciples of Hegel or Marx has maintained or implied that to allow this is crude empiricism, surrender to the forces of darkness, abdication before brute facts, the recognition of things as they are without demanding a rational justification – a conclusion that reason must indignantly reject. And yet it seems no less clear that some positive values are not compatible, that no situation seems conceivable in which truth and happiness, or kindness and justice, or liberty and equality can be guaranteed a priori not to conflict.

For unless we are armed with some a priori guarantee, as some of the philosophers of antiquity thought that they were, of a total harmony of all true values, we are left with nothing but the ordinary resources of empirical observation; and this gives us no warrant for thinking that all good things, or all bad things for that matter, are reconcilable with each other; still less [that] they are all many aspects or modes of a single entity, material or spiritual, in which the appearances, the many, are seen as distortions of the underlying reality of the one. Our everyday means of observation exhibit the world as a field in which we are faced with choices between ends equally ultimate, [J] and claims equally absolute, [C] the [214] realisation of some of which must inevitably involve the sacrifice of others. Indeed, it is because this is their situation that men place such immense value upon the freedom to choose;

for if they had an assurance that in some perfect state realisable by men on earth no ends pursued by them would ever be in conflict, the crucial importance and agony of choice would disappear, and with it the central importance of liberty. If this were true, any method of bringing this final State nearer would then be justified by its purpose, no matter how much freedom were sacrificed in its advance.

It is, I have no doubt, some such a priori belief, whereby all problems are regarded as capable, at least in principle, of some one final universal solution, that has been responsible for the deep, serene, unshakeable conviction in the minds of some of the most merciless tyrants and persecutors in history that what they did was fully justified by its purpose. I do not say that the ideal of self-perfection which consciously animated some of these men and their followers is to be condemned as such, or that the language which they used was necessarily the result of a confused or fraudulent use of words, or of a lack of moral or intellectual insight; indeed, I have tried to show that it is the notion of freedom in its positive sense that is generally at the heart of those demands for national or social self-direction which animate the great public movements of our time; that not to recognise this is to remain blind to the most vital facts and ideas of our age. But equally it seems to me that the belief that some single formula can be found which will harmonise the diverse ends of men is false; and that the belief that follows, according to which whatever resists this process should be sacrificed easily as unreal and unworthy, leads to behaviour that is often gratuitously brutal and iniquitous. The need for choice between absolute claims is inevitable, and one of the characteristics that makes human beings human; it is this that gives its value to freedom as an end in itself, and not as a temporary need arising out of our disordered lives, a predicament which some panacea may presently put right.[1]

[C] [215] No doubt the extent of a man's or people's liberty

[1] [Note 256/1 occurs here in the main text of J.]

to choose must be weighed against the claims of other values. Moreover, as we are rightly reminded by Mr Tawney, freedom for the pike is death for the minnows; liberty for the strong, whether their strength is physical or economic, must be restrained. We respect this principle because the other principles, justice or equality, are as basic in men as a desire for liberty. The need to balance and compromise, the certainty that we shall never reach wholly clear, wholly certain answers, will madden those who seek for final solutions guaranteed to be eternal. Nevertheless [216] the 'negative' liberty [*recording corrupt*] accept the view that I have urged seem to me to strive for a more humane ideal than the goals of those who seek in the great disciplined authoritarian structures the idea of 'positive' self-mastery by classes or peoples or the whole of mankind. More humane because [it] destroy[s] less than the system-builders of what most men have found to be indispensable [217] to their life as human beings.

It may be that the idea of personal liberty, and of the pluralism of values connected with it, is historically conditioned by capitalist civilisation, which alone gives men possessions and a desire to preserve them; that it is an ideal which remote ages and primitive societies haven't known, and one on which posterity will look with interest but little comprehension. Principles are not less sacred because their duration cannot be guaranteed. It seems to me that no scepticism follows; indeed, the very desire for guarantees that our values are eternal and secure in some objective heaven is perhaps only a metaphysical form of the craving for the certainties of childhood. 'To realise the relative validity of one's convictions', said a distinguished thinker of our time, 'and yet stand for them unflinchingly is what distinguishes a civilised man from a barbarian.' That appears to me to be the best statement that has ever been made about the character of our ultimate convictions. To ask for more is perhaps a deep metaphysical need, but to build tactical conclusions on it is a sign of a no less profound moral immaturity.

Editorial Postscript on the Peroration

The famous peroration of the lecture constituted by its last two paragraphs has considerable rhetorical power, but it also contains a number of obscurities that have caused difficulty to commentators. Here I comment briefly on three of these in the light of the drafts.

1. *What does 'entails' entail?*

The penultimate paragraph of the published text begins 'Pluralism, with the measure of "negative" liberty that it entails [...]'. This remark has been fastened on by many participants in the voluminous debate about what logical relationship, if any, exists between value pluralism and liberalism, and therefore about the political implications of pluralism. Do pluralists have to be liberals in order to be rationally consistent? Or is there, rather, a looser connection of some kind (which would allow pluralists to favour a non-liberal political system without inconsistency)? (A third possibility, that pluralism actually rules out liberalism, is not one that Berlin accepted, though some critics have urged it against him.) Berlin's use of 'entails' in this context has been taken by some commentators to show that Berlin saw a full logical entailment between value pluralism and liberalism (or at any rate negative liberty); indeed, it lit the fuse of the debate.

One of the main difficulties is that elsewhere Berlin explicitly rejects the idea of such a link, most notably in Ramin Jahanbegloo's *Conversations with Isaiah Berlin*,[1] where he says 'I believe in both liberalism and pluralism, but they are not logically connected.' To make matters worse, he then immediately goes on to say something that appears to contradict this:

[1] London, 1992. The quotations are at 44.

> Pluralism entails that, since it is possible that no final answers can be given to moral and political questions, or indeed any questions about value, and more than that, that some answers that people give, and are entitled to give, are not compatible with each other, room must be made for a life in which some values may turn out to be incompatible, so that if destructive conflict is to be avoided compromises have to be effected, and a minimum degree of toleration, however reluctant, becomes indispensable.

Of course, what is said to be 'entailed' here is 'a minimum degree of toleration' rather than full-blown liberalism, but it would perhaps be pedantic to depend on this distinction when trying to reconcile Berlin's remarks.

In this context, the phrase 'connected with it' at the beginning of the last paragraph of C perhaps has some significance. This earlier wording suggests that 'entails' may be used here in its looser, informal sense of 'involves'. Berlin arguably uses it in this sense elsewhere, at 184 (twice), 196, 207 and 224(?); and when he uses it in the stricter sense, it is clear from the context that logical entailment is meant, as at 197/1, 236 (and 258), 240 ('necessarily entails'), 243 ('logically entails') and perhaps 256. He may also be using 'entails' informally in the passage quoted from *Conversations.*

In any event, given Berlin's mode of composition and the literary qualities of his text, one should not perhaps put too much weight on a specific formulation if it leaves room for more than one interpretation. Moreover, I assume that when he dictated the lecture he did not ask himself the exact question 'Does pluralism logically entail liberalism?' He certainly thought that it was natural for a pluralist to be a liberal (in some sense that requires clarification), but that is not quite the same thing. It is only in the light of the later discussion that his choice of words acquires importance. (It was George Crowder who started this discussion in 1994 with his article 'Pluralism and Liberalism',[1] and the reply

[1] *Political Studies* 42 (1994), 293–305.

to that article by Berlin and Bernard Williams does throw some light on Berlin's view, without making it entirely pellucid.)[1]

Even if we absolve Berlin of asserting a logical entailment between pluralism and liberalism, it remains, of course, to make clear exactly what connection he saw between them. But this is not the place to join this debate.

2. *'Principles are not less sacred because their duration cannot be guaranteed'*

This oracular and somewhat opaque remark has caused some trouble. If the duration of a principle cannot be guaranteed, why should it be regarded as sacred? Are liberal values applicable only to capitalist societies, while illiberal ones are in order for totalitarian societies? Is value pluralism true universally or only in a specific epoch? Even if we are convinced (as I am) that Berlin regarded value pluralism as an enduring truth about the human condition, a common denominator through all the vicissitudes of cultural history, the difficulty of explaining the sentence in question remains.

I take Berlin's refusal of a guarantee to be more of a theoretical concession than a historical hypothesis. He certainly believed in the historicity of some values, values that might be regarded as not belonging to the hard moral core that endures through time and is found in some form in every known culture. He often suggested that sincerity, integrity and variety, for instance, are values of comparatively recent origin.[2] But he also believed that some central values are appropriate to humanity at all times and in all places – contingently so, but so all the same. The world might

[1] ibid., 306–9.

[2] e.g. in *Against the Current*, 2nd ed. (Princeton, 2013), 420; *Conversations with Isaiah Berlin* (262), 42–3; *The Crooked Timber of Humanity* (xxx/2), 2nd. ed., 204; *The Power of Ideas* (xiv/1), 16; *The Roots of Romanticism* (277), 10; *The Sense of Reality* (London, 1996), 185.

have been different, and might not have contained human beings as we know them, but it is in fact what it is, and has always been so, and human beings have always possessed the same underlying nature since they emerged.[1] If I am right, this is another way of saying what Joseph Schumpeter says in the celebrated remark that Berlin goes on to quote, and to which I now turn.

The occurrence in this quotation of the word 'relativity' is unfortunate, as it can seem to leave Berlin open to the charge of moral relativism. Why should one stand for one's convictions, let alone unflinchingly, if their validity is only relative? However, Berlin's replacement of 'relativistic' with 'empirical' in B, together with the tenor of the rest of the peroration in its various incarnations, seems to me to make his own view clear: namely, that our values are empirical, not a priori – not metaphysically guaranteed against change, for all that many of them may in fact apply through human history. This still leaves us able to stand unflinchingly for our commitments, or at least those among them that we regard as basic requirements of humane conduct: we do not, he believes, need the values we stand for to be part of the fabric of eternity; nor are they.[2] 'Genuine belief in the inviolability of a minimum extent of individual liberty entails [an] absolute stand' (L 210). If there is any relativity here, it is only relativity to (empirical) human nature. Internally to human nature, there is no relativity.

[1] There is a problem about defining this moment, and relating claims of a constant human nature to it, but I do not explore this here.

[2] He captures this point well in describing J. G. Hamann's rejection of all necessary truth: 'No bridge is needed between necessary and contingent truths because the laws of the world in which man lives are as contingent as the "facts" in it. All that exists could have been otherwise if God had so chosen, and can be so still. God's creative powers are unlimited, man's are limited; nothing is eternally fixed, at least nothing in the human world – outside it we know nothing, at any rate in this life. The "necessary" is relatively stable, the "contingent" is relatively changing, but this is a matter of degree, not kind.' *Three Critics of the Enlightenment* (171/1), 2nd ed., 363.

This is certainly a misleading flaw in the quotation when it is used in this context (in its original context it has to do with the claim that democracy is an optimal political system only in certain historical circumstances), but in other ways it evidently expressed with some eloquence the point Berlin sought to make. At any rate, this contextual infelicity should not lead us to impute to Berlin (moral) relativism as usually understood, and as it is often described by Berlin, for instance when he writes: 'Herder believes in the development of each movement of the symphony (each act of the drama) in terms of its own ends, its own values, which are none the worse or less morally valuable because they will pass or be destroyed and be succeeded by others.'[1]

Nevertheless, I think it is fair to say that Berlin fails to express himself as clearly as he might have done. He perhaps elides moral knowledge with moral fact. Historicity may be more a property of the former than of the latter. If we are moral realists, as Berlin seems to have been, we may take the view that the principles in question endure as part of reality although our knowledge of them may not: that would explain the failure of primitive societies to recognise some of our values, as well as the hypothetical incomprehension of posterity. Values may be both intrinsic to human nature, but also discovered only historically, as our understanding of our nature grows. Thus Berlin writes of values 'accepted so widely, and [...] grounded so deeply in the actual nature of men as they have developed through history, as to be, by now, an essential part of what we mean by being a normal human being' (L 210).

Incidentally, the latter formulation embodies another equivocation, between widespread acceptance and a grounding in human nature as the criterion of key values. The latter seems to me a more plausible candidate, and the former often catches up with it as the ages pass: slavery was once widely accepted, and

[1] ibid. 270.

indeed thought to be a condition natural to slaves. Taken at face value, Berlin's formulation appears to suggest that the satisfaction of both criteria is necessary; but again, this may be to put too much weight on his wording.

However this may be, my suggested explanation of what Berlin intends is only a conjecture on my part, an attempt to make sense of a puzzling passage. Whether I am right or not, it is part of the purpose of the present exercise to show that Berlin was feeling his way towards novel insights, about whose precise nature he may not himself have been entirely clear. Inspection of his successive wordings helps us to sense what it was that he may have been trying to say.

3. *It depends on what the meaning of the word 'it' is*

The last sentence of C contains an ambiguity, not eliminated in the published version, which runs: 'To demand more than this is perhaps a deep and incurable metaphysical need; but to allow it to determine one's practice is a symptom of an equally deep, and more dangerous, moral and political immaturity.' To what does 'it' refer? Since this is one of the most important sentences Berlin wrote, it is worth settling this. One critic[1] not unnaturally takes 'it' to refer to 'this'[2] earlier in the sentence, which in turn refers to Schumpeter's criterion of civilisation. On this interpretation, Berlin would be warning against the paralysis that can be induced by excessive awareness – and tolerance – of differing viewpoints:

[1] Nicholas Kristof, 'On Isaiah Berlin: Explorer', *New York Review of Books*, 25 February 2010, 26–7; quotation at 26. A version of the present section was published as a letter to the editor, responding to Kristof: 'Skeptical Isaiah Berlin', ibid., 8 April 2010, 89–90.

[2] It would also be possible to take 'it' to refer to 'more than this', but this would not fit Kristof's interpretation, and is in any case ruled out by the reading of D, given in the next paragraph. Moreover, it would amount to the same as what D says, since the need in question is precisely for 'more than' what Schumpeter says is available.

what in his essay on Turgenev he calls 'the liberal predicament', and recognised as a brake on strong opinion and action in his own case. As Kristof puts it, one must not let 'appreciation of nuance emasculate one's capacity to make strong moral judgements'. This would be essentially a restatement of Schumpeter's point, and as such a somewhat anticlimactic ending to Berlin's peroration, for all that he would have agreed with it.

Fortunately D makes clear what 'it' refers to: 'To demand unity and certainty is perhaps a deep, universal metaphysical need; but not to resist it, and above all to allow it to guide one's practice, is a symptom of a no less profound moral and political immaturity.' Here 'it' plainly refers to the 'deep, universal metaphysical need'.

Since this was unclear in the published text, I have changed 'it' to 'such a need' in later impressions of the piece. This reading gives a much stronger ending, since Berlin is now warning against being guided by what, immediately before his quotation from Schumpeter, he calls 'the certainties of childhood or the absolute values of our primitive past'. He is referring, that is, to the moral and political immaturity of monists, totalitarians, extremists, fanatics, fundamentalists – uncivilised barbarians who have not grown up, and who wreak havoc in the world. These are the worst villains of our age, for Berlin, not the relativists, even though the latter can give succour to the former.

REFERENCES

As in the case of *The Roots of Romanticism*, and for the same reasons,[1] I have collected references for quotations together here at the end of the text, identifying the passages to which they refer by page number and opening words.

The reader should be warned that Berlin's quotations from languages other than English are sometimes very free, and can merge into paraphrase. I have not on the whole tried to make them more accurate, since this would often make them less resonant, but I have occasionally given a more literal version in the note. In a few cases, where I happen to know it, I have given a reference for a close paraphrase even though I have withheld quotation marks in the text.

Once again I have recorded my failure to trace a few ostensible quotations. I shall as always be most grateful to any readers who can fill in the gaps, and in future impressions of this book I shall incorporate any information I receive.

The references often depend on the generosity of experts, to whom I am greatly indebted. I fear I may not have kept a record of every single scholar who has assisted me, and I offer my apologies to anyone I have overlooked. Gunnar Beck has helped enormously with Fichte (see the section on that lecture below), Michael Inwood with Hegel, Ralph Locke and Bruce Tolley with Saint-Simon, and Robert Wokler with Rousseau.

[1] See 2nd ed. of that volume (Princeton, 2013), 182.

The Maistre lecture draws again on the invaluable contribution made by Richard Lebrun to 'Joseph de Maistre and the Origins of Fascism', recorded in my preface to *The Crooked Timber of Humanity*. For assistance with individual problems I thank John Burrow, Andrew Fairbairn, Steffen Groß, Samuel Guttenplan, Ian Harris, Roger Hausheer, Leofranc Holford-Strevens, Andrew Hunwick, Reinhardt Lauth, Richard Lebrun, Ray Monk, T. J. Reed, Philip Schofield, Jonas Steffen and Ralph Walker.

References to multi-volume editions are by volume and page in this form: iv 476.

There are a few editorial remarks interspersed among the references.

Page *Reference*

Introduction

3 **Bertrand Russell once said**
History of Western Philosophy (London, 1946), 226. Berlin greatly enlivens Russell's presentation of this point.

Helvétius

12 **'As one meditates'**
Discours prononcé dans l'Académie Française, le jeudi 21 février 1782, à la réception de M. le Marquis de Condorcet: *Oeuvres de Condorcet*, ed. A. Condorcet O'Connor and M. F. Arago (Paris, 1847–9), i 392.

'As mathematics and physics'
Esquisse d'un tableau historique des progrès de l'esprit humain (Paris, 1795), 365; *Outlines of an Historical View of the Progress of the Human Mind* (London, 1795), 353.

'Morality is the science'
Holbach, *Système de la nature* 1. 11.

13 **'I endow thee with sensibility.'**

Helvétius, *De l'esprit* 3. 9.

17 **'Do not fight prejudice; use it.'**
This formulation untraced, but cf. Vilfredo Pareto, *The Mind and Society* (London, 1935), vol. 1, *Non-Logical Conduct*, §§ 72–3.

18 **'the language of interest'**
De l'esprit 2. 15 (beginning of penultimate paragraph).

'I do not care if men be vicious'
De l'homme 9. 6.

21 **'Woe to us if the masses start reasoning'**
Perhaps a paraphrase of 'when the masses get involved in reasoning, everything is lost', *The Complete Works of Voltaire*, ed. Theodore Besterman and others (Geneva/Toronto/Banbury, 1968–), cxiv 155.

'The people are cattle'
'À l'égard du peuple [... c]e sont des boeufs, auxquels il faut un joug, un aiguillon et du foin.' Letter to Jean François René Tabareau, 3 February 1769. Cf. *Oeuvres complètes de Voltaire* [ed. Louis Moland] (Paris, 1877–85) xix 208, 623, xxiv 413.

23 **'Let us flee from those greedy and cruel animals'**
De l'esprit 2. 2.

25 **'nature binds by an unbreakable chain'**
Condorcet, *Esquisse* (see note to 12 above), 228.

'education is simply'
Holbach, loc. cit. (note to 12 above).

26 **'Euclid is a veritable despot'**
[Pierre-Paul François Joachim Henri Le Mercier de la Rivière], *L'Ordre naturel et essentiel des sociétés politiques* (London, 1767) i 311.

'*bawling* upon paper'
Jeremy Bentham, *Rights, Representation, and Reform: 'Nonsense upon Stilts' and Other Writings on the French Revolution*, ed. Philip Schofield, Catherine

Pease-Watkin and Cyprian Blamires (Oxford, 2002), 187.

'nonsense upon stilts'
ibid., 330.

Rousseau

28 **'Starting from unlimited freedom'**
Dostoevsky, *The Devils* 2. 7. 2.

'had produced more effect with his pen'
Herbert Paul recalling Acton in *Letters of Lord Acton to Mary, Daughter of the Right Hon. W. E. Gladstone*, ed. with an introductory memoir by Herbert Paul (London, 1904), xii.

'Rousseau said nothing new'
Madame de Staël, *De la littérature considérée dans ses rapports avec les institutions sociales*, ed. Paul van Tieghem (Geneva, 1959), ii 280–1.

34 **'slavery [. . .] is against nature'**
Jean-Jacques Rousseau, *Oeuvres complètes* (183/1) [hereafter OC], iii 243.

'To renounce liberty'
OC iii 356.

'death is not an event in life'
'Der Tod ist kein Ereignis des Lebens': Ludwig Wittgenstein, *Tractatus Logico-Philosophicus*, trans. C. K. Ogden, (London, 1922), proposition 6.4311.

37 **'the law of nature'**
OC iii 973.

37 **'graven on the hearts of men'**
OC iii 1001; similarly he says that the laws of custom, morality and public opinion are 'graven, not on tablets of marble or brass, but on the hearts of citizens' (ibid. 394).

'to find a form of association'
OC iii 360.

'in giving himself to all'
OC iii 361.

In a letter to Malesherbes
OC i 1134–8; cf. ibid. 350–1.

42 **'As long as several men in the assembly'**
OC iii 437, 440.

'penetrates into a man's innermost being'
OC iii 251.

46 **'Man is born free'**
OC iii 351.

47 **'the surrender of each individual'**
OC iii 360.

49 **the right of society to force men to be free**
OC iii 364.

Fichte

At some point after he had broadcast his lecture on Fichte, Berlin annotated the transcript with a view to incorporating numerous additional quotations from Fichte's works. He probably used this annotated version, and the sheets of quotations to which his annotations refer (though only some of these sheets, it appears, survive), in lecturing on Fichte on other occasions. When I came to edit the transcript, I discussed the annotations and quotations with Gunnar Beck, an expert on Fichte, who with Berlin's encouragement checked them, and suggested further relevant quotations. He also recommended a reordering of the transcript at one point so that it would follow Fichte's intellectual development more perspicuously. Berlin accepted this recommendation, which is therefore adopted here; but he did not revise the text to include more quotations.

I have not attempted to incorporate the additional quotations myself, if only because this would unbalance this lecture by comparison with the others, and indeed in its own terms; it would also go beyond the limits of my self-imposed general remit. But I give the quotations below, cued by the last few words of the passage on which they bear. An asterisk in the text at the relevant point indicates that supplementary quotations are given hereunder.

References to Fichte's works are to the following editions: *Johann Gottlieb Fichte's sämmtliche Werke*, ed. I. H. Fichte (Berlin, 1845–6), and *Johann Gottlieb Fichte's nachgelassene Werke*, ed. I. H. Fichte (Bonn, 1834–5). These editions are referred to hereafter as SW and NW.

54 **'It is the individual's right'**
Benjamin Constant, *De la liberté des anciens comparée à celle des modernes*: op. cit (187/1, on 188), 593–4.

'My system, from beginning to end'
Letter to Karl Leonhard Reinhold, 8 January 1800: J. G. Fichte, *Briefwechsel*, ed. Hans Schulz (Leipzig, 1925), ii 206.

55 **'To men as they are in their ordinary education'**
NW i 4.

56, 65 **'The nature of things'**
loc. cit. (183/1): more literally 'it is in the nature of man patiently to endure the necessity of things, but not the ill will of others'.

60 **'desires what he is able to perform'**
OC iv 309.

67 **'I am wholly my own creation'**
SW ii 256.

'I do not accept what my nature offers me'
ibid. Cf. 'Every animal *is* what it is. Man alone is originally nothing. What he ought to be, he must become; and since he must be a being for himself, he must become so through himself' (SW iii 80).

they must serve me
'I want to be master of nature, and she must be my servant; I want to have causal power over her, but she must have none over me' (SW ii 192–3). 'The self is to be absolutely independent, whereas everything is to be dependent upon the self. Hence what is required is the identity [Übereinstimmung] of the object with the self' (SW i 260). This self-determination by the self for itself is defined by Fichte as 'absolute independence from all nature' (SW iv 131). 'Autonomy, our ultimate goal, consists [...] in that state of affairs in which everything is dependent upon me and I am not dependent upon anything, where everything that I will occurs in my sensible world simply because I will it to be so, just as in the case of my body, the starting-point of my absolute causality. The world must become for me what my body is for me. To be sure, this goal is unattainable, but nevertheless I should always advance towards it – that is, I should

work upon [bearbeiten] everything in the sensible world so that it comes to be a means for the attainment of this final purpose' (SW iv 229). 'Only through voluntary submission of our prejudices and our opinions to the law of truth [i.e. the law of morality] do we first learn to bow and be silent before the idea of a law as such; this law first restrains [bändigt] our selfishness, which the law of morality has to govern. Free and unselfish love for theoretical truth – because it is truth – is the most fruitful preparation for the ethical purification of our convictions' (SW vi 14). The moral law is revealed to each man by his conscience (*Gewissen*). Each man possesses this basic moral faculty, and it 'commands him to will this and not that, and this freely and of his own accord, independent from all external force' (SW vi 11).

70 **lovable but silly**

Cf. Berlin's *The Roots of Romanticism* (London and Princeton, 1999; 2nd ed., Princeton, 2013), 2nd. ed., 9–10, 139–41. Indeed, in general these later lectures usefully expand the views on romanticism expressed here thirteen years earlier.

nature is simply a collection of dead matter

SW i 412–13.

naturam sequi

'To follow nature', the Stoic principle: see, e.g., Cicero, *Laws* 1. 56, Seneca, *Letters* 66. 3. 9.

71 **not impinged upon by anything else**

'This pure form of our self' alone 'is wholly opposed to the nature of experience' (SW vi 59). Man's will is governed by the inner self if it is 'something original [ein Erstes] which is grounded absolutely in itself and in nothing outside the self' (SW iv 24: 'Das Wollen, als solches, ist ein Erstes, absolut in sich selbst, und in nichts ausser ihm Gegründetes'). 'Our sole happiness [Glückseligkeit] on this earth [...] is free unencumbered self-activity [Selbstthätigkeit], activity [Wirken] springing from our own causal power [eigener Kraft] and according to our own ends' (SW vi 29). '[Man] is and must remain free; no authority may prescribe anything to him other than this law [the moral law – Sittengesetz] within him; it is his sole law, and it contradicts this law if he allows himself to be governed by another – the humanity within him will be annihilated and he will be relegated to the status of an animal' (SW vi 12). 'No one may determine his choice, his direction and his limits other than man himself' (SW vi 23). 'I cannot allow any law to be thrust upon me without thereby forfeiting my humanity, personhood and freedom' (SW vi 13).

71 **has a date and a place**

'Human life and any historical epoch are themselves only necessary epochs of the One time and the One eternal life, [...] the life of the *Gattung* [translation problematic: roughly group, community, species, race]' (SW vii 7). '[The plan of history] is *this*: that the *Gattung* freely transform itself through history into the pure expression of reason' (SW vii 17). 'Individuals now disappear completely from the view of the philosopher, and all fall together into the one great community [Gemeine]' (SW vii 14). The thinking self is 'not that of the particular thinking individual, which could never be independent, but the one and eternal thinking in which all individuals are mere thought' (SW vii 55). '*Religion* consists therein, [...] that all life is viewed and accepted as the necessary development of the one, authentic, perfect, moral and blessed life [of the *Gattung*]' (SW vii 240–1).

72

The group – *Gattung* – alone exists

SW vii 37–8: 'looking at the matter in truth and as such' we find 'that the individual does not exist, he should not count for anything, but must vanish completely; the *Gattung* alone exists'.

'Man becomes man'

SW iii 39.

'Man is destined to live in society'

SW vi 306. Cf. 'The concept of individuality is [never the concept of an isolated being but] a *reciprocal concept* [which] is never merely *mine* but [...] always *mine and his, his and mine*; a common consciousness in which two consciousnesses are united into one' (SW iii 47–8).

73

the moral orders [...] of its inner self

Freedom, man's liberation from necessitation by natural causality, is no longer the rational self-determination of the individual, but that process 'whereby the *Gattung* gradually liberates itself through a succession of individuals' (SW vii 20). 'Man's rational capacity [Vernunftinstinct]', man's drive to liberate himself from domination by the blind forces of nature, 'is manifest only in the life of the *Gattung* as such. It is never manifest in the existence of the mere individual, whose natural drive aims at self-preservation and personal well-being' (SW vii 22). 'This one and unchanging life of reason [Leben der Vernunft] [...] is divided, from an earthly perspective, into a multiplicity of individuals, and therefore appears in its totality only in the one life of the whole *Gattung*' (SW vii 25). 'It is the greatest error and the true basis of all other errors [...] when an individual imagines that he can exist and live, think and act for himself, or when someone believes that he himself, the particular person, is the thinking in his thought, since he is merely a single thought in the one general and necessary thought' (SW vii 23–4). 'Reason is manifest solely in the one life of the *Gattung*; if reason does not guide our life, only individuality and selfishness remain. Thus rational life consists in this: that the individual forgets himself in the *Gattung*, ties his life to the life of the whole and sacrifices his life to the whole; and irrational life consists in this: that the individual thinks of nothing but himself and in relation to himself, and seeks nothing but his own well-being: […] so that there is but one virtue – to forget oneself as an individual – and only one vice – to think of oneself […]. Whosoever […] seeks enjoyment for himself and thinks of himself and of a living and being apart from *within* and *for* the *Gattung* is […] merely a base, little, evil and wretched man' (SW vii 34–5). 'To devote one's life to the *Gattung* means to devote one's life to the idea [by which Fichte refers, interchangeably, to reason or freedom]; […] consequently, the only rational and thus right, good and truthful life consists in man forgetting himself in the pursuit of the idea and seeking no enjoyment other than that of the sacrifice of all other pleasures for the sake of the idea' (SW vii 37).

73 **race, nation, mankind**

'Nothing individual can exist in and for itself; everything can exist only within and for the whole' (SW vii 63). 'The truth of the whole [of the *Gattung*] is confirmed by the fact that its parts are explicable and meaningful solely by reference to the whole, […] solely through this whole do the parts exist at all' (SW vii 118). 'The continuation [of life as such and not as the continuation of evanescent existence] […] is promised solely by the independent continuation of his nation: to save her, he must be prepared to die, so that she can live, and he can live in and through her, which is the only life he has ever desired' (SW vii 383).

'Either you believe in an original principle'
SW vii 374–5. Berlin, as so often, slightly improves on the quotation, though in essence wording and meaning are accurate. Cf. 'To have character and to be German are indubitably the same' (SW vii 446).

75 **'What we need is a leader'**
SW vii 565 (somewhat amplified). Cf. 'Each man who has the knowledge and the power does not only have the right, but the sacred duty, to subject men to the yoke of law by force; a single man [coercing] the whole of mankind, if it so happens' (SW iv 436). 'Who has the right to be Oberherr? [...] The man with the greatest rational insight of his time and people' (SW iv 444). 'Some day one will come and must come who, as the most righteous man of his people, is also their leader; he will find the means to establish a succession of the best' (NW ii 635).

by a so-called 'organic' process
'The multitude of individuals must be construed as one indivisible organic whole' (SW vii 157). The true essence of art, Fichte says, lies in 'its organic unity, as indeed anything that is of genius, limitless and inexhaustible' (SW vii 95). The creative, moulding process whereby man's will and wishes as an individual are brought into unison with his ethical vocation is placed by Fichte in the hands of the State. 'The absolute State [...] is an artefact, designed to direct all individual forces to the life of the *Gattung* and fuse them into one within it'

(SW vii 144). 'The end of the State is [...] none other than that of the human *Gattung* itself, namely that all men's relations be ordered according to the law of reason' (SW vii 161). In the perfect State 'the individuality of all is dissolved in the totality of the *Gattung*' (SW vii 146). 'The end [of the State] is that of the *Gattung*' (SW vii 145). 'The end of the State [...] is no other than that of mankind [der menschlichen Gattung] itself, namely, that all human affairs be governed by the law of reason' (SW vii 161). 'The State, as the highest governor [Verweser] of all human affairs, and as the [...] guardian of the ignorant and recalcitrant [Unmündiger], has the perfect right to coerce the latter for the sake of their own salvation' (SW vii 436).

75 **the shape of a great nation, or of history**
The State now becomes something more than the mere sum of its parts: 'the conception not merely of an *imagined* totality, [...] but of a genuine totality [...]; not merely of all single individuals, but of their indivisible union [nicht bloß Aller, sondern einer Allheit]' (SW iii 202). In and through the State 'all flow together into One, united no longer in an abstract conception, as a compositum, but truly united, as a *totum*. [...] Reason is only one, and its representation in the sensuous world is also only one; mankind is one organised and organising totality of reason. Reason was divided into several independent parts, but already the natural institution of the State ends this independence provisionally and melts the separate parts into one whole, until finally morality recreates the whole species into one.

'The posited conception [of the State] can best be illustrated by the conception of an organised product of nature, for instance, that of a *tree*. [...] [Each part], as much as it wills its own preservation, must will the preservation of the whole tree, because on that condition only is its own preservation possible. [...] The whole, therefore, is to be protected first and foremost' (SW iii 203). Each single individual is part of the greater organic whole of the State: 'In the organic body each part continually preserves the whole, and, in preserving the whole, preserves itself; in this way, too, the citizen relates to the State: [...] every part, and every citizen, in preserving himself in the position assigned to him by the whole, preserves the whole in its position; the whole returns into itself, and preserves itself' (SW iii 209).

77 **'The idea tries to become action'**
Heine, *Zur Geschichte der Religion und Philosophie in Deutschland*, book 3: vii 294–6 in *Heinrich Heines sämtliche Werke*, ed. Oskar Walzel (Leipzig, 1911–20).

'The world is the poem'
Josiah Royce, *The Spirit of Modern Philosophy: An Essay in the Form of Lectures* (Boston and New York, 1892), 162.

'Kantians will appear'
Heine, op. cit. (note to 77 above), vii 351.

'Don't try to suppress or to extinguish the flame'
ibid., 352.

78 **'Thought precedes action'**
ibid.

'For you liberated Germany'
ibid., 353–4.

'amidst the nude deities'
ibid., 354.

Hegel

97 **a slave dragged by the Fates**
Seneca, *Letters* 107. 11, after Cleanthes fr. 91 Pearson.

'slaughter-bench'
Georg Wilhelm Friedrich Hegel, *Sämtliche Werke*, ed. Hermann Glockner (Stuttgart, 1927–51) [hereafter HSW], xi 49.

'history is not the theatre of happiness'
HSW xi 56.

98 **'the cunning of reason'**
HSW v 226, vi 127, viii 420, xi 63.

'sets the passions to work for itself'
HSW xi 63.

99 **'civil society'**
See especially HSW vii 262–328.

100 **'the world-historical'**
See especially HSW xi 59–65.

101 **'God's march through the universe'**
HSW vii 336.

a myriad invisible threads
Probably derives from Taine's 'myriades de fils' in *Discours de M. Taine prononcé à l'Académie française* (Paris, 1880), 24, quoted in Berlin's *Concepts and Categories* (London and New York, 1978; 2nd ed., Princeton, 2013), 2nd ed., 123, though Berlin usually ascribes the image (often 'myriad strands') to Burke.

the living and the dead and those yet unborn
Edmund Burke, loc. cit. (196/1).

102 **'concrete'**
See especially HSW xvii 52–6.

103 **iron ring**
Untraced.

104 **'Gangrene is not cured with lavender water'**
The German Constitution (1802) [not in HSW], § 9: Georg Wilhelm Friedrich Hegel, *Schriften zur Politik und Rechtsphilosophie* [*Sämtliche Werke*, ed. Georg Lasson, vol. 7] (Leipzig, 1913), 113.

'not from the peaceful time-hallowed tradition'
HSW xi 60.

Having quaffed the bitter draught of world history
Paraphrase of HSW xi 119.

105 **'the Emperor – that world soul'**
Hegel to Immanuel Niethammer, 13 October 1806: *Briefe von und an Hegel*, ed. Johannes Hoffmeister (Hamburg, 1952–60), i 120.

Saint-Simon

117 **'I write because I have new ideas'**
Introduction aux travaux scientifiques du dix-neuvième siècle (1808): *Oeuvres de Claude-Henri de Saint-Simon* (Paris, 1966) vi 16; cf. 'Epître dédicatoire à son neveu Victor de Saint-Simon', *Oeuvres de Saint-Simon et d'Enfantin* (Paris, 1865–78) [hereafter *Oeuvres*] i 98.

118 **'Rise, M. le Comte'**

For this anecdote see Louis Reybaud, *Études sur les Réformateurs ou socialistes modernes: Saint-Simon, Charles Fourier, Robert Owen* (Paris, 1840), chapter 2, 'Saint-Simon et les Saint-Simoniens', 43. It also appears in M. G. Hubbard, *Saint-Simon: sa vie et ses travaux* (Paris, 1857), 9.

He had been a pupil

Or so Saint-Simon claimed. According to Frank E. Manuel, *The New World of Henri Saint-Simon* (Cambridge, Mass., 1956), 13, 'there is not a scrap of evidence' for this boast.

132 **Therefore (he says very firmly)**

This sentence and the next, which are exceptionally problematic in the BBC transcript, presented difficulties of reconstruction sufficiently severe to justify reproducing them here in their original form:[1]

oppressive and unncessary, and so he says very firmly what
we need is simply a State which has become a kind of
industrial enterprise, of which we are all members, a kind
of enormous limited liability company, unlimited
liability perhaps precisely what Burke who in a sense was
also historically minded, St. Simon demanded not merely a
partnership in all virtue, a partnership in all science, a
partnership in all art, although he blieves that of course
dispassionately, but also a partnership in the most literal
sense, in the sense in which Burke statement so to speak
decide it was not a partnership - a partnership yes and trade
in calico, exactly what Burke denied, a partnership in trade,
in commerce, a partnership in industry, a partnership in
industry and in the sales of all the human needs of knowledge,
without which men cannot get anything done at all.

I am unconfident about my conjectural version of this passage, but I hope at least that the argument is not seriously impaired. If any reader can supply a better solution I shall incorporate it gratefully in any reprint.

[1] Oxford, Bodleian Library, MS. Berlin 595, fol. 265 (detail): scan © Bodleian Library 2014.

'a partnership in all science'
Burke, loc. cit. (196/1).

'the best application'
Oeuvres iv 193–4.

135 **'From everyone according to his capacity'**
This is the first part of the epigraph that appeared on the title page of *Le Globe* when the Saint-Simonians owned it. It continues 'to every capacity according to its work' (which became 'to each according to his needs' in the Marxist version). See Georg G. Iggers, *The Cult of Authority* (The Hague, 1958), 151/3.

'engineers of human souls'
In a speech on the role of Soviet writers made at Maxim Gorky's house on 26 October 1932, recorded in an unpublished manuscript in the Gorky archive – K. L. Zelinsky, 'Vstrecha pisatelei s I. V. Stalinym' ('A meeting of writers with I. V. Stalin') – and published for the first time, in English, in A. Kemp-Welch, *Stalin and the Literary Intelligentsia, 1928–39* (Basingstoke and London, 1991), 128–31: for this phrase see 131, and, for the Russian original, 'inzhenery chelovecheskikh dush', I. V. Stalin, *Sochineniya* (Moscow, 1946–67) xiii 410. Gorky used the phrase (without 'human') in a 1934 speech to the Writers' Congress: 'the proletarian State must bring up thousands of excellent "mechanics of culture", "engineers of the soul"'. The idea behind the phrase dates back to the early 1920s, when Mayakovsky made analogies with engineering in discussing the role of the writer.

136 **'the divine Smith'**
Untraced. Possibly a misremembering of the use of the phrase by Ludwig von Vincke.

136 **the administration, not of persons, but of things**
See *Oeuvres* xviii 182–91. This way of putting it is due rather to Engels: see Karl Marx, Friedrich Engels, *Werke* (Berlin, 1956–83) xix 195; Karl Marx, Frederick Engels, *Collected Works* (London, 1975–2005), xxv 246–7, where the relevant passage reads: 'In 1816, [Saint-Simon] declares that politics is the science of production, and foretells the complete absorption of politics by economics. The knowledge that economic conditions are the basis of political institutions appears here only in embryo. Yet what is here already very plainly expressed is the idea of the future conversion of political rule over men into an administration of things [eine Verwaltung von Dingen] and a direction of processes of production – that is to say, the "abolition of the State", about which recently there has been so much noise.' (In *Oeuvres* Saint-Simon's remarks are dated to 1817.)

137 **'You are an aspect of me'**
Literally '*you are* an aspect of *my* LIFE, and *I am* an aspect of *yours*'. See Enfantin and H. Saint-Simon, *Science de l'homme: physiologie religieuse* (Paris, 1858), 199.

140 **'There is one thing I wish to say to you'**
All except the first sentence of this 'quotation', like the next, is taken from Reybaud, op. cit. (note to 118 above), 7th ed., i 84. See also 'Notices historiques I: Saint-Simon', *Oeuvres* i 121–2. (The first part of the injunction in the first sentence seems to be the familiar Christian principle, which Saint-Simon endorsed, but which appears not to have been attributed to him on his deathbed.)

Maistre

142 **'a fierce absolutist'**
Émile Faguet, *Politiques et moralistes du dix-neuvième siècle*, 1st series (Paris, 1899), 1.

'his Christianity is terror'
ibid., 59.

'a slightly touched-up paganism'
ibid. ('un paganisme un peu "nettoyé"').

'Praetorian of the Vatican'
ibid., 60.

'Christianity of terror'
S. Rocheblave, 'Étude sur Joseph de Maistre', *Revue d'histoire et de philosophie religieuses* 2 (1922), 312.

'inexorable God aided by the hangman'
E. Quinet, *Le Christianisme et la Révolution française* (Paris, 1845), 357–8.

'slaughter-house'
'[el] matadero del difunto conde José de Maistre'. Miguel de Unamuno, *La agonía del cristianismo*: see *Obras completas*, ed. Manuel García Blanco (Madrid, 1966–71), vii 308.

148 **'the heavenly city of the eighteenth-century philosophers'**
The title of a book (New Haven, 1932) by Carl L. Becker.

149 **'In the vast domain of living nature'**
References for quotations from Maistre are to *Oeuvres complètes de J. de Maistre* (Lyon, 1884–7 and later

unchanged impressions). The reference for this quotation is v 22–5. The French original is printed in full in *The Crooked Timber of Humanity* (xxx/2), 2nd. ed., 178–80, together with a somewhat different translation (181–3, excerpted at 115–16).

151 **'Five or six kinds of intoxication'**
v 34.

154 **The Assyrians invented the nominative**
iv 88.

155 **'What does he mean?'**
ii 338.

sheep, who were born carnivorous
'Dire: les moutons sont nés carnivores, et partout ils mangent de l'herbe, serait aussi juste.' op. cit. (note to 142 above, 'a fierce absolutist'), 41.

Who is this lady?
iv 132–3.

156 **'In the course of my life'**
i 74.

'the two anchors of society'
viii 284.

Nobody can want as violently
viii 288.

'Pugachevs of the University'
viii 291.

159, 162–3 **'la secte'**
e.g. i 407, viii 91, 222, 223, 268, 283, 292 ('une secte détestable qui ne dort jamais'), 311–12, 336, 345, 512–13.

161 **'Who is this inexplicable being?'**
iv 32–3. The Biblical quotation at the end of this passage is from 1 Samuel 2: 8. The French original is printed in full in *The Crooked Timber of Humanity* (xxx/2), 2nd. ed., 183–5, and a somewhat different translation ibid. 119–20.

162 **'It is as if all his works'**
Letter of 8 October 1834 to the Comtesse de Senfft: Félicité de Lamennais, *Correspondance générale*, ed. Louis le Guillou (Paris, 1971–81), letter 2338, vi 307.

163 **the perpetual hideous grin**
iv 208–9: 'Ce *rictus* épouvantable, courant d'une oreille à l'autre, et ces lèvres pincées par la cruelle malice'.

164 **'The principle of the sovereignty of the people'**
ix 494.

INDEX

Douglas Matthews